THE CRYPTO LEGAL HANDBOOK

A Guide to the Laws of Crypto, Web3, and the Decentralized World

JUSTIN WALES

Electric  Connected

Copyright © 2024 by Justin Wales
Published by Electric Connected, LLC

All rights reserved.

No portion of this book may be reproduced in any form without written permission from the publisher or author, except as permitted by U.S. copyright law.

This publication is designed to provide accurate and authoritative information in regard to the subject matter covered. It is sold with the understanding that neither the author nor the publisher is engaged in rendering legal, investment, accounting, or other professional services. While the author has used his best efforts in preparing this book, he makes no representations or warranties with respect to the accuracy or completeness of the contents of this book and specifically disclaims any implied warranties of merchantability or fitness for a particular purpose. No warranty may be created or extended by sales representatives or written sales materials. The advice and strategies contained herein may not be suitable for your situation. You should consult with a professional when appropriate. The author shall not be liable for any loss of profit or any other commercial damages, including but not limited to special, incidental, consequential, personal, or other damages.

The views and opinions expressed in this book are the author's and do not necessarily reflect the official policy or position of his employer.

Book Cover by Mai Sari, maisari.com.

Version 1.1 – April 20, 2024

The Digital Asset Industry Is Evolving Quickly...

The world of cryptocurrency is dynamic, and the legal and regulatory environment surrounding it can shift rapidly. Many of the topics discussed in this book are still being deliberated by courts and regulators across the country. At the same time, entrepreneurs around the world are innovating the technology underlying the industry.

For updates, further insights, and additional resources, visit www.TheCryptoLegalHandbook.com.

Contents

Introduction 1

Chapter 1 Prerequisites to Becoming a "Crypto Lawyer" 9

Chapter 2 A Cyclone of Progress: Developing a Regulatory Perspective ... 15

Chapter 3 Thinking Beyond the Price 23

Chapter 4 Bitcoin in Theory 29

Chapter 5 The Genesis Block and Bitcoin's Early History 43

Chapter 6 Bitcoin in Practice 53

Chapter 7 From Global Ledger to World Computer 73

Chapter 8 Privacy Coins and Stablecoins 89

Chapter 9 The Everything Machines and Decentralized Finance 103

Chapter 10 The Department of Treasury 119

Chapter 11 The States 133

Chapter 12 The Commodity Futures Trading Commission 163

Chapter 13 A Primer on Federal Securities Law 179

Chapter 14 Investment Contracts 191

Chapter 15 The Securities and Exchange Commission 203

Chapter 16 NFTs and Web3 225

Chapter 17 Tax, International Considerations, and Other Legal Intrigue .. 235

Chapter 18 Conclusion and a Plan for Keeping Up 241

Introduction

I started law school a year after Satoshi Nakamoto published the Bitcoin White Paper. A year and a half after that, I stumbled across a mention of it in a Tweet from Wikileaks alerting their followers they would anonymously accept something called "bitcoin" to counteract pressure from the Obama administration on payment companies to stop processing donations.

"What the heck is a bitcoin?" I thought.

As I learned more, I fell down the rabbit hole. I started attending bitcoin meetups in Miami to connect with others who also believed that a technology that enables us to interact directly with one another could be deeply impactful. My initial interest in Bitcoin occurred during its first real bull run, but when I met with other early enthusiasts, the price increases were rarely our focus. Instead, we mostly discussed how a global financial system independent of government control could impact the world. As I was living in Miami at the time, the people who showed up to these early meetups disproportionately had lived under oppressive regimes like Cuba and Venezuela and had experienced first-hand the dangers of asset confiscation and currency inflation. To them, bitcoin was not a financial investment. It was a safety net.

After I graduated from law school in 2012, I took a job at a large law firm working on First Amendment cases without any aspiration of going into "crypto law." At the time, a bitcoin business was most likely to consist of a few friends silk-screening a "₿" on a t-shirt from their garage, and they didn't need to hire me as a lawyer for that. Trying to be a crypto lawyer back then was as realistic a goal as becoming a time travel attorney.

The landscape began to change over those first few years of my career. As the price of bitcoin increased, there was more funding in the space, and new companies were trying to understand what regulations applied to digital assets. I was lucky that several friends I met through meetups needed a lawyer, and since I was the only one they knew, they called me. At the time, my career was focused on constitutional litigation and my role was essentially to translate the crypto to the regulatory lawyers at my firm and then convey their legal advice back to the clients.

By 2015, Ethereum was launched, and within the next few years, a deluge of new blockchains and token projects came to the market, promising to decentralize just about everything. As the industry grew, I found my constitutional law practice replaced by a diverse set of clients operating in nearly every niche of the crypto space. From bitcoin ATMs to global exchanges and celebrities exploring NFT projects to crypto mining pools. My clients ranged from those on the vanguard of the technology, like programmers developing decentralized financial protocols and exploring decentralized governance models, to traditional financial institutions like banks and Wall Street funds just starting to dip their toes in the digital asset space, and about every type of business in between.

My clients all loosely fit under the ever-growing crypto/digital asset/Web3[1] banner, but because the industry is so expansive, I found myself working across a wide variety of legal disciplines. As I grew my practice, I relied on my firm's experts to workshop the regulatory, corporate, and litigation challenges my clients faced. I spent my nights studying off the clock and leaned on my firm's partners to tutor me in their expertise.

After a few years, I had developed a generalist, industry-focused practice that no longer depended entirely on more senior partners for their insight. They were there if needed, but unlike some of my

---

1 I use "crypto" as a broad term encompassing cryptocurrencies, virtual currencies, and digital assets. While each term has a distinct meaning, they are used interchangeably in general discourse and within this book. Unless otherwise specified, "crypto" refers to digital assets that operate on blockchain or similar decentralized technologies and are not managed by a central entity.

Web3 has emerged as a broad, catch-all term for what some describe as the next iteration of the internet. It's typically used to refer to blockchain-based applications that enable users to interact directly with protocols rather than through centralized platforms. *See* Chapter 16 for a broader discussion.

colleagues who had spent their careers developing a single deep well of knowledge, I had gained the experience to competently switch between many types of complex issues. On a given day, I bounced between fundraisings, regulatory inquiries, corporate restructurings, licensing approvals, civil litigations, IP disputes, criminal matters, and product counseling.

When I went in-house to head the U.S. legal team of one of the world's largest cryptocurrency platforms, I found the generalist training I had developed helped me manage the mélange of questions that came across my inbox. I enjoyed the freedom to expand the group of experts I could learn from beyond just my former law firm. The ability to be challenged with new questions and to learn from the best in my profession has given my career a forward momentum and enabled me to take a business-oriented approach to providing legal advice.

Unfortunately for those entering the field, the generalist, industry-focused legal practice I stumbled into is actively discouraged by most law schools and the large law firms that serve as the training ground for many of the brightest young lawyers.

A Problem with Lawyers

A trend over the last few decades in the legal industry has been for lawyers to force themselves into a practice area specialization. I was told to develop an expertise when I was in law school, and after I began seeking out corporate and regulatory attorneys to assist me with my crypto work, I was chastised by a senior partner for not focusing on the litigation path laid out in front of me. But I wasn't interested in becoming very good at one area of law to the exclusion of all other skill sets. I wanted to be able to represent an entire industry no matter the issue. That requires legal dexterity.

Regrettably, most law firms tasked with developing new lawyers do not want their associates to specialize in anything other than the narrow practice area of their direct supervisor. The trend toward specialization is rooted in the economic model of large law firms and tends to benefit the senior partners and firm management more than the developing attorneys or clients.

While it is obviously important for lawyers to develop an expertise, a result of the trend toward hyper-specialization is that a surprising number of lawyers who are subject matter experts in their area of choice have embarrassingly large gaps in knowledge in even adjacent fields of practice. For anyone who has ever worked with a large law firm across multiple matters, this results in an exponentially large bill as more and more lawyers are added to every email and call to opine on considerations outside of the narrow expertise of the lawyer that was initially hired.

While valuable when put to surgical use, hyper-specialized lawyers tend to see all issues before them through the lens of their specialty. To a hammer, everything is a nail, and to a swaps lawyer, every memo needs a section about perpetual swaps regulations. Even when it doesn't.

The challenge of being a crypto lawyer is not that the concepts or regulations at issue are beyond comprehension but that there is so much uncertainty and movement in how legal principles are applied to the industry. This uncertainty, which can result in contradictory legal considerations, is exacerbated by the perpetual innovation by which the space develops. These factors make competent representation within the crypto field difficult because it requires attorneys to be up-to-date with fast-changing developments across multiple areas of law and familiar with the intricacies of an expanding set of technologies and applications.

If I weren't already in the space, I would find it overwhelming to know where to start. That's where I got the idea for this book.

It's a place to start.

Who Is This Book For?

Law Students and Lawyers Wanting to Work in The Crypto Industry

I receive many messages from law students and lawyers looking to start or grow a crypto practice, or who want to go in-house, asking what they can do to succeed. My answer is always the same:

1. Download a wallet and start experimenting with the technology;
2. Learn the industry's history and keep up with the news; and
3. Become fluent in the different areas of law that impact the digital asset space.

That advice is straightforward enough, but unfortunately, there hasn't been a single source that someone starting out can pick up to give them a substantive and practical overview of how to begin their crypto legal journey that assumes no prior technical background, a blank slate as to the history of the industry, and zero knowledge about the multitude of legal concepts and principles that you ought to know before you try to get a job in the field.

Entrepreneurs Not Wanting to Get Screwed by Their Outside Counsel

While this book is admittedly styled as a guide for lawyers navigating a crypto legal practice, I recognize that the groups that may find its lessons most immediately valuable are entrepreneurs and developers building in the space.

When I was in private practice, it always surprised me how many of the founders who hired me lacked a basic understanding of the law and procedures governing their industry and demonstrated almost no interest in learning. Clients who do not educate themselves do not have the ability to rein in costs or, more importantly, judge whether the lawyers they have engaged are providing bad advice.

They're operating with blinders.

This isn't a self-help book and nothing here is legal advice. To be clear, you should not pursue any business or project (especially in the crypto space) without consulting an experienced, knowledgeable lawyer first. But you should know legal work ain't rocket science (or even computer science) and that with the right information, entrepreneurs can become better informed of the legal nuances impacting their business and make better decisions that will save them money and lower their risk.

How To Use This Book

This book is not exhaustive nor a replacement for relying on subject matter experts or hiring outside counsel. It also is not a "law school in a box" and, for the most part, ignores discussions on areas of law that are largely unaffected by developments in digital asset technologies that may nevertheless require consideration as a lawyer representing a company in the space. For example, a crypto company with employees must set up a corporate structure and comply with local and federal employment regulations. Neither is addressed here. For the most part, the book tries to stay focused on areas of law that are specifically relevant to the crypto industry. The section on naming rights deals for NBA arenas has been entirely omitted.

One of the difficulties of just about any work in this space is that it becomes outdated the moment it is published. The relevant cases and regulatory citations outlined throughout this book will need updating in the future as the law catches up with the technology and will need to be further revised when the technology once again surpasses the law. I intend to update this project annually, but that will largely depend on whether this book sells, if people are mean to me on the internet, or if I get hit by a bus. If it is after 2024 and you are reading this, go to www.TheCryptoLegalHandbook.com and check to see if a newer edition is available.

Finally, I have tried to write this book in a way that balances the academic nature of a textbook with the practical advice relevant to someone with a non-theoretical job to do. As you go through this book, you'll notice that each section is filled with footnotes and supplemental resources that you can follow to dive deeper into these complex subjects. I've tried not to make too many references to academic articles or other forms of legal or technical esoterica when explaining the topics discussed in the book and have done my best to curate the type of secondary sources I tend to turn to when trying to make sense of complicated topics: YouTube videos, podcasts and self-published blogs created by actual experts working in the field. To make it easy for you to access the links, I have included all cited resources at www.TheCryptoLegalHandbook.com/Resources.

This Book Is Just a Place to Start

Follow the links, experiment with the technology, read the resources, and enjoy falling down the rabbit hole.

Or, in other words, as we say in the biz:

DYOR.[2]

---

2 Look it up.

CHAPTER 1

Prerequisites to Becoming a "Crypto Lawyer"

I'll start with an opinion that has somehow become controversial in the digital asset space:

A "Crypto Lawyer" Should Use Crypto

I've gotten into many disagreements about this, sometimes with excellent attorneys who represent clients in the cryptocurrency industry at a very high level.

But respectfully...

They aren't crypto lawyers. They're securities lawyers. Or financial regulation attorneys. Or general business lawyers with crypto clients.

But they're not "crypto lawyers."

This isn't a knock on their legal skills, and the argument against my position tends to be that in the same way an aviation attorney doesn't need to be a pilot, a crypto lawyer doesn't need to use crypto. And while I agree that a pilot's license isn't necessary to represent an airline, that experience would bring a valuable practical perspective that shouldn't be discounted.

If I were General Counsel of American Airlines, I wouldn't require my lawyers to know how to pilot a plane, but I would be apprehensive about hiring someone who not only has never been to an airport but doesn't see planes as any different from trains, cars, or even horse and buggies.[3]

---

3 For an often-referenced discussion on whether law should be revised to accommodate new technologies or new technologies should be fit into existing regulations, *see* Frank H.

Similarly, I don't think lawyers in the space need to have computer science degrees or know how to code (although it wouldn't hurt), but they should have hands-on experience with how decentralized technologies are being used and understand how the crypto industry is developing.

My controversial, unchangeable, never-in-a-million-years can be convinced otherwise view is that you cannot provide the best advice possible to clients in the crypto space without a working first-hand knowledge of the technology. There are self-proclaimed crypto lawyers out there who believe the equivalent of "if god wanted man to fly, he would have given him wings," and my experience is those disinterested in the technology, when confronted with the most difficult questions of first impression facing the industry, don't always see the non-obvious arguments that often make the difference.

Early in my career, I was hired by a founder working on developing a non-custodial digital wallet. He had spent more than $50,000 in legal fees working with a senior financial regulatory attorney at one of the world's largest law firms who sold his experience of having practiced law in the space for over 30 years and touted that there was "nothing new about crypto." Cut to several months later, and all the client had for his money was an endlessly long memorandum concluding that there was no direct guidance on the subject, but nevertheless recommended the company undertake a multi-year process of obtaining state money transmitter licenses that was sent with a cost estimate for a million dollars in legal fees. Practically speaking, his professional recommendation for this client amounted to: "Go out of business."

When I met with the founder, he was exhausted from interviewing law firms for a second opinion. As we spoke, he began to give an overview of bitcoin and non-custodial wallets. I stopped him.

Easterbrook, "Cyberspace and the Law of the Horse," 1996 University of Chicago Legal Forum 207 (1996).

The article addresses questions about the regulatory framework that should be developed around the internet by posing the question of whether automobiles fit into regulations on horse and buggies. There is no shortage of articles you can find extending the analogy to digital asset law.

"Not needed. What's the issue?"

My experience using digital wallets, self-custodying crypto, sending transactions, running my own node, and generally being interested in what he was building allowed us to shortcut his issues. I wasn't a programmer like him, but we spoke the same language, which just made things easier.

After I was engaged, I read through the memo from his former attorney. It was obvious that his lawyer fundamentally did not understand what it meant to self-custody digital assets, and that lack of appreciation poisoned his entire legal analysis. As I worked with this client, he was relieved and admitted he tried to explain self-custody to his former lawyer, who refused to understand it.

That lawyer took the position that nothing is new and was, therefore, blind to the new thing in front of him.

Sometimes, you need to experience something to appreciate it. That was the case in the early days, and it has only become truer as technology has splintered and grown in different directions. As the decentralization of all things persists, and experiments with open-source protocols, decentralized financial platforms, NFTs, DAOs, and whatever is in store for us next continue, it becomes harder to develop the right legal and policy arguments about new technologies without understanding the user experience.

No resource can keep up with all the latest iterations of the technology. This book gives a basic primer on some of the most common concepts and projects within the expanding crypto space and provides resources for learning more, but to embrace the moniker of a "crypto lawyer," you'll need to adventure through the crypto ecosystem yourself.

I believe the best way to learn is to set aside an amount of money you are okay writing off as an educational expense and start purchasing digital assets, sending transactions, and interacting with different protocols and the communities that support them. Try to get a feel for what is possible and an opinion on whether there is anything to all this crypto stuff in the first place.

Knowing About Crypto is Not *Sufficient*

An important caveat to the above is that just understanding the technology or being a "degen"[4] with a law degree doesn't qualify you to represent anyone.

There needs to be a balance between understanding the technology and having experience and training as a practicing lawyer. I'll lose some friends saying this, but generally, you should try to work under someone with experience representing crypto clients (or even non-crypto financial services or technology companies) at a high level before setting out on your own or trying to go in-house.

Your personal experience with crypto will be an asset to your group if you are working on crypto matters, but even if you aren't, it is important to realize that the law is experiential, and it is difficult to be entirely self-taught in a way that doesn't require you to eventually alert your malpractice carrier.

Being a Crypto Lawyer Does Not Mean Becoming a Cheerleader

Finally, while I support lawyers being enthusiastic about the industry, we must still be professionally skeptical of the projects entering the space and cognizant of our role as attorneys in bringing them to market. The truth is, as with all financial markets and within all industries, there are bad actors who will want to use your law degree as an insurance policy for their own schemes. Commissioners from both the Securities and Exchange Commission and Commodity Futures Trading Commission have identified attorneys as potential gatekeepers for the industry and have even suggested they may be liable for failing to perform that role properly.

There is no shortage of clients looking to pay a lawyer to sign off on their project, and there is an abundance of lawyers out there who are willing to send a memo giving the opinion that 2+2=5 for the right price. Indiscriminate lawyers are taking a huge risk with their careers for a quick payday and frankly lulling their clients into a false

---

4 "Degen" (short for "degenerate") is a slang term used within the cryptocurrency community to describe a person who engages in high-risk, speculative trading or investing.

sense of security as those letters will not shield them from regulatory scrutiny.

Our role as gatekeepers is to vet those seeking representation and provide legal advice that is unpersuaded by our own financial gain or personal self-interest. This does not mean one must adopt a prudish approach to their practice or ignore the differing opinions and uncertainties as to how the law does or should apply to new technologies, but each opinion provided must be independent and well-reasoned.

CHAPTER 2

A Cyclone of Progress: Developing a Regulatory Perspective

Over the next several chapters, we'll explore how Satoshi Nakamoto designed the Bitcoin network to address the problems he believed were inherent in state-issued money. From there, we can trace how his innovation took on a life of its own and developed from Bitcoin to the broader crypto ecosystem. But before we do, I want to make an obvious point clearer: Nobody knows how this space will develop, no matter how smart they are or how successful they have been in the past.

This includes every founder, regulator, politician, lawyer, CNBC pundit, billionaire investor, hedge fund manager, Bank CEO, Nobel Prize-winning economist, YouTube influencer, Ivy League professor, or anyone else with an opinion on whether crypto will succeed or fail, including the author of this book and Satoshi Nakamoto himself.

While most would admit that they are not clairvoyant, as you make your way through the crypto industry, you'll encounter many with impressive pedigrees who speak as though they can, in fact, see the future when it comes to crypto. Unfortunately, these people tend to have the largest platforms and are the most vocal about what they see as inevitable.

Their confidence is always misplaced, and their pontifications about the industry's success or failure have no bearing on what will actually happen.

Everything is *Evitable*

I make this point because those confident about crypto's success or failure tend to engage in some degree of magical thinking about the industry. Given sentiment about crypto is often directly correlated to the spot trading price of highly volatile assets, problems are underestimated in good markets and overestimated in bad ones. Advocates on both sides also tend to view technology in moralistic terms and see their support or criticism of the industry (or a subset of projects within it) as a character trait rather than a policy position.

The tribalism that has developed around crypto has had the effect of politicizing and inserting emotion into what should be disinterested discussions about the proper role of regulation within the industry. Proponents and critics are pitted against one another such that conversations about the actual nature of the technology and the role regulation should play in its growth are increasingly rare because their support or disdain for crypto has been pre-determined in accordance with their political allegiances or philosophical ideology. Although it is certainly not the case that all politicians, regulators, or advocates behave this way, in my experience, it is common enough that both sides have become reluctant to work together to solve the many still unanswered questions that befuddle the industry. This reluctance to engage in good faith communication is the primary reason the industry is still awaiting guidance on fundamental questions of regulatory application that have been long settled in other jurisdictions.

Throughout the book, we will address some of the current debates about how regulation should develop. For now, five principles should guide any discussion on regulation in the crypto industry.

Regulatory Principle 1: Technology is Neutral

One of the most disturbing trends I've seen develop is the moralization of crypto technology. For supporters, Satoshi Nakamoto is a sacred figure who blessed the world with stateless money, while for detractors, he is the original shadowy super coder who created a tool for terrorists and criminals to transact in secret. The truth is he is neither. Satoshi Nakamoto was a person (maybe a few) who devised an innovative idea on how computers could work together to validate online transactions. In 2008, he wrote a 9-page technical paper outlining his concept for an electronic cash system called Bitcoin and sent it to a handful of people on a cryptography listserv. The project improbably grew from there.

There was no master plan for how Bitcoin would develop or achieve mainstream adoption, and certainly no intention that it would evolve into the broader crypto industry that exists today.

Crypto has become so wide-ranging at this point that it is irresponsible to treat the industry as a monolith. At its core, centralized actors operating in the space need to be given clarity as to what is permissible, and more amorphous concepts like decentralized protocols or the networks and technologies underlying crypto projects must not be vilified as anything other than neutral tools that people can use for good or bad reasons.

Most of the technology we use to describe the "crypto" space comes down to different mechanisms devised to verify a growing array of financial and expressive communications. In the same way that the internet's HTTP protocol is not inherently good or bad based on the websites that utilize it, the technologies discussed in this book are merely tools that can be used for a variety of purposes. Whether it is used for good or bad makes no difference to the tool itself.

Regulatory Principle 2: Existing Regulation Should Be Clarified Before New Laws Are Created

As the technology is itself neutral, regulation must focus on prohibiting and punishing bad actors who use it for unlawful purposes rather than trying to regulate the technology itself. In most cases, the types of bad acts that we would want to see made unlawful through the creation of crypto-specific legislation are already illegal under existing regulations. Accordingly, the goal of regulation should not be to invent new laws for every innovation that develops, but to provide, where possible, clarity on how existing rules should be applied to new technologies.

Regulations addressing specific technologies should be enacted only where existing rules are incompatible.

Regulatory Principle 3: When Existing Rules Are Incompatible, Regulators Must Engage in a Transparent Rulemaking Process

While utilizing existing rules is important, we shouldn't pretend that all new technologies fit into existing regulatory frameworks. Many products and technologies developing within the crypto industry do not fit nicely into current legal models. The approach of some has been to try to regulate the industry through isolated enforcement actions, but this approach fails to provide sufficient clarity to the many good actors building in the space because enforcement cases are either settled before resolution or decided on a particularized set of facts that are not representative of others in the industry.

We must insist that agencies engage in a formal rulemaking process rather than regulation by enforcement in cases where existing rules are inapplicable or incapable of being satisfied.

Regulatory Principle 4: Only Regulate Those Exercising Actual Control

The main idea behind much of crypto is that a network becomes more secure and stable when it replaces centralized intermediaries with a widespread group of participants who contribute to, but do not individually control, the network's activity. This is counterintuitive for many because, until Bitcoin, all financial products and transaction networks necessitated a single issuer or centralized intermediary. As innovators explore the boundaries of these technologies, we must avoid regulations that subject them to perpetual liability for building or running software that allows individuals to participate in the decentralized management of a network.

We must only regulate those who exercise actual network control or custody of a user's funds. There is an incorrect belief by many that the crypto industry is not regulated, but in fact, crypto companies that take on the role of a centralized intermediary and exercise control of customer assets are subject to oversight by state regulators and the federal government. I observe that most people across the industry agree that oversight and some form of registration for centralized money service businesses is appropriate. However, there is a belief among some that the developers of decentralized projects themselves, or even those just running the open-source code needed to support a network, should be regulated even where they exercise no control over the network or a user's funds. Such an approach does nothing but chill innovation without offering any protection to the public.

Regulatory Principle 5: Don't Pick Winners and Losers

We do not want to promote incumbent technologies, including established cryptocurrency networks like Bitcoin or Ethereum, who, because of their time in the market, were able to grow without scrutiny in a way that is no longer possible for newer projects. It's best not to allow regulation to decide winners and losers. Any proposed law must contemplate a pathway for new technologies or projects to achieve the same status as earlier entrants.

Why Thoughtful Regulation Matters: We Can't Think Exponentially

The primary challenge of trying to place guardrails on developing technologies is our inability to accurately predict how things will develop. This, coupled with how slow the legislative process can be, means that regulations need to be written in a way that protects users without stifling innovation. This is difficult under any circumstance, but especially when discussing technologies such as those underlying the crypto industry, which have already grown in unanticipated directions.

The foundational principle that underpins the entire industry—that technology has advanced to a stage where intermediaries involved in financial transactions and communications are becoming increasingly obsolete—signifies a fundamental shift in our society. Whether or not you believe such disintermediation is valid or likely, if successful, it has the potential to change foundational concepts of how our civilization is organized. Unfortunately, humans are very bad at anticipating the unintended consequences or benefits of transformative technology.

The internet is a perfect example of how innovation can change society in unexpected ways over a relatively short amount of time. In only around a quarter century, the information superhighway evolved from a fairly slow and limited application portal to a ubiquitous communicative infrastructure that has altered every aspect of our personal and professional lives. Yet, despite the now obvious success of the internet in reshaping our world and perception of what is possible, the internet archives are littered with dismissive quotes by 1990s-era pundits who interpreted its then-limitations as proof the vision of a globally connected society would never be fulfilled.

As Nobel Prize-winning economist Paul Krugman famously predicted in 1998: "By 2005 or so, it will become clear that the internet's impact on the economy has been no greater than the fax machine."[5]

In retrospect, Mr. Krugman's prediction is hilariously wrong, and, in hindsight, it is easy to think that if given the opportunity to comment on the internet's growth in 1998, we would have made a better prediction. But even if you could have better seen the internet's value, would you have believed that a tool primarily used for e-mails and looking up recipes would change nearly every aspect of your day-to-day life?

Ubiquity is impossible to predict not because of a lack of imagination but because the type of fundamental technological changes that were caused by the internet or which may be caused by this next iteration of technologies tend to impact the culture itself, which then fosters the environment for future innovation, and so on, and so on. It's a cyclone of progress that we don't realize we are in until after we're spinning too fast to stop.

Before you know it, you go from scoffing at how long it takes to sign online to having a supercomputer in your pocket and access to the vacation photos of everyone you ever knew.

Despite countless examples of exponential innovations and their

---

5 Krugman, Paul. "Why Most Economists' Predictions Are Wrong." The Red Herring, June 1998, shorturl.at/el347.

mark on society, it's astonishing how many people I encounter who cannot appreciate that we may be in the midst of the same type of transformative growth right now. The aforementioned technologist Paul Krugman himself has moved on from predicting the internet's irrelevancy to predicting Bitcoin's failure. To Mr. Krugman, who has been foretelling Bitcoin's death since 2013, digital assets are nothing more than just another fax machine.[6]

The most effective crypto lawyers I know embrace the uncertainty of innovation and have made a principled-based, project-neutral approach to regulation a foundation of their practice. I'll save my own best guess on where this all leads, but as we move on to the substantive portions of this book, I caution everyone entering the space to proceed with a healthy dose of humility about the future.

It's probably a safe bet that we won't become a less digital world, but we have no idea how things will grow and must ensure that as we advocate for regulations, we allow for the possibility of the unforeseeable.

---

6 You can peruse over 400 Bitcoin Obituaries dating back to 2010 at 99bitcoins.com/bitcoin-obituaries.

For a collection of Mr. Krugman's thoughts on Bitcoin's inevitable demise, *see* shorturl.at/mvSZ7.

CHAPTER 3

Thinking Beyond the Price

"Crypto" is a catch-all term for many related technologies, but every single one of them started with Bitcoin. There is a culture of tribalism within the crypto space and endless debate over the relative value of different blockchains, consensus mechanisms, and applications, but I believe the starting point to understanding even the furthest iterations of "Web3" is an appreciation of the Bitcoin Network and its philosophy of decentralization.

Crypto People Make Terrible Party Guests

If you hang around the crypto space for any amount of time, you'll witness many insufferable people attempt to explain how Bitcoin works to whoever is unlucky enough to sit next to them at a party. I've been that insufferable person many times, and after staring into the disinterested faces of every one of my wife's friends, I have come to realize these conversations are unhelpful and the reason crypto people are usually seated at the farthest end of the table.

In preparing to write this book, I pulled several primers and textbooks on crypto, all specifically geared to non-technical audiences, and found that they almost always started with *how* Bitcoin or its blockchain work and not *why* we should care about it in the first place.

I think that is the wrong approach.

At this point, let's table the *how* of Bitcoin and focus on its *why*. No one needed to understand the intricacies of packet switching to see the importance of the internet because its potential was demonstrated through its application. The first time someone sent an e-mail and received a response, they understood it was better than paying for postage and waiting for the mail to be delivered. As the application layer of the internet advanced, the public's appetite to get online increased. Comparable to how we discuss crypto today, the "internet industry" of the mid-90s was clouded by regulatory uncertainty. Thankfully, the public's excitement for the technology and its potential to be an economic boon for the United States manifested in a federal policy of protecting an open internet and fostering its growth.[7]

In other words, the policy to support the internet through regulation was rooted in an appreciation of the ways a global communication network could better the world, irrespective of the particular technologies that allowed it to do so. Accordingly, while it is true lawyers in the space should be fluent in the industry's technological foundations, advocates are also served well by understanding the motivation of those who actually use it.

Reframing the Typical Crypto Narrative

A cynical person would say that the motivation of people who own bitcoin, or any crypto, is to speculate on its value. Indeed, most of the conversations occurring in the United States about crypto are focused on its price and volatility, and there are many people, particularly in wealthy democratic countries, who primarily purchase it as an investment. But these people tend to embrace a myopic view of the industry and ignore how a censorship-resistant digital currency that enables users to send, receive, and self-custody value without an intermediary's permission or even knowledge is a defensive tool for those living in less accommodating places.

The Human Rights Foundation has been a strong proponent of Bitcoin adoption precisely because it can be used as a "currency of last resort" for those living in oppressive regimes and conditions.[8]

---

7 *See* Kosseff, Jeff. *The Twenty-Six Words That Created The Internet.* Cornell University Press, 2018. The book explores the history and impact of Section 230 of the Communications Decency Act of 1996, a law that has played a crucial role in shaping the modern internet. Kosseff examines the law's origins and evolution, its role in protecting free speech online, and the ongoing debate over its interpretation and potential reform.

8 Gladstein, Alex. "Currency of Last Resort." Bitcoin Magazine, 4 May 2022, bitcoinmagazine.com/culture/currency-of-last-resort.

We tend to take for granted the relative stability we enjoy in the United States, but throughout even just our very recent history, there are numerous examples of the devastating impacts that come from government-issued money and its dependence on centralized financial infrastructure.

Imagine your home was Ukraine in February 2022, and you wake up to the news that the Russian army had invaded the country. You and your family decide to flee so you run to the bank to withdraw money to fund your getaway. It is closed. You go to the local ATM, encounter a several-hour-long line, and learn that the machine will not have enough funds to satisfy all the withdrawal requests. The value of Ukraine's currency, the hryvnia, crashes before your eyes, so you try to send your funds through an online transfer to the account of a relative to sell it for a more stable currency, only to find out that Ukraine's Central Bank has suspended electronic cash transfers. You're stuck without access to your assets and unable to escape the oncoming siege.

In other words: You're fucked.

This scenario is hardly hypothetical to Ukraine's 44 million residents, and it has been widely reported that many turned to Bitcoin to "blunt the impact" of the total economic collapse of Ukraine's financial infrastructure by seeking out a currency that doesn't depend on it. As one of many examples, it was reported in the news that a 20-year-old was able to fund his escape to Poland with bitcoin and leave his war-torn country with his remaining digital savings without reliance on any bank, government, or centralized institution.[9] Now go ask him if digital assets have any "inherent value."

The importance of digital assets that are not reliant on a centralized infrastructure or controlled by governments is not limited to those living in countries under attack by foreign powers. By the end of 2023, half of the world had experienced double-digit levels of inflation, with Zimbabwe, Lebanon, Venezuela, Syria, Sudan, Argentina, Turkey, and Sri Lanka experiencing near hyperinflation levels. For

---

9 "Ukrainian Flees to Poland with $2,000 in Bitcoin on USB Drive." CNBC, 23 Mar. 2022, shorturl.at/pAGPQ.

residents in these countries, the ability to self-custody and turn to a digital asset that is not at the mercy of their fragile and often corrupt native banking system has provided a level of financial security not otherwise available during times of economic collapse.

It's easy for those of us in the United States or other countries that are perceived to be economically stable to discount these examples, but over a long enough time period every economy and currency fails. Ignore the fragility of supposedly stable economies at your own risk.

Throughout this book, I'll highlight certain thought leaders and encourage you to follow their writings. The first is Alex Gladstein (@gladstein), who serves as the Chief Strategy Officer of the Human Rights Foundation and has numerous articles, podcasts, and videos on his website about how people utilize Bitcoin and other digital assets to hedge against government oppression.[10] He is also the author of *Check Your Financial Privilege*, a must-read book that provides a compelling view of what life is like for the 89% of the world not lucky enough to be living under relatively strong monetary systems like the dollar, euro, or yen, and details how bitcoin is used by those living under unstable financial or politically oppressive regimes as a tool for economic sovereignty.

As a crypto lawyer, I am often called on to speak with regulators and policymakers who are apprehensive about the idea of digital assets and whose primary understanding of crypto is, at best as an investment that periodically booms or busts and, at worst, a tool for criminals with no redeeming social value. I always try to frame my conversations with those I know are not inclined to support the industry's growth with these real-world uses of the technology.

I have found that when crypto is reframed against the backdrop of its most vital use cases the importance of the continued development and support of the technology becomes evident. It is difficult for even the most cynical critic to completely discount the use of the technology when presented with evidence that it is the only method by which an El Salvadorian can receive money from family living abroad without paying predatory remittance fees or Iranian students

---

10 Alex Gladstein's website can be found at alexgladstein.com.

can fund protests against an oppressive political regime without fear of financial surveillance and retaliation.

When the banks in your country fail, the value of an asset capable of complete self-custody becomes intuitive.

It's easy to be distracted by the volatility of digital assets or the industry's splintering uses and to discount the space as frivolous. But no matter the application, whether it is a digital asset used as a lifeboat for freedom fighters or transferrable images of monkeys wearing sunglasses, the entire space is dependent on the same foundational principle that tools that allow us to interact with one another directly and without permission must be fostered and protected for the benefit of humanity.

CHAPTER 4

Bitcoin in Theory

Defining Bitcoin

The best definition of Bitcoin I've heard is from the comedian John Oliver, who described it as "everything you don't understand about money combined with everything you don't understand about computers." That doesn't tell you much about what Bitcoin actually is, but I think it conveys more about the innovation than most off-the-shelf definitions, which tend to go something like: "Bitcoin is a decentralized digital currency that enables peer-to-peer transactions secured through cryptography and maintained by a global network of computers."

While this is true, most singular descriptions of Bitcoin, including the one just presented, fail to capture its full essence. Bitcoin goes beyond being just a medium of exchange and encompasses elements of technology and economics in a way that challenges traditional financial systems and their centralized control. It is also an evolving project that may utilize its global network in as-yet-to-be-determined ways. Its unknown potential uses require any adequate definition to be somewhat open-ended.

Part of the difficulty in defining Bitcoin also comes from the fact that the term has dual meanings. "Bitcoin" with a capital "B" refers to the global, decentralized protocol and communication network used to transact its native digital currency.[11] Lowercase "b" "bitcoin" denotes

---

[11] In the cryptocurrency context, "protocol" refers to the foundational technology and the rules that determine how a digital network operates, including the exchange of data and facilitation of transactions. Blockchains like Bitcoin or Ethereum are protocols because they have specific guidelines for verifying transactions, securing data, and achieving consensus. Similarly, software applications, smart contracts, and secondary networks that build upon or utilize these blockchain frameworks are also considered protocols, as they

the native digital asset used within that network. This dual meaning creates an ambiguity surrounding the term that is exacerbated by Bitcoin's unique nature as an asset intrinsically tied to the technology used to maintain it.

Is it money? A technology? An investment? A network?

Yes.

Before its creation, no asset existed that was so closely connected to its underlying infrastructure. This unprecedented relationship has made it difficult to categorize Bitcoin, leading to varying interpretations and confusion by the general public and those charged with regulating it. Depending on who you ask, B/bitcoin is, among other things, a currency, an investment, a hedge against inflation, a publication tool, a network as potentially expansive as the internet itself, or all these things and more at once.

Perhaps its qualities are so ephemeral that it can only be adequately described in more poetic terms. As Michael Saylor (@saylor), the founder of MicroStrategy and one of the first public company CEOs to convert a material amount of corporate funds to bitcoin, expounded:

> **Michael Saylor** ⚡ ✓
> @saylor
>
>  is a swarm of cyber hornets serving the goddess of wisdom, feeding on the fire of truth, exponentially growing ever smarter, faster, and stronger behind a wall of encrypted energy.
>
> 12:51 PM · Sep 18, 2020

I tend to think of Bitcoin as broader than a mere financial product (though not in the same Grecian terms as Mr. Saylor) and one that is most fascinating because of the potential for the infrastructure and network supporting it to evolve to accommodate a growing

---

follow and expand upon the basic principles established by the underlying blockchain for secure, decentralized digital interactions.

number of use cases. However, because Bitcoin is at once an asset and its infrastructure, and its potential is dependent on its continued development and the market's reaction to a first-of-its-kind technology, there is still a lot of debate around how to best describe it.

Perhaps the best answer is: We're still trying to figure it out.[12]

There are many great resources for learning about Bitcoin, but for those truly starting at the beginning, I recommend watching a short clip of Peter Van Valkenburg (@valkenburgh), the Director of Research at Coin Center, testifying before the Senate Banking Committee in 2018 and providing possibly the best justification for Bitcoin you will ever hear.[13] Coin Center is an important non-profit organization that promotes policies that preserve the freedom and benefits of decentralized technologies. The organization offers numerous educational materials on digital asset policies and regulations on its website at coincenter.org, many of which are referenced throughout this book.

Another important resource for beginners that I rely on heavily is the work of Andreas Antonopoulos (@aantonop), an author and Bitcoin educator, who has created some of the best primers on Bitcoin available. He also has best articulated an expansive view of Bitcoin that I share that it is much more than just digital money: "Saying bitcoin is digital money is like saying the internet is a fancy telephone. It's like saying that the internet is all about email. Money is just the first application."[14]

If you're just starting out on your journey into crypto, I recommend you watch Andreas's presentation *"Introduction to Bitcoin: what is bitcoin and why does it matter?"* published on his YouTube channel.[15]

---

12 Lopp, Jameson. "Nobody Understands Bitcoin (And That's OK)." 11 Mar. 2017, blog.lopp.net/nobody-understands-bitcoin-and-thats-ok.

13 "The Best Explanation of Bitcoin You Will Ever Hear | PV Valkenburgh." *YouTube*, Lets BCS, 20 July 2022, y2u.be/HzxKs-Jd0H4.

14 Antonopoulos, Andreas. The Internet of Money: A Collection of Talks. Vol. 1–3, Merkle Bloom LLC, 2020.

15 "Introduction to Bitcoin: What Is Bitcoin and Why Does It Matter?" *YouTube*, Aan-

I'll leave it to you to decide how to best define Bitcoin, but no matter how you conceptualize it, the technology that underlines it, as well as the subsequent protocols, projects, and tools it inspired, share a common principle: In its simplest form, Bitcoin created a way to make something that exists in an entirely digital environment rare without relying on a centralized authority to maintain its scarcity.

Everything in the space flowed from this breakthrough.

The Double Spend Problem

Before Bitcoin, online payments required centralized processors to act as intermediaries to ensure a transaction's validity. There was no alternative because it was impossible to reliably prove that a digital asset, which is at its core just data that can be infinitely copied or reproduced, hadn't been spent before. For digital asset transactions, this meant that a recipient had to trust that the sender hadn't already spent the funds. As anyone who has interacted with someone online understands, the requirement that you trust the person you are interacting with is an unworkable prerequisite. The inability to verify that a digital asset had not previously been spent before the recipient received it is known as the "double spend" problem.

Because trust can never be assumed online, payment processors like Visa and PayPal have become the dominant infrastructure for settling all online commerce. For their part, centralized processors charge a fee for each transaction and are able to exercise a high degree of control over the parties, including the ability to censor transactions made by those they disfavor. As a result, lawful organizations and entire industries have found themselves blocked from digital commerce based on nothing more than a bias against them. Perhaps unironically, the crypto industry itself has been the object of numerous attempts by banks and payment networks to censor lawful activity.

Beginning in the 1990s, computer scientists set out to solve the problem of intermediated digital transactions, or how to send value without the need for a middleman. While many of the tools

---

tonop, 25 Sept. 2016, y2u.be/l1si5ZWLgy0.

employed by Bitcoin can be traced back to earlier projects like Adam Back's Hashcash or Wei Dai's B-Money, it was not until a pseudonymous computer programmer called Satoshi Nakamoto outlined his conception of how to integrate these technologies and other concepts in Bitcoin's White Paper that a solution to the double spend problem that was not dependent on a central authority was first articulated.

The Bitcoin Whitepaper

On October 31, 2008, Satoshi posted a nine-page research paper to a small mailing list of cryptographers proposing a novel solution to the double spend problem he called "Bitcoin: A Peer-to-Peer Electronic Cash System."

The Bitcoin White Paper is a technical document that proposes a method for carrying out trustless digital transactions using a public ledger (what we now call a "blockchain"). The ledger contains a record of every bitcoin transaction made using the network and is accessible to anyone who downloads it. Computers across the network, called "nodes," validate the integrity of new transactions by tracing the history of all prior transactions on the network to ensure the sender has sufficient funds. Participants called "miners" then expend computing power and compete in a sort of computational lottery for the right to confirm these new transactions utilizing a "Proof of Work" consensus mechanism. Once a miner confirms a block of transactions, the nodes update the confirmed transactions to the blockchain. To encourage miners to act honestly and direct their computers to compete for the right to confirm new blocks, the network programmatically rewards successful miners with newly minted bitcoin.

In this book, we'll break down several ideas that are core to Bitcoin and cryptography in general, but I encourage you to follow the links to the resources listed in each section to better understand these subjects.

I think it's natural to begin your supplemental reading for this section with Satoshi's Bitcoin White Paper.[16] As Bitcoin is an evolving open-source project, the community has upgraded it over the years, so the White Paper shouldn't be viewed as a roadmap for its current iteration. While it still effectively describes much of the core architecture of the Bitcoin network, I see its educational value not for its technical description but as a reminder of the nature of Bitcoin's original proposal.

As you read the White Paper, note that the economic principles that advocates so closely associate with the project, including the potential price of a bitcoin or a strategy for growing adoption, are absent. Instead, the White Paper is merely a technical proposal on how a group of people may work together to validate information as a collective. As will become clear throughout the book, it is often an underappreciation of the role of the protocol in supporting a crypto asset that causes one to view projects throughout the space in purely financial terms rather than as hybrid products that combine technological and financial characteristics that require a more thoughtful analysis.

There Is No CEO of Bitcoin

There is a joke within the Bitcoin community that is posted whenever a news story critical about Bitcoin is published: The CEO of Bitcoin could not be reached for comment.

While this observation is obviously a ploy, it illustrates Bitcoin's most important characteristic: No one "owns" the Bitcoin network.

Bitcoin is not formally organized, has no board of directors, and lacks a centralized governance structure. Instead, and integral to discussions over the proper regulatory perspective of Bitcoin and the technologies it inspired, Bitcoin's network is merely a communal piece of software that empowers and rewards individuals who contribute to maintaining its integrity. Anyone can download and run Bitcoin's software and is free to propose amendments to the protocol.[17] Once

---

16 I recommend this annotated version for added context. *See* fermatslibrary.com/s/bitcoin.

17 There are several iterations of the Bitcoin software. The original and most popular is

most of the "nodes" (computers) connected to the Bitcoin network agree to a change, it changes, regardless of whether Satoshi or any other singular figure or association approves of the change.

When describing Bitcoin, people often ignore or discount the role of nodes within the network's infrastructure or conflate it with miners. But they are distinct. The way Bitcoin solves the double spend problem and eliminates the need for a centralized intermediary is by allowing anyone to run a node and download a full copy of the Bitcoin blockchain, which contains the complete history of all prior Bitcoin transactions. Each time a bitcoin is sent there is a reference to every previous transaction of that bitcoin dating back to when the network created it. This means that when Alice attempts to send a transaction to Bob, every node can confirm by checking the blockchain that Alice has not already spent the same bitcoin or created it out of thin air. Bob does not have to trust that Alice is being honest.

After a transaction is sent by Alice, it is propagated through the network of nodes who verify that the blockchain's public transaction history does not contradict the transaction. In other words, the nodes check to see if Alice's wallet did, in fact, control a bitcoin that could be sent to Bob. As the network of nodes verifies this information, the transaction is considered "pending." At this point, miners worldwide compete by using specialized computers to confirm the pending transaction (which is grouped together in a "block" of other pending transactions). Once a miner confirms a block of transactions, the nodes update the public ledger to account for the now confirmed block (which is "chained" to previously confirmed blocks) and the miner is paid a reward of newly minted bitcoin from the network. This process is repeated approximately every 10 minutes.

Understanding the way in which Bitcoin maintains consensus requires more effort than reading the few pages dedicated to its design in this book. I have included a number of resources at the end of this Chapter that will enable you to learn more, but I recommend starting with the Andreas Antonopoulos playlist linked below and the online course Bitcoin for Everybody offered for free by Saylor Academy. Both do a good job of breaking down the method through

---

"Bitcoin Core." *See* bitcoin.org/bitcoin-core.

which Bitcoin transactions are made. Some of these concepts will be touched on in more detail elsewhere in this book, but I encourage you to stop after this Chapter and take some time to explore the footnotes and supplemental materials. Understanding how the Bitcoin network works is essential to understanding how other projects and concepts in the space are designed and whether differing regulatory approaches are appropriate as applied to the wider crypto ecosystem.

Bitcoin, Not Blockchain

Bitcoin is a unique asset because it is integrated with the infrastructure that maintains it, which many people incorrectly assume means its "blockchain." Before we move on, I want to discuss the relationship between Bitcoin and its "blockchain," as it is often misunderstood, such that the importance of the blockchain is overstated relative to the network of users that maintain it.

Occasionally, you'll hear someone say that they are interested in "blockchain, not bitcoin" or, even worse, that they are supportive of the catchall corporate-speak concept of "distributed ledger technologies." There isn't a person alive who has uttered these phrases in earnest that understands the purpose of Bitcoin in the first place.

A blockchain is merely a data-management tool. That may be useful, but what makes Bitcoin and other projects within the crypto space innovative is the ability to manage that database without a central authority figure overseeing the process. As soon as you implement a level of control over the integrity of a database, whether through the creation of a permissioned or private blockchain or because a project failed to sufficiently distribute control over its network, the reason for using a blockchain in the first place is undermined. In other words, the notable aspect of Bitcoin is the number of people continuously working to maintain its integrity. Simply copying Bitcoin's design to start a new currency will fail unless you also have a distributed base of supporters to ensure the network's long-term viability. This is a major hurdle that all emerging projects face and a key point of critique regarding centrally managed tokens such as Central Bank Digital Currencies (CBDCs), which are, as their name suggests, prone to the type of centralized control that Bitcoin was designed to eliminate.

I don't consider myself a "Bitcoin Maximalist," meaning someone who believes that Bitcoin is the only digital asset capable of surviving or having any value, but I believe it has been the digital asset that has most convincingly demonstrated how the management of a public database can be successfully distributed. Bitcoin utilizes its community of nodes and miners to sustain its blockchain. What is often lost on those first learning about Bitcoin is that without the nodes and miners that make up the Bitcoin network the blockchain itself is just a database. It is the difference between the World Wide Web and a company intranet used for sharing folders among those with permission to log on. One is a revolutionary new tool that changes how we are capable of interacting with each other and the other is just an information management tool a company may decide to implement in the next fiscal year.

Bitcoin strengthened its network by eliminating a central point of failure. That is itself innovative, but the genius of Satoshi's design is that in finding a way to incentivize people across the world to run nodes and expend resources to confirm new transactions, he created a digital asset with monetary principles that cannot be artificially inflated.

The network and the asset are reliant on each other.

There is no upper-case "B" Bitcoin network without the lower-case "b" bitcoin digital asset. This symbiotic relationship between the network and asset is a feature of many projects within the space, including some that abandon Satoshi's miner-driven Proof of Work consensus mechanism for alternative structures. As you encounter alternatives to Bitcoin, I urge you to consider whether the implementation of a different methodology for maintaining a blockchain's network should have an impact on how the network itself, or at least the digital asset used to maintain it, is treated under the law.

Hard-Coded Monetary Policy

While Satoshi's vision for a decentralized currency was initially presented as a technical solution to a computer science problem, the project's supporters quickly understood that Bitcoin's design could also potentially address the broader shortcomings of central banks and their inability to manage the global monetary supply responsibly.

The monetary supply of fiat currencies like the U.S. dollar or Euro can be expanded or constricted by the governments that manage them. While there are reasons why a government would want, and some argue need, to exercise this type of power over the currency, an inflationary money supply devalues the spending power of the currency over time.

Fear of currency debasement had concerned many in the United States since the abandonment of the gold standard permitted central banks to print money without restraint. The 2008 bailout brought the concern of fiat devaluation to the mainstream when the U.S. Federal Reserve attempted to stimulate the economy through the creation of new dollars. Satoshi felt history confirmed that central banks, subject to the whims of political leaders, could not control unbridled spending and envisioned a technical solution to the problem. As Nathanial Popper explained in Digital Gold:

> This apparently small detail in the system carried potentially great political significance in a world worried about unlimited printing of money. What's more, the restraints on Bitcoin creation helped deal with one of the big issues that had bedeviled earlier digital moneys—the matter of how to convince users that the money would be worth something in the future. With a hard cap on the number of Bitcoins, users could reasonably believe that Bitcoins would become harder to get over time and thus would go up in value.

Satoshi designed Bitcoin to be deflationary with a capped total supply of 21 million bitcoin, although in the same way that a dollar can be divided into pennies, each bitcoin can be subdivided into a smaller unit called a "satoshi" or "sat."[18] Bitcoin's supply cap ensures the cryptocurrency will not experience the same inflationary pressures as fiat currencies, which can be printed at the discretion of central banks. As the demand for bitcoin increases over time and the supply

---

18 Each bitcoin can be subdivided into 100 million sats.

remains capped, the value of the currency should theoretically rise and increase its purchasing power.

New bitcoins are created programmatically by the network and awarded to miners who successfully validate new blocks of transactions. This distribution process is an essential part of Bitcoin's economic policy, and it assumes that Bitcoin's adoption will continue. As the value of each incremental bitcoin increases, the rate by which new bitcoins are created will decrease until the last bitcoin is mined around the year 2140.

The block reward is, therefore, not constant and is programmed to decrease over time. Approximately every four years, or every 210,000 blocks, the block reward is halved. When Bitcoin was first introduced in 2009, the block reward was 50 bitcoin (BTC) per block. After the first halving in 2012, it dropped to 25 BTC, then to 12.5 BTC in 2016. In April 2024, the block reward became 3.125 BTC. It will continue to halve every four years for another hundred and sixteen years.[19]

As Satoshi posted on the website of the P2P Foundation, an organization dedicated to peer-to-peer technology, "[t]he root problem with conventional currency is all the trust that's required to make it work . . . [t]he central bank must be trusted not to debase the currency, but the history of fiat currencies is full of breaches of that trust."[20] The central theory behind Bitcoin's monetary policy is that the temptation to manipulate the monetary supply for a central bank's short-term gains is too great, and therefore, the only way to prevent it is by transitioning to a currency system that is programmatically incapable of being manipulated by the whims of centralized leadership.

---

19 A natural question arises about the sustainability of Bitcoin after 2140, when the block rewards cease. The prevailing hypothesis is that transaction fees, paid voluntarily by Bitcoin users, will be sufficient to incentives miners to continue supporting the network. For more on this topic, see "Bitcoin Q&A: Mining Incentives After 2140," *YouTube*, Aantonop, Nov. 19, 2019, y2u.be/LNSlIiKyZJM.

20 Nakamoto, Satoshi. "Bitcoin Open Source Implementation of P2P Currency." *P2P Foundation: Forum,* 11 Feb. 2009, shorturl.at/cCDE1.

Supplemental Resources – Understanding Bitcoin[21]

- *Explain Bitcoin Like I'm Five*, **Custodio, Nik.** *Medium,* **12 Dec. 2013,** shorturl.at/nvNP9.

- *Bitcoin Nodes vs. Miners: Demystified,* **Braiins, 14 May 2021,** braiins.com/blog/bitcoin-nodes-vs-miners-demystified.

- *Bitcoin Mining Is Not Solving Complex Math Problems [Beginner's Guide]: Braiins,* **14 Apr. 2021,** braiins.com/blog/bitcoin-mining-analogy-beginners-guide.

- "Bitcoin Documentary | The Trust Machine." *YouTube,* **28 May 2018,** y2u.be/ZKwqNgG-Sv4.

- **Antonopoulos, Andreas.** *The Internet of Money: A Collection of Talks.* **Vol. 1–3, Merkle Bloom LLC, 2020.** These books contain transcribed speeches on numerous technical and philosophical topics, mostly focused on Bitcoin and decentralization. I find it a great resource, but the *free* recordings of the speeches can be found within a series of playlists on Andreas's YouTube channel. *See* **Antonopoulos, Andreas.** "**Collection of Videos from 'The Internet of Money Volume 1' Book.**" *YouTube,* playlist by Aantonop, shorturl.at/zAGJY.

- **Antonopoulos, Andreas M.** *Mastering Bitcoin: Programming The Open Blockchain.* **O'Reilly Media Inc., 2024.** This book is a helpful physical resource for learning more about Bitcoin's technological infrastructure. It isn't a beginner's book but offers a more technical examination of Bitcoin's architecture.

- **Bitcoin for Everybody and other online courses** - A cottage industry of online classes and certifications has emerged over the last few years that will charge

---

21 For ease of reference, all Supplemental Resources and footnote links are available at www.TheCryptoLegalHandbook.com/Resources.

you thousands of dollars for a class that teaches you the basics of Bitcoin or crypto. For the most part, I would caution you to stay away from these types of classes as there are plenty of free alternatives out there. "Bitcoin for Everybody," offered by Saylor Academy, is the best free non-technical course, in my opinion, but there are plenty of other options. You can check out a list of classes at lopp.net/bitcoin-information/online-offline-classes.

- **Lopp.net – Bitcoin Information and Resources** - Self-custody business Casa's founder, Jameson Lopp, has collected a well-vetted repository of Bitcoin-specific resources that you should certainly bookmark. The website contains everything from basics on how to get started using bitcoin to advanced technical documents. *See* lopp.net/bitcoin-information.

Supplemental Resources - Bitcoin's Monetary Philosophy

Many resources are available to learn about Bitcoin's economic principles or, perhaps more broadly, how money works. In my view, resources written specifically about Bitcoin by Bitcoin advocates tend to be somewhat absolutist in their thesis. Before reading the Bitcoin-specific material, my advice is to focus on the history of our monetary supply outside the context of Bitcoin or digital currencies.

- **Graeber, David, and Thomas Piketty.** *Debt: The First 5000 Years.* **Melville House, 2021.** This is a must-read book that traces the history of money and debt and challenges long-held assumptions about their roles within society. First published in 2011, it makes no mention of Bitcoin and is focused on the impact of debt, value, and money on society. It has obtained a somewhat cult status among many crypto advocates.

- **Murphy, Robert P. "Understanding Money Mechanics."** *Mises Institute,* **Jan. 2020,** mises.org/library/periodical/understanding-money-mechanics. A free and easy-to-digest overview of money and banking, covering topics such as the abandonment of the Gold Standard and the development of Modern Monetary Theory.

- **Ammous, Saifedean. *The Bitcoin Standard: Sound Money in a Digital Age.* John Wiley & Sons, 2018.** This is one of the more influential books on economics within the Bitcoin community. The book explores the history of money and the problems of centralized economic control and advocates that Bitcoin could become an alternative monetary standard.

- **Bhatia, Nik. *Layered Money from Gold and Dollars to Bitcoin and Central Bank Digital Currencies.* 2021.** A spiritual successor to The Bitcoin Standard that takes a broader historical and economic view on the current status of central bank monetary systems and Bitcoin's growing role within that broader economy.

CHAPTER 5

The Genesis Block and Bitcoin's Early History

The Genesis Block

On January 3, 2009, two months after the publication of its White Paper, Bitcoin went live. Satoshi mined Bitcoin's first block, what we now refer to as "The Genesis Block," and for his effort was rewarded by the network with the first 50 bitcoins. At the time, they had no market value, and it wasn't until May 22, 2010, when, after a member of the Bitcoin Talk internet forum named Laszlo Hanyecz agreed to pay 10,000 bitcoin for two pizzas, that the world had its first indication of the value of a bitcoin. Depending on the day, those two pizzas have a present-day price of upwards of a half-billion dollars, information made somehow more upsetting by the fact that the pizzas were from Papa John's.

The early days of Bitcoin and its growth from a theoretical solution to the double spend problem to a potential new global currency are fascinating examples of the unexpected ways through which new ideas are adopted. There is a saying within the crypto community that things happen "slowly, then suddenly," which I think is demonstrated by Bitcoin's early history and how the project monetized and grew. So, while today Bitcoin is legal tender in El Salvador and treated as a safe-harbor currency for several publicly listed companies, the earliest uses of bitcoin involved people agreeing to purchase pizza (or drugs) on internet forums or exchanging the asset on a website originally set up to trade Magic cards.[22]

---

[22] The first online bitcoin exchange was "Mt. Gox," which stood for "Magic the Gathering Online Exchange." The website was initially a place to trade Magic cards but was repurposed in 2010. It collapsed in 2014 following a security breach and has been in bankruptcy proceedings since. The story is detailed in *Digital Gold*, referenced in the Supplemental Resources.

Bitcoin's critics will sometimes point to its colorful history as a way of discounting its long-term viability, but in my view, the fact that Bitcoin's beginnings were so frivolous directly contributed to the project's survival. A central premise behind Bitcoin is that the integrity of a network that is not controlled by a centralized authority is stronger than one that is centrally managed. That foundation is only true when the network becomes disintermediated enough that a bad actor cannot overtake it with superior resources. In practice, "decentralization" is not a binary objective that a network either has or has not achieved. It is a characteristic that is strengthened over time until the point where a takeover of the network becomes less and less likely.

On the day Satoshi first published Bitcoin's code the project was centralized. Two days later, when a computer scientist named Hal Finney became the second person to run Bitcoin, it was less centralized than at its launch, but still lacked the distribution required for a trustless monetary system. As more people joined the network, it hardened, and the miracle of Bitcoin was that it was able to grow slowly at a time when there wasn't an incentive from those who knew about it to dedicate the resources needed to attack it successfully. After all, why waste time or energy or money trying to destroy an experimental digital currency worth basically nothing and whose primary use was to purchase weed on online message boards?

Destroying Bitcoin when it was vulnerable enough to be destroyed wasn't worth the trouble.

Satoshi's Disappearance

For Satoshi and many of Bitcoin's earliest supporters, there was a fear that growing too fast would be detrimental to the project and would tempt those with the resources to disrupt the network to attack it. The last public message from Satoshi is a warning not to promote adoption too quickly. It was directed at WikiLeaks after the organization started asking supporters to donate to them using Bitcoin after traditional payment networks stopped processing its transactions.

"No, don't bring it on," Satoshi pleaded in his penultimate message to the world. "I make this appeal to WikiLeaks not to try to use Bitcoin. Bitcoin is a small beta community in its infancy. You would not stand to get more than pocket change, and the heat you would bring would likely destroy us at this stage."

Satoshi's warning to Wikileaks and the broader Bitcoin community was ignored. In his final public message, posted on December 10, 2010, Bitcoin's creator cautioned that there are "still more ways to attack [Bitcoin] than I can count."

And with that, Satoshi vanished.

But the project didn't die. Perhaps the attention brought on by WikiLeaks was not enough to tempt capable actors to attack the network. Or maybe having a well-known organization like WikiLeaks support Bitcoin provided a real-world example of the need for censorship-resistant money that attracted new supporters who joined and strengthened the network. I first learned of Bitcoin after WikiLeaks tweeted a call for bitcoin donations and became interested in digital assets through learning WikiLeaks had been cut off by traditional payment processors in retaliation for its reporting.

No matter the reasons why Satoshi's concerns never manifested, what I find most interesting about this period in Bitcoin's early history is that by the time Satoshi left the project, the Bitcoin community had grown to the point where the network could be sustained without him. Other programmers would contribute to Bitcoin's code, the number of individuals worldwide running nodes increased, and more people would invest resources to mine new bitcoin. To this day, entrepreneurs and supporters contribute to growing Satoshi's network without regard for Satoshi's vision for the project or reliance on his or anyone else's efforts.

The Mythology of Satoshi

As I write this, we are almost fifteen years removed from Bitcoin's creation and still grappling in the United States with the basic question of how to appropriately classify a growing variety of crypto assets. There are many open legal questions in the crypto space we'll discuss in this book, but the most debated is the precise characteristics of a digital asset that would result in the asset itself being a "security" under U.S. law.

We'll spend a significant portion of this book on how to determine whether something constitutes a security, which is a special classification of investment whose sales are subject to additional oversight, and the implications of that classification. But the one point of consistency in analyzing this question is an agreement that whether or not a digital asset is a security has at least something to do with its connection to the identity of a founder or company or ascertainable set of early supporters of a project.

According to Gary Gensler, the current Chair of the Securities and Exchange Commission, every digital asset other than bitcoin is a security that should fall within his agency's remit. Chair Gensler's view is hardly settled, and only an act of legislation could make his answer so simple, but it's important to appreciate the opinion of many that Bitcoin is somehow characteristically different from everything that is not Bitcoin.

In Chapter 15, we'll attempt to parse through the often contradictory case law and statements, some by Chair Gensler and his own colleagues at the SEC, about how to determine if a token is a security. For now, the only thing anyone can seemingly agree upon is that Bitcoin is not one.

Considering Bitcoin's Special Status

There are tens of thousands of crypto assets in the market, encompassing a huge diversity of purposes and technological characteristics. This begs the question of what it is about Bitcoin that makes it so fundamentally different from everything else and if it is possible for a new project to acquire a similar status.

When pressed during a Senate hearing by former Senator Pat Toomey on what he sees as the difference between bitcoin and other cryptocurrencies, Chair Gensler said that with bitcoin there was "no group of individuals in the middle" and that "in essence, investing in bitcoin is not betting on the group of people in the middle."

Senator Toomey remarked about his answer: "So you didn't use the term 'decentralized,' but that is what you're saying."[23]

Gensler refused to agree to this characterization, although others within the Securities and Exchange Commission have said as much.[24]

Decentralization is a continuum. Although we have little guidance other than that Bitcoin is "decentralized," we do not know at what point it became decentralized enough to satisfy this standard or whether this amorphous standard is even the relevant test.

The fact that Bitcoin is accepted as being decentralized begs the question of whether any other project can be similarly labeled or if it is even possible for anything other than Bitcoin to achieve this status. One would think the law could not be such that only one project can satisfy the decentralization criteria. However, it appears, at least according to some, including the Chair of the Securities and Exchange Commission, that may be the case.

A common response of those supportive of Bitcoin's special status is that its Proof of Work (PoW) consensus validation mechanism and the fact that there was no "pre-mined" bitcoin distributed to early adopters is determinative of the question and that the lack of consolidation among Bitcoin's current stakeholders is demonstrative that no individual person or entity's efforts are material to the potential profit-seeking motivation of new bitcoin purchasers.

It is undeniable that the architecture of the Bitcoin network contributes to, and incentivizes, broad network participation that undercuts the argument that bitcoins are securities, but perhaps not in a way that is fundamentally different from other projects and certainly, as I hope becomes clear throughout this book, not in a way that should foreclose other projects from achieving the same regulatory status. Indeed, there are other crypto assets utilizing PoW consensus mechanisms and alternative systems, which have

---

23 "Watch GOP Senator and SEC Chair Spar over Definition of Bitcoin." *YouTube*, CNET Highlights 16 Sept. 2022, y2u.be/3H19OF3lbnA.

24 Hinman, William, Director, Division of Corporation Finance, SEC. "Digital Asset Transactions: When Howey Met Gary (Plastic)." 14 June 2018, bit.ly/2l8t5dB.

achieved a level of decentralization such that its founding teams can no longer reasonably be said to have managerial control over the project's future. Yet, taking Chair Gensler at his word, those projects have not yet achieved Bitcoin's special status and likely never will.

So, what is the fundamental difference?

My theory is that in the absence of a precise definition of "decentralization" or a method by which a project could demonstrate that they have empirically achieved that standard, the relevant characteristic distinguishing Bitcoin from everything else is simply the anonymity of its founder and the amount of time that has passed since he disappeared. Law enforcement cannot easily charge an anonymous issuer of a popular project who has not been heard from in over a decade, so the guidance has developed such that the activities of the long-absent founder are separated from ascertainable creators trying to achieve similar goals. It is unfortunate that under the current regime's treatment of digital asset innovation anonymity has emerged as a founder's greatest defense against enforcement, a strategy that discourages open dialogue, pushes what would be otherwise legitimate innovative activity into the shadows, and causes downstream consequences for both the project's team and society in general.

As we examine Bitcoin's progeny, I encourage you to keep in mind its special status under the law and to consider whether, if Satoshi Nakamoto's identity were known and the project was launched today, it would be possible for Bitcoin to achieve the same regulatory treatment it currently enjoys. My guess is it wouldn't.

Satoshi is Irrelevant

We don't really know much about Satoshi Nakamoto, who hasn't been heard from publicly since December 2010. In fact, the world of primary sources we have about Bitcoin's founder is limited to Bitcoin's White Paper and a collection of postings and emails written before he vanished. Given the unpredictable longevity and popularity of Bitcoin, as well as the potential broader applications of its underlying blockchain, Satoshi has emerged as an almost messianic figure. He is so revered by some that a collection of his messages is published as "The Book of Satoshi," which has become a fixture on the shelf of every good Bitcoin Maximalist.[25]

I think there is certainly something to be learned from Bitcoin's history, and there is admittedly something fascinating around the narrative of Bitcoin's virginal birth that is made more curious by the fact that Satoshi's own untouched bitcoin holdings are valued well into the 11-figure range. Still, I encourage you not to place too much significance on the intent or identity of Bitcoin's lost founder.

The way Satoshi Nakamoto designed Bitcoin makes his opinion of how it should develop entirely irrelevant to the direction the global community has taken the project. I find it ironic that Satoshi's name is so often invoked as an appeal to authority by Bitcoin's supporters, or, as often, detractors claiming that their project is better aligned with "Satoshi's vision" than Bitcoin's current iteration. As I write this Chapter, there is a debate within the Bitcoin community over whether the use of "Ordinals," which are used to inscribe non-financial data such as pictures or documents into Bitcoin's blockchain, is aligned with Satoshi's original vision. This is the latest in a history of internal debates over the use and size of data stored through the Bitcoin network.[26]

As with all religious fights, the words of the Father are used to support all positions. Those who support the Ordinal movement point to the fact that Satoshi inscribed the first mined Bitcoin block with a non-financial message alluding to the 2008 financial crisis occurring during Bitcoin's birth: "The Times 03/Jan/2009 Chancellor on brink of second bailout for banks." Meanwhile, those who want to preserve Bitcoin's blockchain as a purely transactional network will point to Satoshi describing the project as a "Peer-to-Peer Electronic Cash System" in his White Paper and argue that non-financial uses of the underlying blockchain are an attack on Bitcoin itself. Each of these camps is further subdivided on a variety of other issues, including whether to grow, shrink, or keep the current amount of data that

---

25 Champagne, Phil. *The Book of Satoshi: The Collected Writings of Bitcoin Creator Satoshi Nakamoto*. e53 Publishing, 2014.

26 Bier, Jonathan. *The Blocksize War: The Battle Over Who Controls Bitcoin's Protocol Rules*. 2021.

is capable of being stored in each block to either accommodate or suppress non-financial data from being sent. Each faction can point to Satoshi's words to support their intended outcome.

However, Satoshi's vision for Bitcoin is irrelevant because Bitcoin allows anyone to propose improvements that can be adopted by a majority of those running Bitcoin's software. *That is the point of Bitcoin*. No one person owns it or can control it, yet its collective community of supporters is constantly developing it. The Bitcoin network that exists today is not the same as the one Satoshi first proposed in 2008, and that's a good thing. Bitcoin has evolved and is still evolving.

Supplemental Resources - Exploring Bitcoin's Early History[27]

- **Popper, Nathaniel.** *Digital Gold: Bitcoin and the Inside Story of the Misfits and Millionaires Trying to Reinvent Money.* **Harper, 2016.** There are many resources for exploring Bitcoin's origins, but Digital Gold is my favorite. Former New York Times reporter Nathanial Popper does a wonderful job telling the story of Bitcoin's earliest days. The book takes a neutral stance on the technology, neither advocating for adoption nor criticizing the premise of digital assets. Published in 2016, the book is benefitted by the fact that it was published at a time when Bitcoin's long-term success was less certain than it is now. Because it was published so early in Bitcoin's history, it presents a focused narrative that traces Bitcoin's technical and philosophical origins through 2015, when traditional finance and Wall Street first started to consider whether the digital asset movement was worth exploring.

- **"The Rise and Rise of Bitcoin: Bitcoin Movie: Documentary: Blockchain."** *YouTube,* **Moconomy, 26 Sept. 2023,** y2uo.be/A06qdTpOYcg. A 2016

---

27 For ease of reference, all Supplemental Resources and footnote links are available at www.TheCryptoLegalHandbook.com/Resources.

documentary that chronicles Bitcoin's origins.

- **Bier, Jonathan.** ***The Blocksize War: The Battle Over Who Controls Bitcoin's Protocol Rules.*** **2021.** This book traces the debate within the Bitcoin community between 2015 and 2017 over whether to upgrade Bitcoin's code to accommodate larger block sizes. Proponents argued increasing the block size would make bitcoin transactions faster and cheaper. Opponents believed doing so could make the cost of running nodes too expensive and result in Bitcoin becoming more centralized. Ultimately, Bitcoin remained a "small block" blockchain, with a minority of defectors forcing a "hard fork" of the chain to create an alternative version of Bitcoin called "Bitcoin Cash."

CHAPTER 6

Bitcoin in Practice

> "If you don't believe it or don't get it,
> I don't have the time to try to convince you, sorry."
> -Satoshi Nakamoto

So far, we have mostly spoken of Bitcoin in hypothetical terms. If you have gotten to this point in the book and explored the supplemental resources, you should have a fairly fluent understanding of how Bitcoin works and hopefully have developed an opinion on whether you think it's worth more of your time.

Try to be honest with yourself before moving on. Is stateless money an area of interest you want to continue to pursue?

Not everyone does. Warren Buffet *hates* the stuff.

In my view, if you still don't see the value of Bitcoin (in societal terms, not necessarily as reflected in today's market price), now is a good opportunity to rethink the focus of your career and explore a different high-growth area.

Perhaps A.I.?

I'm being facetious, but in my experience, the best lawyers in the space are fully bought into the central premise that what the industry is building is for the broader good of society. That doesn't necessarily mean they are focused on Bitcoin specifically; in fact, many of them are not and believe there are more exciting projects in the space that deserve their attention. However, the principles behind the development of Bitcoin, such as the value of a network-backed asset or the benefit of self-custody, are persistent through much of the wider crypto ecosystem and an appreciation of these concepts is core to developing an industry-focused practice.

So, assuming you're still with me, let's spend some of your money and examine how regulation impacts common bitcoin transaction flows.

Your First (Fraction of a) Bitcoin

Bitcoin is the most readily purchasable digital asset and a good introduction to crypto commerce in general. Many of the practical mechanics of buying, holding, and sending bitcoin are directly applicable to other digital assets discussed later in the book.

The first thing you'll notice when trying to "opt-in" to the digital economy is that, for the most part, doing so lawfully in the United States is almost entirely dependent on your ability to access traditional banking and financial systems. This strikes many as counterintuitive to the premise of decentralized money and contradicts the narrative that the crypto industry is entirely unregulated. Under current U.S. regulations, one's ability to purchase a digital asset from a centralized U.S. platform using fiat dollars requires you to provide identifying information to the exchange and to link your account to an existing financial system or, at the very least, to connect a debit or credit card in your name.

Sellers of virtual currencies are primarily regulated at a state level under the money transmission laws of each jurisdiction. The states vary *significantly* as to how and even whether virtual currency sales are regulated. However, beyond each individual state's approach, there exists a set of requirements imposed on all "money services businesses" by the Department of Treasury's Financial Crimes Enforcement Network (FinCEN). We'll explore the details of federal and state-level oversight in Chapters 10 and 11, but for now, note that FinCEN sets forth numerous obligations on "exchangers" and "administrators" of virtual currencies, including recordkeeping, reporting, and anti-money laundering program obligations under the Bank Secrecy Act. Notably, pure "users" of virtual currencies are not subject to regulations that obligate the purchasers of digital assets to provide at least some identifiable information to the business selling them virtual currencies, depending on the amount transacted.

Accordingly, the only ways to trade in your fiat dollars for bitcoin lawfully and in a way that is completely unconnected to existing financial systems is to earn bitcoin by selling a good or service, mine bitcoin directly from the network, or engage in a peer-to-peer cash transaction. While I think each of these is an unlikely path to one's first bitcoin, they deserve addressing.

Earning Bitcoin – For the entrepreneurially minded, one can sell goods or provide services in exchange for bitcoin or other virtual currencies. Such activity falls outside the scope of money services regulation at both the state and federal levels, although income received in bitcoin is taxable.[28]

Mining – As of this writing, about 19.5 million of the 21 million bitcoins that will ever exist have been mined. In the early days, it was possible to mine new bitcoin from a personal computer or relatively small home setup, but the effort is no longer practical given the cost of electricity and equipment relative to the difficulty caused by increased competition to add new blocks to the network.

Mining can still be profitable at scale, and even smaller mining operations can succeed by joining a "mining pool" that combines the efforts of many miners across the world and pays a pro-rata share of any rewards earned by a member of that pool based on the computing power contributed, but doing so requires capital and upfront costs and is not practical for most.[29]

Peer-To-Peer Transactions – Before centralized trading platforms became mainstream, a popular way to purchase bitcoin with cash was via a peer-to-peer transaction. Typically, a person who wanted to purchase bitcoin would find a counterparty in their area willing to sell their bitcoin directly and would meet in person to effectuate the transaction. Several platforms were set up to facilitate these matches, but the most popular was LocalBitcoins.

As you may imagine, there is a danger inherent to meeting a stranger who is aware you are holding a wad of cash, and eventually,

---

28 See tax discussion in Chapter 17.

29 For an article premised on the belief that my discouragement is wrong, *see* Econoalchemist. "Home Mining for Non-KYC Bitcoin." *BTB Blog*, 18 Feb. 2022, shorturl.at/lpyO3.

LocalBitcoins and other platforms pivoted from in-person transactions to an online escrow system that collected information about each counterparty. This pivot resulted from guidance published by FinCEN in 2019, which we'll discuss in Chapter 10, that characterized peer-to-peer marketplaces as money services businesses. My understanding is this pivot drove away many of LocalBitcoin's privacy-minded users, and in February 2023, the company closed after ten years, citing regulatory pressure.[30]

While it is usually lawful for one to act as a purchaser of virtual currencies through a cash peer-to-peer transaction, I advise you to be cautious if seeking out a stranger in your area willing to sell you bitcoin.[31] If you are interested in exploring peer-to-peer bitcoin transactions, I encourage you to learn more about Bisq (bisq.network), a desktop software that enables a decentralized peer-to-peer exchange that connects bitcoin buyers and sellers. Note that buying bitcoin on Bisq with USD still requires you to fund the transaction with a traditional financial institution.

We'll discuss decentralized financial exchanges in Chapter 9, which, in the broader crypto context, can allow for transfers of digital assets in a way that doesn't require integration with the traditional financial system. While DeFi is touted by many privacy advocates as a less permissioned way to utilize digital assets, the challenge remains of how one first obtains the digital assets required to engage with a decentralized ecosystem without at some point doxing (identifying) themselves by going through a centralized platform.

Centralized Trading Platforms

The easiest way for most people to purchase digital assets is through a centralized trading platform such as Crypto.com, Coinbase, or Kraken.[32] Centralized platforms in the United States are subject

---

30 Kharif, Olga. "LocalBitcoins Matching Exchange Cited by US in Bizlato Case to Close After 10 Years of Operation." *Forbes*, 9 Feb. 2023, shorturl.at/uvzFR.

31 Generally, simply buying bitcoin would not classify the purchaser as a money services business. However, the specifics of the transaction can make the situation more complex. See Chapter 10.

32 When I reference buying bitcoin, I am talking about owning bitcoin directly and

to federal and state regulations on money services businesses and require you to provide information about your identity before being able to use their services. These types of platforms are often called "exchanges" as a shorthand, although most of the time when we discuss "exchanges" we are not referring to their intermediated exchange services that connect buyers and sellers together through a central order book, but their retail platform which acts more like a digital asset store through which the company sells crypto directly to its customers for a fee. Many platforms will allow you to use a bank card or connect your account to your bank in order to fund your purchase.

Centralized platforms often will let you withdraw digital assets to external wallets, including non-custodial wallets, but will, by default, act as a custodian of your funds. Digital assets held on centralized platforms are not subject to government insurance like FDIC or SIPIC, which guarantee fiat funds held in banks or securities held with regulated financial institutions up to a certain amount. This means you must have faith that that company is capable and trustworthy enough to hold your assets on your behalf. I encourage you to sign up for a few centralized platforms to explore their features. Be sure to do your due diligence before sending funds as there have been instances of centralized custodians failing either due to technical exploits or as a result of bad behavior.[33]

Bitcoin ATMs

Bitcoin ATMs (BTMs) look similar to a regular ATM and permit users to deposit cash or use a bank card to purchase bitcoin (or other digital assets) directly from the terminal. Most BTMs only allow a person to purchase bitcoin. This one-way functionality is primarily due to the time it takes to fully confirm an on-chain transaction. The best practice is that following an initial confirmation, you

---

not purchasing exposure to bitcoin through an exchange-traded product like an exchange-traded fund (ETF). In January 2024, following years of litigation, the SEC approved several Bitcoin ETFs. For more on the history that led to Wall Street providing a Bitcoin product, *see* shorturl.at/INQX2.

33 The two most prominent failures of digital asset platforms are Mt. Gox in 2014 and FTX in 2022. These platforms failed for different reasons, but both caused a tremendous fallout in the market. Mt. Gox is in Chapter 5. FTX's collapse is discussed in Chapter 15.

should wait for 3 to 6 additional confirmations (which at around 10 minutes a block means 30 to 60 minutes) before being confident the transaction is permanent. Because most users don't want to hang around a bodega waiting for the BTM to spit out cash, and the cost and complexity on the BTM operator that comes from integrating a withdrawal mechanism is high, most BTMs don't offer the option.

Centralized trading platforms are typically geared toward an investor class, which I don't think represents how most people who *use* bitcoin actually obtain it. One thing that always struck me from my work with BTM operators is that the demographics of BTM users skew toward non-white and immigrant customers living in poorer communities. Through my experience in the industry, I learned that BTM users are overrepresented by populations that are underbanked or who work in cash businesses and who use bitcoin as a supplement to their cash savings or to send money to family overseas without having to pay high remittance fees. The BTM customer profile and use case is much more aligned with the view taken by bitcoin users around the globe who have turned to digital assets as a financial tool rather than a discretionary investment.

Moreover, while centralized trading platforms are fantastic resources for buying digital assets, they are in some ways too easy to use to get a sense of how Bitcoin actually works. When you sign onto a centralized platform to purchase bitcoin with your debit card or through a bank transfer, the bitcoin is available in your account to use on the platform instantly and held on your behalf. I think these services are necessary for widespread adoption and don't have an issue with someone using them (I, in fact, work for one), but there is a high degree of trust being incorporated into a trustless system when you allow a company to hold crypto on your behalf. The common phrase among self-custody maximalists is "not your keys, not your bitcoin."

So, stepping back off of my soapbox, let's send you out into the world to find a BTM. It's hard to get an accurate number, but I've seen estimates that there are 30,000 to 60,000 machines in the United States. You can search for one near you at coinATMradar.com.
Before heading to a machine, I recommend doing your due diligence. Is the company registered as a Money Services Business

with FinCEN? They should be. Most operators that are FinCEN registered have their registration number listed on their website, and you can confirm it at fincen.gov/msb-state-selector. Depending on the state you are in, other registrations may be required (see Chapter 11).

Setting Up a Mobile Wallet

The ability to self-custody is one of Bitcoin's core features. In the United States, centralized platforms that sell digital assets will allow you to hold your crypto with them. Relying on an intermediary to hold your assets is convenient, but there are drawbacks to doing so, and the management and trustworthiness of the platform pose a counterparty risk to your digital asset holdings. For larger digital asset holdings, it is recommended that you purchase a hardware wallet such as a Trezor or Ledger and set up advanced security procedures such as multi-signature authentication.[34] But for most day-to-day transactions, and certainly for your use of a BTM, the preferable method of transacting with Bitcoin is through a non-custodial mobile software wallet.[35]

Assuming you have found a BTM operator you are comfortable using, the next step is to download a mobile digital wallet that allows you to receive bitcoin from the terminal. The process of setting up a mobile wallet is simple and usually doesn't involve much more effort than downloading the wallet onto your cell phone and following the in-app directions of setting up a pin and writing down the wallet's "seed phrase" which is a series of 12 or 24 randomly generated words that you can use to recover the wallet in the future. Be sure to write these down, put them in a safe place, and hope your house doesn't burn down.

My favorite Bitcoin wallet is Muun, which is available through the Apple and Google Play stores. It does not require you to input any

---

34 "Ledger vs Trezor: Best Crypto Wallets?" *YouTube*, MoneyZG, 1 May 2023, y2u.be/WpA1QP6yhU4.

35 Keep in mind that many wallets that enable you to transmit funds are custodial wallets offered by companies that hold digital assets on your behalf. For this exercise, be sure to download a non-custodial wallet.

personal data or sign up for an account.[36] A mobile Bitcoin wallet allows you to receive bitcoin through your on-chain public address.[37] Most ATMs will allow you to type your destination address in manually, but the easier method is to scan a QR code generated by your mobile wallet through a camera on the BTM.

Using the Bitcoin ATM

The transaction onboarding flow at a BTM varies, but don't be surprised if, before being able to purchase bitcoin, you have to provide some level of identifying information such as a phone number or state-issued ID. The requirements may vary depending on your state and the amount of bitcoin you wish to purchase, as well as how conservative the BTM operator is with its "know your customer" obligations. Once onboarded with the ATM, you'll be asked to deposit cash or use a bank card to purchase the bitcoin. Fair warning: Bitcoin ATMs tend to charge a non-immaterial service fee and also implement a very large spread on the price of bitcoin that is above the market rate. This makes BTMs an economically inefficient way to purchase large amounts of bitcoin, but for the $20 or so you should be purchasing on this first transaction consider it the price of a hands-on education.

After depositing your cash or using a bank card and scanning the QR address code from your mobile wallet, the ATM should provide you with a receipt for the transaction with a transaction ID. It should only take a minute or so for your mobile app to register that bitcoin has been sent to your wallet, but it will take about 10 minutes before the transaction receives its first confirmation and another 20-50 minutes before the bitcoin is considered fully settled. Because transaction data is public, you can use a "block explorer" to search for your public address or transaction ID to see the real-time confirmation status of your transaction.[38] Hitting refresh on the block explorer an

---

36 Muun allows both on-chain and Lightning Network transactions. For a tutorial, *see* "A Beautifully Designed Bitcoin & Lightning Wallet in One." *YouTube*, uploaded by All Things Bitcoin, y2u.be/rQJ8JEWOYHg.

37 For a guide to Bitcoin addresses, *see A Practical Guide to Bitcoin Addresses* at bitcoinbriefly.com/practical-guide-bitcoin-addresses-explained.

38 Blockchain.com/explorer is my preferred block explorer. Block explorers provide a

obnoxious number of times and waiting for your transaction to fully confirm is a necessary rite of passage for anyone in crypto.

Once settled, you should see the bitcoin in your mobile wallet. Congratulations, you have your first fraction of a bitcoin and are ready to start sending it.

A Note About "Holding" and "Sending" Bitcoin

It is often said that a user "holds" bitcoin in their digital wallet, which is secured by a private key. However, the notion that one can even take "custody" of bitcoin is misleading because it is a purely digital asset that exists only as a reflection of Bitcoin's community-managed public ledger. A more accurate description is that a digital wallet is just software that keeps track of the holder's crypto and maintains a private key that grants its holder control over the bitcoin that the network recognizes that they own. When one wishes to "send" bitcoin to a digital address, he or she affixes a digital signature to the transaction that, once confirmed valid by the network, starts the process of adding the transaction to the blockchain. When a transaction is made and subsequently authenticated by a consensus of participants on the network, a record of that transaction is etched permanently onto Bitcoin's public ledger. Nothing is literally "held" or "sent."

The general view is that because non-custodial wallets are just software that allows a user to self-custody digital assets and does not take actual custody or control of the assets, they fall outside of the type of regulations generally applicable to financial intermediaries, including FinCEN registration requirements. There is an effort by some in the United States to expand recordkeeping requirements to "unhosted", or non-custodial wallets, such that centralized institutions will be required to obtain information about the recipient of the unhosted wallet. This type of recordkeeping is already required in other parts of the world, but as of this writing, it is not in the United States. For

---

lot of information about a transaction's history, and an entire industry of forensics has developed around interpreting this public data. For a block explorer tutorial, *see* "How Cryptocurrency Transactions Work - Blockchain Explorer Tutorial." *YouTube*, Nugget's News, 3 Oct. 2019, y2u.be/Q-X4MgoKGPg.

further information, see the discussion on the Funds Travel Rule in Chapter 10.

Sending A Transaction

With bitcoin in hand, let's now make a few transactions that will help us further understand some additional concepts related to bitcoin and the broader crypto ecosystem. To do this, download a second wallet application onto your phone so you can send and receive transactions to yourself. I like using the Muun Wallet, but any self-custodial wallet integrated with the Lightning Network will work.

You should have noticed from your BTM transaction that there is a fair amount of friction present when making an on-chain transaction both in terms of the time and cost involved in receiving the digital assets. Bitcoin ATMs pass network fees to the user, and the transaction can take up to an hour to fully settle on network. These facts seemingly contradict the narrative of Bitcoin advocates that it enables fast and cheap digital transactions. I'll be the first to admit that sending on-chain transactions for relatively small amounts of bitcoin can be frustrating, but I think the generalized criticism is misplaced when comparing the Bitcoin network to fully settled traditional financial channels, particularly when transmitting in higher values. For example, one can send and fully settle a million dollars of bitcoin internationally in under an hour for usually a few bucks depending on network congestion. That's more efficient than any traditional financial network, but on its face, a bitcoin transaction can seem slower and more expensive than, say, a Visa transaction.

The relative "inefficiency" of on-chain bitcoin transactions is often pointed to as a failure of the Bitcoin network. Because network fees are dynamic and aren't directly correlated with the amount of bitcoin being sent, at times of great on-chain congestion, when fees are high, critics will argue that Bitcoin cannot succeed as a currency because the fees for purchasing something like a cup of coffee can be higher than the actual purchase price of the drink (to say nothing about the time it takes to settle and the price volatility of the asset).

Exploring Bitcoin's "Coffee Problem"

I believe Bitcoin's critics tend to miss a fundamental point when comparing the price and time it takes to send an on-chain bitcoin transaction with a Visa transaction, because the latter is not fully settled. When you swipe your bank card at a coffee shop, the money in your account is not sent in real-time to the merchant, and it often takes several days for the funds to make their way to their account. For the privilege of being able to accept payment via bank cards, the card networks charge a fee to the merchant and act as a continuous intermediary that can disrupt the permanence of the transaction should the customer initiate a chargeback.[39] Accordingly, comparing an intermediated transaction that subjects the recipient to a clawback months after the fact with an irreversible transaction as soon as it is fully settled in less than an hour is not exactly apples to apples.

However, even considering the value of fully settling a digital transaction in less than an hour, the point is well taken that the time and cost of an on-chain bitcoin transfer are impractical for most retail commerce. Bitcoin's "Coffee Problem" illustrates several practical concepts about its network and helps explain the current state of Bitcoin and the broader crypto ecosystem. There have been several proposals for how to solve the so-called "Coffee Problem.

Change Bitcoin

The original vision of Bitcoin was as an electronic cash system, and in the earliest days of the network, before there were enough users to materially impact network fees, a bitcoin could be sent for basically nothing. The irony of those halcyon days was that it was cheap to send bitcoin, but no one wanted to accept it. As bitcoin grew in popularity and more people began using the network, the cost to send bitcoin

---

[39] The Fair Credit Billing Act (FCBA) and the Electronic Fund Transfer Act (EFTA) provide consumers the right to dispute unauthorized transactions, with the former applying to credit card accounts and the latter to bank transfers and debit card transactions. The FCBA generally gives consumers 60-days to dispute a charge. The EFTA's timeline can vary on when the charge is disputed but allows up to 60 days for a dispute. In addition to these regulations, card networks like Visa and MasterCard have established their own rules—commonly referred to as the "120-day chargeback rule"—that extend the dispute period up to 120 days. Upon receiving a chargeback notification, the merchant's bank will typically debit the amount from the merchant's account and may assess a chargeback fee.

increased such that low-value transactions became unviable for the sender.

Every transaction made on the Bitcoin network requires data about that transaction to be written to a block on Bitcoin's blockchain. When Satoshi created Bitcoin, he designed each block to be mined approximately every 10 minutes and to contain a maximum of 1 MB of data. These parameters, including capping the total number of bitcoins at 21 million, are revered by many within the Bitcoin community but are arbitrary in design. There is nothing inherently special about these limits, and had Bitcoin been designed to allow, for example, twenty or fifty times the data per block or more, the network would still need to address scalability challenges at some point if Bitcoin is to achieve global adoption.[40] As Bitcoin adoption grows and the potential use cases for the network increase, its ability to scale to accommodate the unknown and potentially exponential future needs of the public is not something that could have been accomplished at the time of its design, no matter what block size Satoshi decided to use.

The desire to increase Bitcoin's ability to process transactions faster and with lower fees resulted in a movement within the Bitcoin community to push for a technical change to Bitcoin's design parameters. In some cases, this resulted in so-called "soft forks," such as the SegWit upgrade, which allowed more transaction data to be added to a block without increasing the block size limit. A soft fork allows a blockchain network to be upgraded without splitting the chain and creating a new cryptocurrency.[41]

In contrast to a soft fork, which can be implemented in a manner that keeps the network intact, a "hard fork" requires the network to split, leading to the creation of a separate chain and, therefore, a separate native digital asset. Anyone can create a hard fork of Bitcoin, but the new chain is only as viable as the community of people willing to dedicate resources to support it. In 2017, the debate within the

---

[40] *See* "Will Bitcoin Fail to Scale?" *YouTube,* Aantonop, 2 Apr. 2016, y2u.be/ bFOFqNK-Kns0.

[41] *See* "Soft Fork vs Hard Fork in Crypto." *YouTube*, Whiteboard Crypto, 11 Aug. 2021, y2u.be/Bu1GcyyFZ7w.

Bitcoin community over whether to increase the protocol's block size gained traction, and Bitcoin forked into a different chain dubbed Bitcoin Cash (BCH), which employed an 8 MB (and later increased to 32 MB) block size. While Bitcoin Cash enjoyed modest initial support, the network has not been able to match the support of the original Bitcoin protocol (BTC), and support for BCH has itself been cannibalized by additional hard forks of the Bitcoin Cash protocol, resulting in several other fringe assets in the market.

I think that when most people first learn of the blocksize debate the natural reaction is to side with the "Big Blockers" who seek to increase the number of transactions and lessen the cost of Bitcoin in a way that permits more people to utilize it as a cash replacement. Ultimately, it was the "Small Blockers" who ended up prevailing, and Bitcoin (BTC), the chain created by Satoshi with a mere 1 MB per block data limit, remains the dominant chain. Details of the merits of keeping the block size low are beyond the scope of this book but largely boil down to a concern that increasing the block size would make it too expensive for individuals to run nodes on home computers and could result in the Bitcoin network becoming more centralized. For a full review of the history and debate over increasing the blocksize, *see "The Blocksize War"*, discussed in Chapter 5.

Use a Different Coin

In the same way that one can fork the Bitcoin protocol to create a new version of Bitcoin like Bitcoin Cash, one can also create a new digital asset altogether. There are thousands of different digital assets and protocols in the market today, many implementing different features designed to address what the developers believe to be faults or limitations with Bitcoin's code. Some are based on copies of Satoshi's code, such as Litecoin, while others are bespoke protocols designed to increase the blockchain's functionality and facilitate faster transactions and more complex transaction types. We'll discuss the creation of Ethereum, a protocol created to address some of the perceived functional limitations of Bitcoin, in Chapter 7, but other examples are also explored throughout this book. As we will discuss, the strength of the Bitcoin Network is the infrastructure that has developed since its creation, which hardens the network and acts as a protective factor against attack. Because Bitcoin has had the chance to strengthen its network over such a long period of time, it will be challenging for any digital asset network created after Bitcoin to rival its network security.

While many Bitcoin alternatives (sometimes called "altcoins") aim to enhance or modify Bitcoin's transaction mechanism or broaden its functionality, a distinct category of digital asset known as "Privacy Coins" exists whose primary objective is to reduce the traceability of transactions. These coins are designed to obscure the record of the digital asset's transaction history and are subject to additional legal and regulatory considerations as compared to other digital assets, which can usually be traced pseudonymously by law enforcement. See Chapter 8 for further discussion.

Second Layer Solutions

Bitcoin's security is rooted in the strength and longevity of its network. For its advocates, the network's proven resilience should not be discarded for alternatives that compromise security for efficiency or ease of use. Many who see bitcoin as a safe-harbor currency actively discourage attempts to innovate the protocol in ways that, in their view, could result in centralizing the Network or undermining its security model. As was seen during the Blocksize War, "Small Blockers" that resisted increasing Bitcoin's blocksize did so at least partially out of a concern that increasing it would require more expensive hardware that could make it more difficult for individuals to run their own node, which, hypothetically, could lead to network centralization.

There is an argument that as hardware advances and the cost of data storage becomes less expensive, the concern that increasing the block size will lead to catastrophic centralization is overstated. Yet, for staunch Bitcoin supporters, even a theoretical compromise to Bitcoin's network security, regardless of actual centralization risk, is unacceptable. To those who see Bitcoin as the most important monetary advancement in our lifetime, there is no increase in efficiency worth even a hypothetical decrease to the network's security. This same instinct has sometimes seen Bitcoin advocates cheer higher network fees, even at the cost of disincentivizing usage, under the view that higher fees motivate miners to join and maintain the network.

I'll leave you to decide who's right, but for some who believe Bitcoin's existing structure cannot be matched and should not be materially adjusted, a potential solution to Bitcoin's scaling challenge is to use a payment layer that utilizes and leverages Bitcoin's existing network configuration. This type of infrastructure, which builds on and relies upon the base protocol, is called a "second layer."

The Lightning Network (LN) is the most popular second layer within the Bitcoin ecosystem. It operates on the notion that the security offered through Bitcoin's base layer is unparalleled but that the network cannot by itself meet global demands. LN is premised on the idea that you can decongest Bitcoin's network by allowing parties to pre-fund "payment channels" that move transactions off-chain. This allows parties to send cheap and near-instant transactions to each other because incremental transactions do not need to be recorded on-chain. Only when the parties close a payment channel is an on-chain transaction of the net transfer amount recorded.

As an analogy, imagine a gambler exchanging her cash for a casino's chips and then being able to use those chips to exchange value with the casino after each hand. As the gambler wins or loses, she exchanges chips with the casino but isn't required to wait in line to settle or record the number of chips she has with a cashier. When one sends bitcoin through the Lightning Network, the specific details of that transaction aren't immediately recorded on Bitcoin's blockchain. Instead, only the net outcome of all transactions made within that channel is written to the blockchain once the channel is closed.

Casino chips are very handy while gambling, but what if Alice wants to spend those chips at a nearby restaurant before heading back to the poker table? It would be inconvenient for her to have to cash out to exchange the funds back for chips after her meal. The Lightning Network addresses this by allowing Alice to pay Bob through any connected channel, whether they're directly linked or not. Think of it like this: Alice can spend chips at any restaurant partnered with the casino. That restaurant can then use the chips or exchange them for cash with the casino. As more places partner up, Alice can spend her chips even with businesses connected to her casino's partners. As more businesses partner with the casino or the casino's partners, Alice's ability to spend the casino's chips, even at establishments completely unconnected to the casino, increases. The Lightning Network similarly relies on a network effect that lets payments pass through numerous open payment channels such that a user like Alice can send a transaction to Bob even if they haven't opened a direct channel with each other so long as they are connected to each other through the network.[42]

I'll leave more details about the Lightning Network to the experts listed in the Supplemental Resource section, but one of the reasons I think it's important to highlight it is because it is illustrative of how difficult applying existing regulations or adopting new ones can be within the crypto ecosystem. It also demonstrates the challenges of explaining things by analogy because, while my casino example can help explain how the Lighting Network operates, it is imperfect and mischaracterizes the role of those operating payment channels in a critical way. Casinos are regulated to ensure the establishment has enough cash to exchange all outstanding chips. However, because the Lightning Network relies on pre-funded nodes secured through cryptographic multi-signature contracts, those who open a payment channel do not have the same ability to misuse funds as a casino entrusted with a player's assets. This raises the question of whether payment channels are technically or functionally custodial in nature and, therefore, whether those routing LN payments should (or even could) be regulated like a custodian or transferer of value.[43]

The current assumption by most is that simply operating an LN channel does not implicate payment regulations or trigger accompanying compliance obligations. At the very least, going after those participating in the Lightning Network's infrastructure does

---

[42] "Non-Technical: Lightning Network Explained." *YouTube*, Aantonop, 30 July 2020, y2ube/XCSfoiD8wUA.

[43] I should note the Lightning Network does not enjoy universal support. Some criticize LN channels as custodial in nature and less optimal than on-chain transactions. There is also a concern that routing transactions through large payment channels could lead to centralization. My experience with it is it works well but is still a niche payment method that hasn't been tested at scale. More information about LN is provided in the Supplemental Resources.

not seem to be a priority. Yet, there are emerging rules and guidelines that could be applied, including those that seek to regulate mixing devices like tumblers that obfuscate a transaction's history under the theory that the Lightning Network similarly pools or aggregates funds from multiple persons, wallets, addresses, or accounts. We'll explore these regulations in Chapter 10, but at this point, clarity is elusive.

Sending A Lightning Transaction

Initiating a bitcoin transaction through the Lightning Network looks a lot like making an on-chain bitcoin transaction. Within a Lightning-enabled Bitcoin wallet, you can generate a QR code or copy the destination address to receive funds as either an on-chain Bitcoin transaction or through the Lightning Network. To send bitcoin using the Lightning Network, copy your "Lightning Address" from the receiving wallet and paste it as the destination address in the mobile wallet you have bitcoin in. Then, send a small amount of BTC. I usually send $0.25 worth of BTC to illustrate the point. Once sent, you'll notice that the transaction is complete in only a few seconds for a usually pretty nominal fee.

If you took part in this little exercise, you just sent a quarter's worth of BTC to yourself almost instantly at virtually no cost.[44] While LN can be used to send much larger amounts, the potential of the Lightning Network shines at the micro level. For the first time, LN enables transactions as small as fractions of a penny worth of bitcoin for negligible fees in a way that broadens the use cases for crypto beyond mere savings and commerce. This technology introduces novel methods for us to engage with money. For instance, through LN, you could stream payments in bitcoin to an employee for every second they work, eliminating the need for bi-weekly payroll. LN can also be integrated into video games for micropayments or embedded within social media platforms, enabling users to reward content creators directly with sums that would otherwise be uneconomical

---

44 Bitcoin company Strike uses LN to facilitate near-instant international fiat transactions by transferring fiat to bitcoin, sending it internationally through LN, and converting the received bitcoin back to fiat. *See* "Jack Mallers vs the World." *YouTube*, What Bitcoin Did, 2021, y2u.be/7rExf6EKHW4.

to process.

As innovation across numerous sectors continues, the uses for fast, cheap, and decentralized payments will grow. We don't feel too far off from a future where two self-driving cars negotiating the right of way can initiate LN transactions with each other based on their owner's predetermined time and cost preferences—a notion that would have been dismissed as science fiction not long ago.

Reimagining Value

As we conclude our discussion on Bitcoin and transition to other digital assets, I'd like to reiterate a key takeaway from Chapter 2: Predicting the trajectory of this technology is impossible. Since Bitcoin gained mainstream recognition, many have predicted its downfall, citing scalability issues and perceived limited commercial viability. However, like all transformative technologies, Bitcoin has evolved over time. Its current form has been shaped by, among other things, enhancements to its protocol, the introduction of supporting technologies like LN, the availability of user-friendly digital wallets, and the growing acceptance of digital commerce alongside the recognition of many of the limitations of fiat currencies. The digital asset domain has undergone rapid change, and the ripple effect of continued innovation could be profound.

Being part of this ecosystem offers the opportunity to explore and understand its potential impacts firsthand. To illustrate, consider the fundamental nature of a Bitcoin transaction. When one transmits bitcoin, nothing is "sent" in a literal sense. It's merely an update to a ledger that signifies an agreed-upon change in value. Thus, the Bitcoin Network is not just a payment platform; it's the world's premier record-keeping tool. It just so happens to excel in documenting financial exchanges denominated in bitcoin. As Bitcoin and other decentralized systems expand, their applications extend beyond finance, encompassing other forms of expression. This raises interesting questions:

Does an LN transaction in which a nominal amount of bitcoin is used to signal support of an online publisher's content constitute a financial exchange?

Is using a digital asset to mint art to a blockchain a commercial transaction?

If one uses Bitcoin to immutably embed a revolutionary message within a block's data, does that turn an otherwise pecuniary action into a political one?

The broader and more innovative uses of Bitcoin and decentralized networks generally transcend commercial intent. If digital assets can be utilized both as money and as gateways to more innovative behaviors, how do we regulate the dual uses of digital currencies to facilitate both commerce and broader expressive capabilities?[45]

For the first time, Bitcoin and other related technologies enable the expression of value in a way that is no longer tethered to the medium of fiat currencies or the inefficiencies of its centralized processors. This breakthrough allows the full spectrum of transactional sentiments to be used for the first time. As a society, we are just starting to appreciate its ramifications.

Supplemental Resources[46]

The Supplemental Resources referenced in Chapter 4 provide practical and technical details on sending and receiving bitcoin on-chain. Additional resources about the Lightning Network are provided below.

- **O'Brien, Matt. "The History of Lightning: From Brainstorm to Beta."** *Bitcoin Magazine* bitcoinmagazine.com/technical/history-lightning-brainstorm-beta.

- **Antonopoulos, Andreas M., et al.** *Mastering the Lightning Network: A Second Layer Blockchain Protocol for Instant Bitcoin Payments.* O'Reilly

---

45 I explore the potential First Amendment implications of non-financial bitcoin use cases in *Bitcoin is Speech: Notes Toward Developing the Conceptual Contours of Its Protection Under the First Amendment*. Justin S. Wales and Richard J. Ovelmen, 74 U. Mia. L. Rev. 204 (2019) available at: repository.law.miami.edu/umlr/vol74/iss1/6.

46 For ease of reference, all Supplemental Resources and footnote links are available at www.TheCryptoLegalHandbook.com/Resources.

Media, 2022. This book by Andreas Antonopoulos provides a technical deep dive into the concept of Layer 2s and the Lightning Network.

- **Antonopoulos, Andreas. "The Lightning Network."** *YouTube,* **playlist by Aantonop,** shorturl.at/hmnST.

CHAPTER 7

From Global Ledger to World Computer

Bitcoin's functionality is constrained by its design. The network is specialized for processing and recording bitcoin transactions, and though it offers additional capabilities, they are currently narrow and not particularly user-friendly. Advocates of Bitcoin value its simplicity, associating a limited scope with increased security. They contend that Bitcoin's strength is its focus on being a financial system that resists censorship and central control. However, decentralized networks can have broader applications. The Ethereum network was the first to capitalize on this potential by providing an infrastructure designed to accommodate an array of digital activities beyond financial transactions.

Ethereum ranks second by market capitalization among digital asset networks, but it wasn't the immediate successor to Bitcoin. In the years following Bitcoin's emergence, several cryptocurrencies debuted, each altering or expanding on elements of Satoshi's design. These early alternatives to Bitcoin, some of which are discussed below, largely aimed to mirror Bitcoin's function as a parallel payment system.

- **Litecoin (LTC)** was founded in 2011 by Charlie Lee (@SatoshiLite). It was designed to be a 'lighter' and more experimental version of Bitcoin and is often described as the silver to Bitcoin's gold, although that description tends to overstate its present standing in the market. It is a direct fork of Bitcoin's core blockchain code, meaning it shares much of the same foundation. Like Bitcoin, Litecoin uses a Proof of Work consensus mechanism, although it allows for transactions to occur faster and cheaper than with Bitcoin. The digital asset has remained modestly popular since its creation.[47]

- **Namecoin**, launched in 2011, aimed to enhance Bitcoin's utility by using a Proof of Work mechanism to establish a censorship-resistant domain name system for the ".bit" top-level-domain. It was designed to allow information about the .bit domain's ownership to be recorded and maintained on its blockchain and aimed to serve a broader function than as a purely transactional network. The .bit domain never really took off and the project is largely inactive.[48]

- **Peercoin**, launched in 2012, was the first cryptocurrency to use both a Proof of Stake (PoS) and Proof of Work consensus mechanism. This hybrid system aimed to reduce the energy consumption associated with Bitcoin's PoW system. Peercoin's introduction of PoS allowed users to "mint" new coins by holding onto existing ones. This approach marked a shift in the way cryptocurrencies could achieve distributed consensus and security. Peercoin has not maintained a significant presence in the market.

- **XRP** was created by Ripple Labs, Inc. in 2012 and is the native digital asset of the Ripple payment protocol. It was designed to enable quick, cost-effective cross-border payments. Unlike Bitcoin's decentralized consensus mechanism, in which anyone can join the network and validate transactions, XRP transactions are verified by a network of independent servers trusted by Ripple Labs. In Chapter 15, we will explore XRP in the context of a lawsuit by the Securities and Exchange Commission that alleged XRP sold by Ripple Labs and its executives were unregistered securities. In July 2023, Judge Analisa Torres of the Southern District of New York held that XRP tokens, in and of themselves, are not securities and issued summary judgment against the SEC on several of its claims. The SEC has indicated it

---

[47] "Litecoin (LTC): A Beginner's Guide to the Peer-to-Peer Cryptocurrency." *Cointelegraph*, shorturl.at/fpx59.

[48] NFTing. "History of Namecoin: A Token Forked from Bitcoin's Blockchain." *Medium*, 8 Nov. 2022, shorturl.at/uJPW5.

will appeal the ruling.[49]

- **Dogecoin (DOGE)** was created in 2013 as a joke inspired by an internet meme featuring a Shiba Inu dog. Unlike Bitcoin's finite supply, Dogecoin was created with no cap on the number of coins that can be created. Despite its playful beginnings, the project has retained a significant market cap and enjoys an active community of supporters that include financial luminaries like Elon Musk and Snoop Doggy Dogg.[50]

Bitcoin's initial progeny all shared, for the most part, Satoshi's goal of creating a network that facilitated the transaction of its native digital asset, usually with the added objective of making transactions faster and cheaper than possible with Bitcoin. Even a digital asset like Namecoin, which enabled information about domain name registration for .bit domains to be written into its blockchain, were narrowly designed. It was with this background in mind that a 19-year-old computer programmer named Vitalik Buterin shared his vision to repurpose Satoshi's innovative design for the loftier ambition of creating what he thought of as a "World Computer."

Vitalik Buterin and the Ethereum Network

The Ethereum network was created by Vitalik Buterin (@VitalikButerin), who, along with several co-founders, launched the network and its native currency, ether (ETH), on July 30, 2015. Like bitcoin, ether can be used as a digital currency that is capable of being sent, received, or self-custodied without reliance on an intermediary. At launch (and until a 2022 change to a Proof of Stake consensus mechanism), the Ethereum network employed a Proof of Work structure similar to Bitcoin in which a global set of participants were rewarded with new ether for expending energy required to validate transactions. However, where the Bitcoin network functioned primarily as a way to track ownership of its native currency, Vitalik envisioned ether as primarily a resource that holders could employ to execute "smart contracts" or run "decentralized applications"

---

49 "What Is Ripple: Overview, History and XRP Cryptocurrency." *Cointelegraph,* shorturl.at/koO69. *See* discussion on the SEC's case against Ripple Labs in Chapter 15.

50 Copeland, Tim. "A Brief History of Dogecoin." *The Block,* 18 Sept. 2023, rb.gy/7j359p.

(dApps).

The history of Ethereum's founding is a fascinating story that is detailed in the supplemental resources section of this chapter. *The Cryptopians: Idealism, Greed, Lies, and the Making of the First Big Cryptocurrency Craze* by Laura Shin (@LauraShin) is a particularly good read that chronicles the many efforts of Vitalik and his co-founders to not only develop the Ethereum network, but to grow, protect, and promote it. This included not only the network's technical development, but also selling ether to investors before launch to raise capital that went into the project, facilitating secondary markets for the asset, setting up foundations and businesses to promote its growth and functionality, and, as discussed below, exerting influence on network participants to fork the network following a hack of a decentralized application called "The DAO."

The continuing role of the Ethereum founders in the lasting success of their project raises a number of interesting questions about the policy and rules implicated by the issuance of digital assets. A network requires a critical mass of participants in order to achieve a meaningful degree of decentralization. Satoshi's innovation was to create a mechanism in the form of a native digital asset that incentivizes participation in the network. While Bitcoin was able to grow somewhat organically, most founders desire to take on a more lasting and active role than Satoshi did in their project's growth. It remains an open question not only what role a project's founders can take before regulations on the unregistered issuance of securities are implicated but also to what degree early efforts taint a native token's ability to be lawfully traded in the future.

The World's Computer

In order to have a meaningful discussion about the legal ramifications of either the initial or subsequent sales of ether, it is vital to understand the role the digital asset plays within the Ethereum network and the broad and ever-expanding variety of activities it can facilitate for its users. I encourage you to start by reading the opening pages of Vitalik Buterin's 2014 Ethereum Whitepaper, titled "*Ethereum: A Next-Generation Smart Contract and Decentralized Application Platform*," which details how Ethereum sought to improve upon Bitcoin's design for a more expansive vision.[51] As the title itself indicates, Ethereum was designed to be a more versatile and functional platform than Bitcoin's *"Peer-to-Peer Electronic Cash System."*

While the Bitcoin network can support a number of non-monetary functions, and ether can indeed be transferred as a form of digital cash, each project has been optimized to achieve its core purpose. Bitcoin prioritizes monetary soundness and network security, while Ethereum is designed to allow for expansive functionality. Each network caters to distinct objectives and user communities. The divergence of Ethereum from Bitcoin's core principles is creatively explored in a short speech by Andreas Antonopoulos called "The Lion & the Shark: Bitcoin vs Ethereum: Divergent Evolution in Cryptocurrency" which offers a helpful perspective for how to conceptualize Ethereum within the broader digital asset ecosystem.[52]

The Ethereum network allows users to interact with a diverse and expanding array of smart contracts without the permission of any centralized company or person. A smart contract is a self-executing code deployed on a network that automates processes or agreements. Despite its name, smart contracts are not 'smart' in that they can't learn or adapt, nor are they 'contracts' in the traditional legal sense. But it sounds cool.

The Ethereum Network employs a decentralized computational engine called the Ethereum Virtual Machine (EVM) that interprets and executes a smart contract's code independently of any centralized intermediary. For every computation on the network, users must compensate the EVM and, by extension, the validators maintaining the network, by paying a "gas fee" in ether. The complexity of the action determines the gas fee, so the more steps or computations an action requires, the more that action will cost.[53]

---

51 The original 2014 Ethereum White Paper and an updated version from 2015 are available at ethereum.org/whitepaper.

52 "Remastering the Lion & the Shark: Bitcoin vs Ethereum: Divergent Evolution in Cryptocurrency." *YouTube*, Aantonop, 7 Jan 2022, y2u.be/y-S8hOQIBnI.

53 As an example, a simple action like sending ether from one wallet to another requires 21,000 gas units. To calculate the fee, multiply the number of gas units (21,000) by the

The Ethereum network relies on a community of users worldwide to validate transactions, which are themselves required to execute actions on the network. Transactions made through the Ethereum network are grouped into blocks and confirmed by a validator before being written into Ethereum's blockchain. Blocks are validated approximately every 12 seconds, and nodes around the world maintain the record of all validated blocks. Validators are rewarded with newly minted ether and transaction fees for their role.

Note that requiring users to pay a fee to interact with the network acts as a crucial security measure, deterring malicious actors from overloading Ethereum's system. This fee mechanism can lead to increased costs during periods of high demand, potentially making some functions less economically feasible. To address these challenges, various strategies have been proposed for scaling the Ethereum network, including technical improvements and the implementation of layer 2 solutions, which aim to enhance transaction throughput and reduce costs. Additionally, the limitations of the Ethereum network have opened up opportunities for alternative smart contract platforms, such as Solana and Cardano, among many others, which offer different approaches to scalability and have emerged as potential competitors.

The Merge

When Ethereum launched, it utilized a Proof of Work consensus mechanism like Bitcoin's that compensated miners who validated transactions by expending computational energy with newly created ether. With Bitcoin's rising popularity and its increasing energy demands for transaction validation, criticisms about the amount of energy required to maintain the Bitcoin network developed. Discussions regarding Ethereum's shift to an eco friendly Proof

---

price of gas, which the user sets based on how quickly they want their transaction processed. Gas prices are denoted in "gwei", a unit of ether equal to one billion "wei", which is the smallest divisible unit of ether. Assuming a user sets a gas price of 100 gwei, the transaction would require 2,100,000 gwei, or 0.0021 ether, to complete.

For a deeper dive into how gas fees are calculated, see "What Is Ethereum Gas? (Examples + Easy Explanation)." *YouTube*, Whiteboard Crypto, 25 Apr. 2021, y2u.be/3ehaSqwUZ0s. The Ethereum Foundation also provides an explanation of gas fees at ethereum.org/gas.

of Stake model have been present since its inception. This model supplants energy-intensive mining with a system where validators are chosen to process transactions and form new blocks based on the amount of ether they lock up or 'stake' as collateral, thereby reducing energy consumption. Ethereum finalized its transition to a PoS consensus mechanism on September 15, 2022, an event known as "The Merge." Since the transition, the network has rewarded validators with new ether proportional to the amount of Ethereum they have staked as collateral.[54]

The Merge reminds us of the evolutionary potential of decentralized networks. It also underscores how Ethereum's founders, especially Vitalik Buterin, who played a crucial role in advocating for the PoS transition, remain key figures in ether's development. The continued influence of its founders, in contrast to the anonymous creator of Bitcoin, brings complexity to the regulatory analysis of these two assets. Identifying the material differences between ether and other tokens that have been alleged to be securities has perplexed the industry and underscores the need for meaningful guidance.[55]

Going to the Moon

Ethereum was first announced to the public at a Bitcoin conference in Miami on January 23, 2014. I encourage you to watch the announcement, which, despite being more than ten years old, provides a prescient image for much of the development within the broader digital asset industry.[56] This book touches on some of the uses for decentralized networks, but its scope is limited, describing only those uses that have resulted in either significant legal or regulatory developments.
The vision for what Ethereum could become resonated with many in that Miami auditorium, and as word spread, people around the

---

54 "Ethereum Merge - the Most Anticipated Event in Crypto Explained." *YouTube*, Finematics 3 Aug. 2022, y2u.be/EEuPmA8w0Kc.

55 Opinions are divided regarding PoW's environmental impact. For an overview of the debate, see "Breaking down the Bitcoin Energy Debate w/ Nic Carter (Castle Island)." *YouTube*, Coinbase, 27 Aug. 2022, y2u.be/w1MW5iS43jU.

56 "Vitalik Buterin Reveals Ethereum at Bitcoin Miami 2014." *YouTube*, Ethereum 1 Feb. 2014, y2u.be/l9dpjN3Mwps.

world were eager to support it. Because the Ethereum network was designed such that the digital asset ether was needed to run all sorts of advanced functions, many were keen to get their hands on ether even before the network's launch. Given that the price of bitcoin had already grown exponentially, a significant amount of the interest in Ethereum was likely due to a belief that the value of ether would experience a similar growth.

Between July 22 and September 2, 2014, the Ethereum Foundation, a Swiss non-profit incorporated to support Ethereum's development, offered and sold supporters the opportunity to purchase pre-mined ether at a discount to its price at launch. The pre-sale of ether raised 31,591 bitcoin (valued at $18.4 million dollars at the time), which the Ethereum Foundation used to fund the development of the project. The success of the ether pre-sale and the demonstration of an alternative funding model that did not require giving up equity to venture capitalists inspired countless projects to raise capital through what would be termed "Initial Coin Offerings" or "ICOs." These initial token sales became the first source of regulatory activity in the digital asset space by the Securities and Exchange Commission and are explored in Chapter 15.[57]

The Ethereum network launched on July 30, 2015, introducing a blockchain designed for more than just processing cryptocurrency transactions. This innovation opened up a world of possibilities for decentralized applications, sparking significant interest and investment from both the crypto community and mainstream audiences. As experimentation on the network progressed, the value of ether grew.

This period saw the launch of numerous new projects and tokens. While some projects released tokens with minimal practical use, serving mainly as a new fundraising method, others introduced tokens that were, at least theoretically, necessary for a decentralized application to function. A technical standardization for Ethereum-

---

[57] "Token" typically refers to a digital asset that exists on a pre-established blockchain, such as those created using the Ethereum network. "Cryptocurrency" generally describes the native digital asset of a blockchain, such as bitcoin or ether. "Coin" is used more flexibly, encompassing both.

based tokens called ERC-20 was introduced in 2015 that simplified the token creation process and allowed developers to create new tokens that could be sold to the public easily.[58] In 2017, nearly $5 billion dollars in capital was raised through ICO sales. Because most of the new tokens entering the market were ERC-20 tokens, interest in these assets increased the demand for ether. By the end of 2017, at the peak of what we now call the "ICO bubble," the price of one ether surged from less than $3 to over $1,400.

Token Sales and Regulatory Gymnastics

Many (maybe most) tokens sold during the ICO bubble were pure money grabs. I'm aware of many projects that were well into development that added a token for the sole purpose of being able to sell it to the public through an ICO. Putting the opportunists aside, there are clearly at least some instances in which a token is necessary for a project's success because it provides a network with an economic incentive that attracts supporters. If a meaningful level of decentralization is a requirement for network security, and the distribution of tokens across a wide population is needed to increase decentralization, how can a project's creators attract enough initial supporters to the project to make the network viable? This is a challenging question for any project, but one made even more difficult in the United States, which has rules restricting the sale of securities to the public.

Many projects, enticed by the promise of easy money, threw caution to the wind and sold pre-mined tokens directly to the public with a promise that their value would increase. Others recognized that the direct public sale of tokens into the U.S. market could trigger scrutiny from U.S. regulators. While there are many novel theories on how to get a token to market, it is important to understand that actually registering the token with the SEC is not one of them. There are numerous reasons why, many of which are outlined in Paradigm's multi-part article "Due to SEC Inaction, Registration is Not a Viable

---

58 ERC-20 is an "Ethereum Request for Comment" proposal that created a standard for fungible tokens on the Ethereum blockchain. For more information *see* "Marcobello, Mason. "What Are EIP and ERC and How Are They Connected?" *CoinDesk*, 11 May 2023, shorturl.at/pqCUZ.

Path for Crypto Projects."[59] In short, the registration of securities in the United States is a long and expensive process under the best circumstances, but because the registration process was designed primarily to accommodate the listing of shares of company stock, the process is unsuitable for most tokens, as it presumes an issuer-security relationship that does not exist in decentralized systems. As explained in Part 2 of the Paradigm article, nearly every project that attempted to register a token with the SEC has failed to either become registered or has failed as a result of their registration.[60]

Many projects attempted to avoid U.S. restrictions by actually, or at least cosmetically, blocking the initial sale of tokens to U.S. persons under the Regulation S exemption of the Securities Act, which exempts securities sold outside of the United States from registration. For others, including those eager to raise money from U.S.-based venture capitalists, there was a theory that a project could sell a promise to deliver tokens in the future under Regulation D of the Securities Act, which permits the unregistered sale of securities in certain instances to "accredited investors" that meet a wealth threshold.[61]

A popular strategy to leverage Reg D was the "SAFT," an acronym for "Simple Agreement for Future Tokens." The rationale behind SAFTs was that although the agreement to sell tokens to an investor might be a security, the tokens themselves, which would be delivered when a related network was fully operational, are not themselves securities. The theory was that as the tokens had some utility potential because they were needed to interact with a network, the tokens themselves had the characteristics of a commodity.[62] SAFTs gained popularity during the ICO boom and, with it, the characterization of a generation

---

[59] "Due to SEC Inaction, Registration Is Not a Viable Path for Crypto Projects." *Paradigm Policy*, policy.paradigm.xyz/writing/secs-path-to-registration-part-i.

[60] "Lessons from Crypto Projects' Failed Attempts to Register with the SEC." *Paradigm Policy*, policy.paradigm.xyz/writing/secs-path-to-registration-part-ii.

[61] To qualify as an accredited investor, individuals must are generally required to have an annual income exceeding $200,000, or a net worth exceeding $1 million, either alone or together with a spouse, excluding the value of their primary residence. *See* sec.gov/education/capitalraising/building-blocks/accredited-investor.

[62] The original SAFT proposal is available at saft-project.org.

of digital assets as "Utility Tokens," a phrase that has fallen out of fashion but was intended to signal that the token would serve some practical purpose within a network.

Since their introduction, the legal community has debated the usefulness of SAFTs in avoiding U.S. regulatory scrutiny. At least three courts have pierced the instrument to attach liability to its issuers, which has caused the use of SAFTs to decline. However, while the industry has largely stopped using SAFTs, its underlying premise, that a token might not itself be a security even when sold as part of a broader securities offering, has found some judicial support. We'll discuss these cases at length in Chapter 15.

The DAO

Of the thousands of projects launched on Ethereum, the DAO was the most impactful for Ethereum and the crypto industry at large. DAO stands for "Decentralized Autonomous Organization," a structure enabling the decentralized governance of a project through the distribution of tokens that give its holders a vote in a project's direction. Information about DAOs is generally available in Chapter 9, but the focus here is on *the* DAO, a project launched in April 2016 that would nearly destroy Ethereum by June of the same year.

The DAO was a decentralized venture capital fund. It operated through smart contracts and allowed investors to send ether to the DAO in exchange for DAO tokens, which granted voting rights on proposed projects. The project was wildly successful in terms of funding, raising over $150 million of ether at the time. However, in June 2016, the DAO's smart contract was exploited, leading to the theft of approximately one-third of the DAO's funds. This incident sent shockwaves through the Ethereum community and raised serious concerns about the security of smart contracts and the long-term viability of Ethereum itself.

In response to the DAO hack, Ethereum's founders proposed a divisive solution: a "hard fork" of the Ethereum blockchain to return the stolen funds. This decision sparked mixed reactions within the community. Supporters of the fork argued that, given the hack's occurrence early in Ethereum's history, intervention was crucial to preserve network confidence and ensure the project's longevity. In contrast, critics contended that this move contradicted the principle of immutability and signaled a worrying potential for centralized influence, conflicting with Ethereum's foundational vision.

Ultimately, a hard fork was implemented in July 2016, resulting in two separate blockchains: a new chain that refunded the DAO investors that took on the Ethereum (ETH) name, and the original Ethereum blockchain that would be renamed "Ethereum Classic" (ETC).[63] On July 25, 2017, the Securities and Exchange Commission published its first substantive analysis of the application of securities regulations to digital assets in a report about the DAO that determined that the sale of DAO tokens constituted the sale of unregistered securities under the Securities Act of 1933 and Exchange Act of 1934.[64]

I encourage you to read *The DAO Report* carefully as it is viewed by the SEC as a "line in the sand" moment which the Commission believes put the industry on notice of its position on digital assets. I also urge you to read it critically and consider how applicable the guidance published in *The DAO Report* is to the broader industry. The DAO was envisioned as a decentralized venture capital fund that provided DAO token holders with a share of the collective profits earned from investment activities. That arrangement is uniquely characteristic of a security, and the fact that DAO tokens were tokens and not, say, shares in a traditional venture capital fund does not materially change the analysis. We'll discuss *The DAO Report* more in Chapter 15, but, as you read it, note that while it provides the SEC's perspective on the DAO Token specifically, and perhaps primary token sales by issuers generally, the more persistent question facing the industry of how to characterize secondary market sales of tokens is not addressed.

---

63 Note the naming conventions that followed major forks. When Bitcoin underwent a fork that resulted in Bitcoin Cash, the original chain kept the name 'Bitcoin.' In contrast, following Ethereum's hard fork, the original chain was named 'Ethereum Classic,' while the new chain took the name 'Ethereum.'

64 United States Securities and Exchange Commission. Report of Investigation Pursuant to Section 21(a) of the Securities Exchange Act of 1934: The DAO. 25 July 2017, bit.ly/3IpiWDt.

Is Ether A Security?

Ethereum demonstrated that a decentralized blockchain can serve purposes beyond just being a transaction ledger, an innovation that has led to significant developments within the crypto ecosystem. The extensive utilization of smart contracts has driven notable growth across the sector, not only on Ethereum, but also on networks like Solana, Cardano, and others that have developed their own smart-contract-enabled ecosystems. In each instance, a token is required for users to interact with an underlying network to take advantage of their full range of capabilities.

Unlike Bitcoin, whose founder is unaccounted for, the Ethereum founding team is still active. Vitalik Buterin still acts as the spiritual spokesperson for Ethereum and often speaks and writes about the direction of the network.[65] The rest of the founding team also remains active and influential.[66] Whereas we have very little indication that Satoshi Nakamoto took any material actions to promote Bitcoin beyond his posts, the early days and influence of Ethereum's founders are well documented. As you read about Ethereum's early history, note that the founders took an active role in selling and marketing ether to the public, establishing foundations and businesses whose goal was to develop Ethereum-based products, persuading exchanges to list ether for secondary sales, and working with lawyers and regulators to address the potential legal implications of distributing and promoting the network's token.

The Ethereum founders' endeavors to grow Ethereum and popularize ether have introduced a challenging regulatory question with respect to whether to classify ether as a security or not. As we'll discuss in detail in Chapter 14, a Supreme Court decision called *Howey* from the 1940s involving the sale of contracts for the maintenance of orange groves in Florida set forth the test for determining whether an asset fits into the Securities Act's catch-all designation of an

---

65 Vitalik's website, which is where he often comments on Ethereum's direction is vitalik.eth.limo.

66 Ethereum's co-founders include Gavin Wood, founder of Polkadot; Charles Hoskinson, creator of Cardano, Anthony Di Iorio, developer of the Jaxx wallet; and Joseph Lubin, founder of ConsenSys, a company that builds Ethereum-based tools and infrastructure.

"investment contract." Under the *Howey* Test, something is an investment contract if it involves 1) an investment of money; 2) in a common enterprise; 3) with the expectation of profits; 4) resulting from the efforts of others. Each factor has been the subject of judicial determinations that can differ from one jurisdiction to another.

There is a debate over whether the *Howey* factors could be met with respect to the direct initial sales of ether made to U.S. persons in 2014. Luckily for the founders, the federal statute of limitations on the sale of unregistered securities is 5 years. But even before that expiration, in a 2018 speech by its then Division of Corporate Finance Director William Hinman, the SEC indicated that while the *initial* sale of ether may have been an investment contract under *Howey*, the network had achieved a sufficient level of decentralization such that secondary market sales of ether do not constitute securities because the efforts of the Ethereum founders or other third parties are no longer the primary factor in the profitability of ether as an investment. As Director Hinman explained:

> So, when I look at Bitcoin today, I do not see a central third party whose efforts are a key determining factor in the enterprise. The network on which Bitcoin functions is operational and appears to have been decentralized for some time, perhaps from inception. Applying the disclosure regime of the federal securities laws to the offer and resale of Bitcoin would seem to add little value. And putting aside the fundraising that accompanied the creation of Ether, based on my understanding of the present state of Ether, the Ethereum network and its decentralized structure, current offers and sales of Ether are not securities transactions.[67]

While Mr. Hinman's words would appear to put the question of ether's classification to rest, the SEC has never *officially* conceded that ether is not a security. In fact, the Commission and its Commissioner, Gary Gensler, have gone out of their way to avoid answering this

---

67 Hinman, William, Director, Division of Corporation Finance, SEC. "Digital Asset Transactions: When Howey Met Gary (Plastic)." 14 June 2018, bit.ly/2l8t5dB.

question directly.[68] Despite this reluctance, the SEC has never alleged that ether is a security.

Supplemental Resources[69]

- **Shin, Laura. *The Cryptopians: Idealism, Greed, Lies, and the Making of the First Big Cryptocurrency Craze*. Public Affairs, 2023.** Laura Shin (@LauraShin) is a well-regarded reporter and host of the Unchained Podcast (@UnchainedCrypto). This book details the development and early history of Ethereum's founding and is, in my view, the best place to start for an understanding of Ethereum's history and the direction it led the broader crypto industry.

- **Antonopoulos, Andreas M. *Mastering Ethereum*. Stanford University Press, 2021.**

- **Antonopoulos, Andreas. "Ethereum Q&A." *YouTube*, playlist by Aantonop,** shorturl.at/gCKX4.

- **"Ethereum Documentary." *YouTube*, 11 July 2021,** y2u.be/oai9_Bw2baM.

---

68 *See* clip from April 2023 hearing before the House Financial Services Committee, in which Chair Gensler refuses to answer the question directly. y2u.be/aIcNGfF8FDA.

69 For ease of reference, all Supplemental Resources and footnote links are available at www.TheCryptoLegalHandbook.com/Resources.

CHAPTER 8

Privacy Coins and Stablecoins

Since Bitcoin's launch, numerous alternative assets have been introduced that are designed to enable faster transactions at cheaper fees. Some of these are forks of Bitcoin itself, like Bitcoin Cash, or based on Bitcoin's code, like Litecoin. Generally speaking, projects that have competed with Bitcoin by offering a "payment coin" that is differentiated primarily in that it offers more efficient or cheaper transactions have, over time, trended downward and the market has prioritized Bitcoin's robust security infrastructure over transactional ease.

There are two categories of "payment coins" that have differentiated themselves from the Bitcoin clones and have drawn a material share of the market: privacy coins and stablecoins.

I. Privacy Coins

Privacy coins are a class of cryptocurrencies that promote anonymity for their users. Unlike cryptocurrencies like Bitcoin, which while pseudonymous, are still traceable on the blockchain, privacy coins use a variety of methods to obscure the details and histories of transactions.

The emergence of privacy coins can be traced back to concerns over the transparency and traceability of cryptocurrencies. While the blockchain technology underlying assets is praised for its transparency, it also means that all transactions are publicly visible and permanently recorded. This openness, coupled with the development of a robust industry of crypto forensic firms and tools, raises privacy concerns that led to the development of anonymity-focused alternatives. Notable examples of privacy coins include:

- **Dash (DASH)**: Originally launched as XCoin in January 2014, it was later rebranded to Darkcoin and ultimately Dash in March 2015. Dash is a cryptocurrency that began as a fork of Bitcoin. Its goal was to improve upon Bitcoin, aiming to provide faster transaction speeds and enhanced privacy features. This is accomplished primarily through an optional service Dash offers called PrivateSend, which enables senders to obscure the origins of a transaction.

  While Dash and Bitcoin share certain technological and historical similarities, Dash introduced a mechanism called Masternodes into its infrastructure that allows users to use DASH as collateral in exchange for network governance rights and other functionalities. As you'll recall, the SEC has determined that bitcoin is not a security subject to SEC jurisdiction. However, the SEC, in an action against digital asset platforms Coinbase and Bittrex, has argued that Dash's use of Masternodes distinguishes it from Bitcoin and that the privacy coin should be treated as a security.[70] The case against Bittrex was settled in August 2023 without a judicial ruling on the SEC's theory, and the Coinbase case is pending. The SEC has not directly brought any action against Dash's issuers.[71]

- **Monero (XMR)**: Launched in April 2014 by a Bitcointalk forum user known as "thankful_for_today," Monero was taken over and led by a group of community members including Riccardo Spagni, alias "Fluffypony" (@fluffypony). A focus on decentralization and scalability drove Monero's creation, and it has since become renowned for its privacy capabilities. It employs features such as Ring Signatures, Stealth Addresses, and Ring Confidential Transactions to promote complete privacy in transactions. This approach makes Monero unique among the privacy coins listed here, as it offers inherent and non-optional

---

70 *SEC v. Bittrex Inc.* No. 2:23-cv-00580, Complaint, DOC 1, pp. 37-40. WD Wash. 17 Apr. 2023. CourtListener, shorturl.at/MRTY0; *SEC v. Coinbase, Inc.* No. 1:23-cv-04738, Complaint, Doc 1, pp. 73-76. SDNY. Filed 6 June 2023. CourtListener, shorturl.at/gstxR.

71 *See* "Dash 101 - Why Do We Need Digital Cash?" *YouTube*, Dash, 23 Jan 2018, y2u.be/DzH7cMbZQHI.

privacy for all users and transactions on its network.[72]

- **Z-Cash (ZEC)**: Z-Cash, originally known as "Zerocoin" and later "Zerocash," was launched in October 2016 by Zooko Wilcox-O'Hearn (@zooko) in collaboration with cryptographers from institutions like MIT and Johns Hopkins. Z-Cash is distinguished by its implementation of zk-SNARKs, a form of zero-knowledge cryptography, enabling transaction validation without revealing any sensitive information. This technology allows Z-Cash users to choose between private and transparent transactions, offering the flexibility to maintain privacy or opt for transparency as needed.[73]

Privacy coins have been scrutinized by regulatory bodies concerned about their use in illicit activities. There have been formal and informal efforts to restrict the use of privacy coins in numerous jurisdictions, including the United States. In some cases, this is the result of indirect pressure by regulators on banks, auditors, and insurance companies to stop providing services to companies that support privacy coins. As a result of these pressures, some digital asset platforms have restricted the ability to purchase certain privacy-enhanced assets.

Putting aside for a moment the question of what restrictions the government can, or should, place on the ability to transact privately, a preliminary challenge in developing regulations on "privacy coins" is the difficulty of defining what constitutes a "privacy coin" in the first place. Privacy is not a binary concept but exists on a continuum, with projects occupying different positions on this spectrum.

Consider a Bitcoin transaction from a self-custodied wallet; while not typically thought of as a "private" transaction, it is pseudonymous and, therefore, offers more privacy than swiping a bank card or sending a wire. Z-Cash and DASH transactions can be more private

---

72 *See* Get Started: What Is Monero?" *Monero*, getmonero.org/get-started/what-is-monero.

73 *See* "Zcash 101" at z.cash/learn. For an introduction to zero-knowledge cryptography, which is being experimented with across numerous networks, *see* "Zero Knowledge Proofs." *YouTube*, Computational Thinking, 25 Oct. 2022, y2u.be/5qzNe1hk0oY.

than Bitcoin, provided their optional privacy features are activated, yet they also allow for transparent transactions. Monero stands out for its design, which is focused on consistent privacy, though recent developments in crypto forensic tools claim to provide some level of insight into transaction histories.[74] Arguably, none of these payment mechanisms provides as robust a privacy feature as cash, which remains legal and is still the primary currency used by criminals who value anonymity.[75]

As the crypto landscape evolves, so do the tools and technologies that govern privacy.[76] Bitcoin and Ethereum have undergone technical enhancements that bolster transactional anonymity, and there's discussion about future upgrades that could further enhance their privacy features. This continuous development presents a regulatory challenge inherent to evolving technologies: How does one effectively regulate something designed to change over time?

Regulating cryptocurrencies based on the privacy they offer to users is made more difficult by the evolving nature of both the technology behind these assets and the tools used to trace them. Privacy, in this context, is not a static feature but a point of contention, constantly influenced by improvements in the technologies that enhance anonymity and the forensic tools designed to penetrate it. The evolving landscape of technology and traceability makes the task of regulation particularly complex. As privacy-enhancing technologies advance, so do the forensic capabilities aiming to monitor and trace these transactions. This results in a fluctuating definition of what constitutes a "privacy coin" that is always being reshaped by the arms race between privacy technologies and investigatory advancements. When considering major cryptocurrencies like Bitcoin and Ethereum, the regulatory challenges intensify. Both communities are exploring

---

74 *See* "CIPHERTRACE Announces Monero Tracing Capabilities." *Ciphertrace*, 4 Aug. 2021, ciphertrace.com/enhanced-monero-tracing.

75 "Financial Criminals Target Fiat More than Crypto - Blog: UNIT21." 15 Sept. 2023, unit21.ai/blog/combat-crypto-fraud-via-fiat.

76 Crypto forensic firms like Chainalysis, Elliptic, and TRM Labs offer analytics tools and provide training to law enforcement to enhance their ability to trace crypto transactions. These tools have become practically required for digital asset platforms to comply with regulations aimed at combating illicit activities. *See* "Cross-Chain Investigations: Tracing Crypto across Blockchains." *YouTube*, TRM Labs, 29 Nov. 2022, y2u.be/5sHOAZnJQVM.

the integration of enhanced privacy features through technical upgrades. Regulating mainstream assets that have been modified to include advanced privacy is considerably more challenging and likely to encounter significant legal and industry pushback, compared to current efforts aimed at marginalizing privacy-focused alternatives with smaller market capitalizations. The potential incorporation of privacy features into leading cryptocurrencies necessitates the development of regulatory frameworks that can adapt to the evolving landscape of privacy technologies and forensic capabilities.

II. Stablecoins

Stablecoins are a class of digital assets that are pegged to the price of an external marker like the U.S. dollar, Euro, or other fiat currencies. Their primary advantage lies in enabling swift and cost-efficient global transactions, allowing users to bypass the often prohibitive fees and time delays associated with traditional banking systems while also avoiding the price volatility inherent in digital assets.

An important aspect of stablecoins is their role in financial empowerment, especially for those who are unbanked or underbanked. As discussed by Alex Gladstein of the Human Rights Foundation, stablecoins have emerged as crucial tools for financial independence around the world.[77] They provide an accessible means for individuals in regions with unstable currencies or limited access to traditional banking to engage in global financial activities. This ability to securely store and transact value independently of local financial institutions or volatile national currencies has profound implications for economic freedom and empowerment, particularly in developing regions. The significance of stablecoins in such contexts cannot be overstated, as they not only offer a stable store of value but also open up opportunities for participation in the broader digital economy.

Stablecoins also play a crucial role in the emergence of decentralized finance (DeFi) by enabling transactions across different blockchain networks, which often have incompatible protocols and native

---

[77] "Alex Gladstein on the Importance of Stablecoins | E14." *YouTube*, Kevin Rooke, 2022, y2u.be/lIjfsX6j958.

tokens. This functionality is essential because each blockchain operates under its own set of rules and supports specific tokens. For instance, consider a user who holds USDC, a stablecoin, on the Ethereum blockchain and wants to use a DeFi application built on the Binance Smart Chain. Without stablecoins, they would face a complex process: selling Ethereum for fiat currency and then buying BNB (Binance Smart Chain's native token) to access the desired application, all while bearing the risk of market volatility for both assets.

However, with stablecoins, this practice is streamlined through 'bridging,' a process that, in our example, would involve 'locking' the stablecoin on the Ethereum blockchain in a smart contract and then 'minting' an equivalent amount of the stablecoin on the Binance Smart Chain. This bridging process bypasses the need to convert assets back to fiat and then to another cryptocurrency, reducing transaction complexity and exposure to market risk.[78]

The interoperability facilitated by stablecoins enhances the user experience in the DeFi ecosystem. It allows users to easily navigate and engage with various platforms and applications without being confined to a single blockchain network or having to undergo cumbersome and risky asset conversions. Stablecoins thus not only offer stability in value but also significantly contribute to the fluidity and accessibility of the DeFi space.

For more information about stablecoins, two valuable resources are "A Primer on Stablecoins" by Austin Campbell (@CampbellJAustin)[79] and the report Cryptodollars: The Story So Far co-authored by Nic Carter (@NicCarter).[80]

---

78 For a more detailed explanation of how bridges work, *see* "What Is a Crypto Bridge? (Examples + Purpose for Blockchains)." *YouTube*, Whiteboard Crypto, 24 June 2021, y2u.be/nT26cIz8HjI.

79 *See* Campbell, Austin. "A Primer on Stablecoins." Colossus, shorturl.at/gtvZ4

80 Carter, Nic. "Cryptodollars: The Story So Far." *Niccarter.info*, Castle Island Ventures, shorturl.at/nGOU3; *See* also "Nic Carter's Bull Case for Stablecoins." *YouTube*, Bankless, 16 Oct. 2023, y2u.be/iecFhe2THeo

Fiat-Backed Stablecoins represent the largest segment of the stablecoin market. They are centralized, and therefore subject to a level of control and potential censorship by their issuers.[81] Their value is typically anchored to fiat currencies like the U.S. dollar. The stability of these coins is ensured by reserves held by the issuer, which commonly include a variety of assets such as cash, cash equivalents, short-term government securities, or commercial papers. These backings aim to match the number of stablecoins in circulation with an equal or greater value in reserve assets, providing stability to their value. Prominent examples of fiat-backed stablecoins include:

- **Tether (USDT):** Launched in 2014, Tether is the most widely used stablecoin. It is operated by Tether Limited, which the owners of the Bitfinex exchange control. Each token is purported to be backed by one U.S. dollar worth of assets which are verified by an independent auditor.[82] The sufficiency of Tether's reserves has been the subject of ongoing controversy and U.S. enforcement actions.[83]
  - NY AG Settlement: In February 2021, Tether and Bitfinex entered into an $18.5 million settlement with the New York Attorney General's office over allegations of improper financial activities. The settlement centered on accusations that the companies had acted unlawfully to conceal reserve losses and mislead customers and included a commitment to provide regular reporting on their reserves and business operations for two years and to cease trading activities with New York residents.[84]
  - CFTC Settlement: In October 2021, the CFTC reached a $42.5 million settlement with Tether and Bitfinex for alleged violations of the Commodity Exchange Act. The settlement was connected to allegations that Tether and Bitfinex had

---

81 Per the Terms and Conditions of centralized stablecoins like USDC and USDT, issuers can censor transactions at their sole discretion. *See*, e.g., shorturl.at/nLSXZ (USDC Terms); shorturl.at/hsxFY (USDT Policy).

82 *See* "Tether Transparency: Reports." *Tether*, tether.to/transparency.

83 For a history of the controversies surrounding Tether's reserves, *see* Lopatto, Elizabeth. "The Tether Controversy, Explained." *The Verge*, 16 Aug. 2021, shorturl.at/itwG4.

84 "Attorney General James Ends Virtual Currency Trading Platform Bitfinex's Illegal Activities in New York." *New York State Attorney General*, shorturl.at/luGIK.

made misrepresentations to the public regarding the amount of reserves they held between 2016 and 2018.[85]

- **USD Coin (USDC)**: USDC was introduced in September 2018 by the Centre consortium, co-founded by Circle with support from members including Coinbase. It is pegged to the U.S. dollar, with its reserves held in audited and regulated financial institutions. USDC provides monthly attestations from accounting firms to verify its reserves.[86]

- **Binance USD (BUSD)**: Binance USD (BUSD) was established in 2019 through a collaboration between its issuer, Paxos, a New York State-chartered trust company, and the Binance exchange. The stablecoin held reserves in regulated financial institutions, similar to USDC, but faced added scrutiny due to its association with Binance.

In late 2023, Binance announced it would discontinue support for BUSD as a result of pressure exerted by the New York Department of Financial Services (DFS) on its issuer Paxos. The DFS expressed concerns about Binance's compliance with financial regulations and anti-money laundering requirements, as well as the minting of BUSD on unauthorized networks. In its notice requiring Paxos to cease minting new BUSD, DFS found that Paxos had been authorized to issue BUSD only on the Ethereum blockchain and that allowing BUSD to be bridged to other networks was unauthorized.[87] Paxos's inability to mint new BUSD effectively killed the project and precipitated Binance to discontinue support of the stablecoin globally.

Crypto-Backed Stablecoins use a pool of cryptocurrency assets as collateral. This category of stablecoins is typically overcollateralized,

---

85 "Release Number 8450-21 - CFTC Orders Tether and Bitfinex to Pay Fines Totaling $42.5 Million." *CFTC*, shorturl.at/bclnB.

86 For more information about USDC, *see* circle.com/usdc.

87 Adams, Josh. "Binance Stablecoin BUSD Will Leave the Stage Just as Market Ticks Upward." *CCN*, 30 Nov. 2023, tinyurl.com/ym5hmu46; "Notice Regarding Paxos-Issued BUSD." *Department of Financial Services*, dfs.ny.gov/consumers/alerts/Paxos_and_Binance.

meaning the value of the crypto assets held as collateral exceeds the value of the stablecoins issued. This over-collateralization is needed to buffer against the volatility of the cryptocurrency markets. A few examples of crypto-backed stablecoins:

- **DAI**: Created in 2017, DAI is a decentralized stablecoin governed by the MakerDAO protocol, a Decentralized Autonomous Organization. Unlike fiat-backed stablecoins, DAI's stability isn't derived from reserves of fiat currency. Instead, it uses overcollateralized assets, primarily ether, locked up in smart contracts. Users of the MakerDAO protocol can deposit ETH or other approved cryptocurrencies into these smart contracts, known as Maker Vaults, to generate new DAI. The peg of DAI to the U.S. dollar is maintained through a system of smart contracts overseen by MakerDAO.[88]

- **Wrapped Bitcoin (wBTC)**: Wrapped Bitcoin is an example of a crypto-backed asset, though not a stablecoin in the traditional sense. It represents and tracks the value of bitcoin (BTC) on the Ethereum blockchain. Essentially, wBTC is a tokenized version of bitcoin that conforms to the ERC-20 standard used by the Ethereum blockchain, allowing bitcoin to be used in the Ethereum ecosystem. This process requires a BTC holder to send their bitcoin to a custodial smart contract which will then issue a new ERC-20 compatible wBTC token at a 1:1 ratio. Many assets can be wrapped, allowing them to be used across different blockchain networks. The wrapped assets typically take on the name "w[ASSET]," so ETH wrapped for use on the Solana network would be designated "wETH."

There is an ongoing debate as to whether wrapping an asset is the swap of one asset (BTC) for a different asset (wBTC) or whether wBTC acts as merely the receipt of a deposit allowing a wBTC holder to redeem BTC in the future. The answer to this question will have a significant impact on both the regulatory treatment of wrapped assets and the tax liability of engaging with the product. The IRS has not issued guidance on the matter, and the only

---

88 *See* makerdao.com/whitepaper; "Makerdao - Creation of Dai." *YouTube*, Campbell Harvey, 17 Nov. 2021, y2u.be.com/t0R94tfhssM.

court to examine whether a wrapped token is a security did not analyze the impact of wrapping and applied the same analysis for a wrapped asset as its underlying asset.[89]

Algorithmic Stablecoins are an experimental class of digital currencies that use algorithms and smart contracts to maintain a stable value. Unlike fiat-backed or crypto-backed stablecoins, algorithmic stablecoins often operate with minimal or no collateral. Instead, they rely on a system of "balancer" or "share" tokens to absorb market volatility and maintain their peg.

For example, the Terra blockchain system used its algorithmic stablecoin, TerraUSD (UST), in conjunction with the governance token Luna to stabilize its value. The mechanism was designed so that when the value of UST rose above $1, Luna holders could profit by exchanging their Luna for UST. Conversely, when the value of UST fell, traders could exchange it for Luna, thereby reducing the supply of UST to increase its price. The premise is that the market would utilize the arbitrage opportunity between the two assets to keep the value of UST at $1.

The long-term viability of algorithmic stablecoins is unproven, as the peg often relies on market demand. If demand decreases significantly, the entire system can falter, as evidenced by the collapse of UST in May 2022. This event, which led to over $40 billion in losses, occurred when the price of UST fell below $1, causing a massive sell-off and a consequent drop in the price of Luna. Following the collapse of UST and Luna, the viability of algorithmic stablecoins has been questioned. However, other algorithmic stablecoins still remain in the market.

Regulating Stablecoins

As demand for stablecoins has increased, the question of how stablecoins will impact the broader economy has been frequently

---

[89] "What's a Wrapped Token? | WBTC, Weth Explained." *YouTube*, Whiteboard Crypto, 12 May 2022, y2u.be/ hhuJRsv9ao8. *See also, SEC v. Terraform Labs Pte Ltd.* No. 1:23-cv-01346, Memorandum & Opinion, Document #149 at 40 n. 10. *Southern District of New York*, Filed 28 Dec 2023. CourtListener, rb.gy/2zwe98 ("the analysis of LUNA applies equally to wLUNA.").

debated. Austin Campbell and others have theorized that the U.S. should embrace the use of U.S. dollar-backed stablecoins as a mechanism for extending the currency's global influence. This is explored in "A Primer on Stablecoins," linked above. Still, others maintain that stablecoins may create an instability risk in the dollar.

Given the concern about the impact of stablecoins on the broader economy, there has been a legislative effort in the United States to regulate them. New York and Nebraska have legislation in place affirmatively regulating the issuance of stablecoins under their state's banking regulations. Other states have incorporated stablecoin guidance within their money transmitter or equivalent regulations.

Federally, in 2023, the *Clarity for Payment Stablecoin Act* made its way out of a Congressional committee but appears to have since stalled. The Bill sought to create a framework that would leave much of the individual regulation of stablecoins to the states but would establish a federal floor with respect to the capitalization, reporting, and types of assets held in reserves by an issuer.[90] It would also clarify that stablecoins are outside of the jurisdiction of securities regulators.

As the expectation of profits is a necessary component of an investment contract, many legal observers believe an asset designed not to rise in value would be difficult to characterize as a security. Nevertheless, the SEC and its Chair have inferred a view that stablecoins may resemble money market accounts or some other asset-backed security and, therefore, could be subject to the SEC's jurisdiction.[91] Notably, the SEC has yet to bring an action based on those theories but has instead brought several actions alleging that a stablecoin was sold as part of a securities offering, in part based on its role in a larger profit-generating scheme.

For example, in December 2023, Judge Rakoff of the Southern District of New York, found the collapsed TerraUSD (UST) was sold as a security because the use of UST within the larger Terra ecosystem resulted in an integrated scheme that allowed UST holders to profit

---

90 H.R. 4766, *Clarity for Payment Stablecoins Act*, 25 Sept. 2023, shorturl.at/uyJKL.

91 Gensler, Gary. "Prepared Remarks of Gary Gensler on Crypto Markets." *Penn Law Capital Markets Association Annual Conference*, 4 Apr. 2022, bit.ly/41azGqb.

as a result of their purchase of the stablecoin.⁹² The SEC is pursuing a similar theory that fiat-backed stablecoin BUSD is a security because of its role in the broader Binance ecosystem that promoted the potential for profits that could be accessed by holding BUSD.⁹³

At the time of this writing, the SEC's case against Binance is pending, and it remains unclear whether UST or BUSD, even if sold by its issuers as part of an integrated securities offering, means the stablecoins are themselves securities, including when sold on the secondary market. Judge Rakoff noted the SEC did not assert that UST was, on its own, a security and made clear his ruling was based on UST's role within the broader Terra ecosystem.

Judge Rakoff's view is, on its face, consistent with the view of many that a digital asset can be sold by its issuer as part of a securities offering even where the digital asset itself is not a security. While this view has found some judicial support, it remains one of the larger open questions for the industry. The case is explored further in Chapter 15.

Supplemental Resources – Privacy Coins⁹⁴

- **"Zcash, Monero & Privacy Coin Regulations W/ J.W. Verret Epi #266."** *YouTube,* **Monero Talk, 4 June 2023,** y2u.be/ ujPpS_LI27s. J.W. Verret (@JWVerret) is a law professor at George Mason University and a privacy advocate. While we will examine the crackdown on economic privacy in Chapter 10, I suggest you first listen to this conversation for an overview of privacy coins and the regulations

---

92 *See SEC v. Terraform Labs Pte Ltd.*, No. 1:23-cv-01346, Memorandum & Opinion, Document #149. *Southern District of New York,* Filed 28 Dec 2023. CourtListener, rb.gy/2zwe98.

93 *See SEC v. Binance Holdings Ltd.*, No. 1:23-cv-01599, Complaint, Document #1. *District Court for the District of Columbia.* Filed 5 June 2023. CourtListener, rb.gy/llawli; For an analysis of the SEC's arguments with respect to BUSD, *see* Wise, Aaron. "Explained: How Binance's Stablecoin BUSD Can Be a Security." *Protos,* 28 Nov. 2023, shorturl.at/suwMY.

94 For ease of reference, all Supplemental Resources and footnote links are available at www.TheCryptoLegalHandbook.com/Resources.

impacting them.

Supplemental Resources - Stablecoins

- **Landy, Douglas, et al. "Blockchain & Cryptocurrency Laws and Regulations: The Regulation of Stablecoins in the United States: GLI."** GLI - *Global Legal Insights - International Legal Business Solutions, Global Legal Group*, 30 Oct. 2023, rb.gy/t99h80. This is a well-done summary of the government's efforts to regulate or provide guidance on using and issuing stablecoins. It is authored by a collection of White and Case attorneys and published for free by Global Legal Insight.

- **"A Conversation on Stablecoins."** *YouTube*, **Office of the Comptroller of the Currency, 13 Apr. 2022,** y2u.be/ywawsIqlS7o. A conversation with Michael Hsu, Acting Comptroller of the Currency. The video provides an administrative perspective on the future impact and uses of stablecoins and the role of regulation in the future of technology.

- **"Circle's Jeremy Allaire on Where Stablecoin Regulation Is Headed - EP. 543."** *YouTube*, **Unchained, 12 Sept. 2023,** y2u.be/bxMdBL0Fees. A conversation with Jeremy Allaire, CEO of USDC issuer Circle, on the future of U.S. stablecoin regulation.

CHAPTER 9

The Everything Machines and Decentralized Finance

Until this point, we have mostly concentrated on understanding the development and technology of Bitcoin and Ethereum. These two projects account for over 50% of the total market capitalization of digital assets but are just the tip of the iceberg in a vast sea of tens of thousands of blockchain projects. In my view, Bitcoin and Ethereum embody the two foundational pillars of the crypto world. Bitcoin introduced the concept of digital scarcity, while Ethereum originated the idea of smart contracts as a means of accessing permissionless applications. Most projects within the ecosystem can trace their roots back to at least one of these innovations.

Attempting to detail every project that emerges in the crypto space is impractical considering the rapid pace of development. Therefore, a more manageable approach is to provide categorical definitions and overviews of key projects, supplemented with links and further resources for your exploration and learning. I encourage you to experiment with some of the projects listed below.

Before your experimentation begins, keep in mind that different networks typically need their own unique wallets or software for you to interact with them. It's crucial to double-check that you're sending your crypto to the correct address. A mistake like sending crypto to the wrong address is irreversible and can lead to a permanent loss of your funds. Although the basic process of sending and receiving cryptocurrencies is quite similar across most digital assets, things get more complex when you start exploring advanced features like executing smart contracts on networks like Ethereum. Delving into these advanced functions requires you to become familiar with a variety of tools and software. Be prepared for a learning curve as you navigate through these more sophisticated aspects of blockchain technology.

Ethereum Alternatives

The introduction of Ethereum in 2015, with its innovative smart contract functionality, spurred the development of numerous projects aimed at refining and enhancing the original concept for more scalable and user-friendly decentralized application ecosystems. Listed in order of their development, these blockchain networks all share the fundamental idea of smart contracts with Ethereum but differ in their consensus mechanisms, scalability solutions, and specific applications.

- **Cardano (ADA):** Launched in 2017 by Ethereum co-founder Charles Hoskinson (@IOHK_Charles), Cardano aimed to position itself as a blockchain with a more environmentally friendly approach compared to Ethereum, which launched as a Proof of Work chain that required miners to expend electrical energy to validate transactions. Cardano employs a consensus protocol called Ouroboros, a Proof of Stake mechanism allowing ADA holders to stake their assets as collateral for securing and validating transactions. Proponents of Ouroboros have advocated for its secure and energy-efficient consensus model as compared to PoW chains.

However, it's important to note that since Ethereum's transition to its own PoS model in September 2022, the distinction between Cardano and Ethereum in terms of energy efficiency has become less pronounced. Cardano has faced challenges in distinguishing itself from Ethereum and other energy-efficient blockchain alternatives and now predominantly tries to differentiate itself on the basis that the Cardano Foundation funds significant research into the further development of blockchain technologies.

The SEC has alleged in cases against digital asset platforms that Cardano's native token, ADA, is a security. As of this writing, no legal action has been taken against ADA's issuers.[95]

---

[95] "What Is Cardano? ADA Explained with Animations." *YouTube*, Whiteboard Crypto, 28 Aug. 2021, y2u.be/UMUztLQNqSI; The Cardano Foundation has also published numerous research papers about the Cardano network at iohk.io/research/library.

- **Algorand (ALGO)**: Launched in June 2019 by Silvio Micali (@silviomicali), Algorand utilizes a consensus mechanism it calls Pure Proof of Stake (PPoS). Unlike PoS, which provides validators who stake their digital assets with rewards for maintaining the network, PPoS allows all ALGO token holders to collect rewards from the network without having to actually stake their tokens.

The ability to passively earn network rewards has attracted investors to the project and has also drawn the attention of the SEC, who has alleged in cases against digital asset platforms that Algorand's native token, ALGO, is a security. As of this writing, no legal action has been taken against ALGO's issuers.[96]

- **Solana (SOL)**: Launched in March 2020 by Anatoly Yakovenko (@aeyakovenko), Solana is a high-performance blockchain that prioritizes rapid transaction processing and scalability. It has emerged as a primary alternative to Ethereum. Solana utilizes a unique consensus mechanism, known as Proof of History, in combination with Proof of Stake, allowing it to process thousands of transactions per second. This architectural advantage enables Solana to validate a transaction block approximately every 400 milliseconds, in contrast to Ethereum, which validates blocks every ten seconds. Due to its increased throughput and efficiency, Solana transactions incur significantly lower fees compared to Ethereum.

The SEC has alleged in cases against digital asset platforms that Solana's native token, SOL, qualifies as a security. As of this writing, no legal action has been taken against SOL's issuers.[97]

- **Polkadot (DOT)**: Established in May 2020 by Dr. Gavin Wood (@gavofyork), a co-founder of Ethereum, Polkadot was specifically designed to enhance blockchain interoperability. It achieves this through the utilization of parachains, which are specialized blockchains that can connect to the central relay

---

96 "What is Algorand? ALGO Explained with Animations." *YouTube*, Whiteboard Crypto, 20 Nov. 2021, y2u.be/XtKTk-ebyQE; *see* also algorand.foundation/the-algo.

97 "What is Solana? SOL Explained with Animations." *YouTube*, Whiteboard Crypto, 13 Sept. 2021, y2u.be/1jzROE6EhxM; *see* also docs.solana.com/introduction.

chain. These parachains enable different blockchain networks to collaborate seamlessly, offering an alternative to Ethereum's single-chain model.

Polkadot employs a consensus mechanism known as Nominated Proof of Stake (NPoS) and incorporates "Grandpa finality." NPoS involves DOT token holders nominating validators, who are responsible for producing and validating blocks. Grandpa finality means that once a block is added to the chain, it is irreversible, enhancing security and trust in the network. An advantage of Polkadot's architecture is it can handle a high volume of transactions, which leads to lower transaction fees and efficiency compared to Ethereum.[98]

- **Binance Smart Chain (BNB)**: Binance Smart Chain (BSC) was launched in September 2020 as an integral part of the Binance ecosystem. It is closely linked to its sister blockchain, Binance Chain, and operates with its native token, Binance Coin (BNB).

While Binance Chain primarily focuses on enabling fast and cost-effective cryptocurrency transfers, BSC expands its capabilities by providing a platform for decentralized applications and smart contracts. BSC employs a consensus mechanism known as Delegated Proof of Stake (DPoS), in which BNB token holders can vote for a select group of delegates or validators who validate transactions and produce new blocks. DPos enhances scalability and transaction processing efficiency compared to traditional PoS systems, where validators are typically chosen based on their cryptocurrency holdings.

Although BSC is closely associated with the Binance exchange and Binance actively contributes to its development, the network is purported to be operated independently of Binance's leadership and operations. Binance remains active in supporting the network's development and regularly purchases BNB from

---

[98] "What is Polkadot? DOT Explained with Animations." *YouTube*, Whiteboard Crypto, 18 Sept. 2021, y2u.be/YlAdEQp6ekM; *see* also "Polkadot Behind the Code." *YouTube*, Polkadot, 26 May 2020, y2u.be/GcOKXAOh4Xw.

the open market through planned buybacks but maintains that it does not exercise direct control over the BSC network.

The SEC has alleged in its case against Binance that the Binance Smart Chain's native token, BNB, is a security.[99]

- **Avalanche (AVAX)**: Launched in September 2020 by Ava Labs and founded by Emin Gün Sirer (@el33th4xor), Ava Labs plays a central role in the continuous development of the Avalanche platform, with a primary focus on delivering a highly scalable blockchain solution. Avalanche supports the creation of customized private and public blockchains, referred to as "subnets," and utilizes the Avalanche Consensus Protocol. This protocol introduces a novel approach to blockchain architecture, incorporating a gossip-based protocol that allows participants to share information in a decentralized and efficient manner, leading to rapid decision-making and transaction finalization.[100]

- **Polygon (MATIC)**: Formerly known as the Matic Network and rebranded as Polygon in October 2021, this project was initially conceived as a Layer 2 scaling solution for Ethereum. The Polygon team, which includes key figures like Jaynti Kanani (@_jdkanani), Sandeep Nailwal (@sandeepnailwal), and others, dedicated their efforts to improving Ethereum's scalability and interoperability. Polygon employs a set of Ethereum-compatible blockchains, referred to as "sidechains," which are connected through a system of validators and bridges. These sidechains allow for faster and more efficient transactions by offloading a significant portion of the processing load from the Ethereum mainnet, thereby alleviating congestion issues. Like Ethereum, Polygon utilizes a PoS consensus mechanism, which is responsible for securing its network and maintaining consensus among validators. In practical terms, Polygon functions as

---

99 "What is the BNB? Binance Smart Chain Explained with Animations." *YouTube*, Whiteboard Crypto, 1 Oct. 2021, y2u.be//G0gmPW8N88M; "A Beginner's Guide to the BNB Chain: The Evolution of the Binance Smart Chain." *Cointelegraph*, shorturl.at/cnw-CV.

100 "What is the Avalanche Network? AVAX Explained with Animations." *YouTube*, Whiteboard Crypto, 4 Sept. 2021, y2u.be//CbM2jidEn0s; *see also* academy.avax.network.

a comprehensive framework for building and deploying decentralized applications on its interconnected sidechains. This approach not only facilitates faster transaction processing but also provides developers with a scalable environment for creating Ethereum-compatible dApps.

The SEC has alleged in cases against digital asset platforms that Polygon's native token, MATIC, is a security. As of this writing, no legal action has been taken against MATIC's issuers for unregistered securities sales.[101]

Networks like Ethereum and the alternatives mentioned above enable creators to develop smart contracts for a broad range of applications. To interact with these platforms and the applications built on them, developers and users must use the native token of each respective network.

The SEC has shown reluctance to categorize Ethereum's native token, ether, as a security. However, they have alleged that the native tokens of many Ethereum alternatives are securities. This perspective confounds many experts, given the similar development, functionality, and market introduction of these tokens compared to ether. Some believe that the SEC's differential treatment of ether may stem from constraints related to previous administration statements, which posited that ether does not currently meet the characteristics of a security.[102] If so, then the distinction between ether and its counterparts is not one based on fact or law but on timing.

The classification of network tokens is crucial to the long-term adoption of decentralized applications. As explored in Chapter 13, the determination that a digital asset is a security would significantly impact the ability of U.S. individuals to engage with the token's network.

Despite the ongoing debate over the classification of ether and its

---

101 "What is Polygon (MATIC)? Explained with Animations." *YouTube,* Whiteboard Crypto, 9 Nov. 2021, y2u.be/GWUwFDFOipoNote.

102 Hinman, William, Director, Division of Corporation Finance, SEC. "Digital Asset Transactions: When Howey Met Gary (Plastic)." 14 June 2018, bit.ly/2l8t5dB.

alternatives, ether remains readily accessible, and the development of decentralized applications continues across various networks. These applications range from crowdfunding platforms, decentralized autonomous organizations, voting systems, informational oracles, decentralized financial tools, social media platforms, file storage solutions, games, and more. While some projects issue their own tokens, others operate without one. For a robust list of projects on different blockchain networks, visit thevalueprop.io.

While a wide array of projects can be developed on decentralized networks, in this initial discussion, I want to highlight a category that has attracted considerable attention and faces distinct legal and regulatory issues: Decentralized Finance.

Decentralized Finance (DeFi)

Decentralized Finance represents a broad spectrum of products and concepts that operate outside of centralized financial institutions. DeFi encompasses any financial activity, protocol, or asset operating independently of central authorities, which could, in a broad sense, include any self-custodial financial asset. However, DeFi is more commonly associated with blockchain-enabled platforms and protocols that facilitate transactions such as lending, borrowing, and trading.

DeFi isn't confined to a single blockchain but spans various networks, including Ethereum and the "Ethereum Alternatives" mentioned previously. The range of financial activities achievable through DeFi without intermediaries is extensive. DeFi applications are typically accessed by connecting a user's in-browser digital wallet to a decentralized application or dApp. Because these applications enable direct interaction through a smart contract protocol, they require users to "sign" transaction commands before any activities are authorized. In-browser wallets are typically self-custodial and allow users to hold digital assets and authorize transactions. Users should exercise extreme caution when connecting their wallet to unknown applications or authorizing signatures, as there is a risk of loss from malicious actors.

There are many in-browser wallet options for connecting to DeFi applications. My preferred wallets are MetaMask for Ethereum-based transactions and Phantom for transactions on the Solana network.[103]

Decentralized Exchanges (DEXs) enable users to trade cryptocurrencies without an intermediary. Most DEXs operate as "automated market makers" (AMMs), allowing trading to occur automatically through liquidity pools rather than traditional market order books.[104] In an AMM, liquidity providers deposit token pairs into a pool, establishing a market for those tokens. Trading prices are determined by a mathematical formula based on the token ratio in the pool, allowing asset pricing to adjust with supply and demand. Users trade against the liquidity pool, with prices adjusting algorithmically as token ratios change after each trade.

Every major blockchain network hosts one or more DEXs. Because different blockchain networks are not directly compatible, "bridges" or "wrapped assets" are required to exchange assets across networks. DEXs charge a transaction fee to traders, a portion of which is allocated to those who stake assets in liquidity pools. Most DEXs have introduced tokens that provide holders with governance rights and, in some cases, a share of the trading fees to incentivize participation within the ecosystem. Below are some examples of DEXs across different networks:

- **Uniswap** – A leading DEX on the Ethereum network, Uniswap features a governance token, UNI, that grants holders voting rights on protocol changes and a share of trading fees.[105] Other Ethereum-based AMMs include SushiSwap (SUSHI)[106]

---

103 "Metamask: Step-by-Step Guide to DEFI's Best Wallet!!." *YouTube*, Coin Bureau, 6 Mar. 2021, y2u.be/MfkqgXNPiHg; "Phantom Wallet: Beginner's Crypto Guide!! Step-by-Step!!." *YouTube*, Coin Bureau, 12 Feb. 2022, y2u.be/zI-Xd9vVnwY.

104 "What Is a Dex? How a Decentralized Exchange Works." *YouTube*, Whiteboard Crypto, 15 Aug. 2021, ytu.be/2tTVJL4bpTU; "What is an Automatic Market Maker? (Liquidity Pool Algorithm)." *Youtube*, Whiteboard Crypto, May 22, 2022, y2u.be/1PbZMudPP5E.

105 "What Is Uniswap? (Animated) Decentralized Exchange + Uni Token." *YouTube*, Whiteboard Crypto, 1 May 2021, y2u.be/DLu35sIqVTM; *see* also uniswap.org.

106 "What Is Sushiswap? (Animated) Sushi Token + Kashi + Miso Explained." *YouTube*, Whiteboard Crypto, 22 June 2021, ytu.be/NTYbVnENeVo; *see* also sushi.com.

and Curve Finance (CRV).[107]

- **Jupiter** – The primary DEX on the Solana network, acting as a "liquidity aggregator" to source liquidity from various DEXs within Solana for optimal trading routes and prices. It has a governance token called JUP.[108]

- **PancakeSwap** – An AMM DEX operating on the Binance Smart Chain, featuring its token, CAKE, which users can earn and stake for governance participation or to receive trading fees.[109]

Decentralized Lending is another significant DeFi use case. DeFi loans are typically overcollateralized, requiring borrowers to deposit more with a smart contract than the amount borrowed. This exposes them to margin calls or the need to add additional deposits should the value of their collateral decrease. There are numerous decentralized lending platforms across different blockchain networks, including Aave[110] and Compound.[111]

Like banks, decentralized lending platforms' loan capabilities rely on users locking up assets to be lent out. Borrowers pay interest to the protocol, while depositors earn interest for providing their funds. This economic incentive encourages users to deposit money, either for lending by the protocol or as liquidity for a decentralized exchange, a practice sometimes referred to as "yield farming."

DEXs and decentralized lending platforms just scratch the surface of the broad range of DeFi applications. The Supplemental Resources section provides additional materials for further learning. I recommend at least experimenting with a DEX to appreciate the

---

107 "What is Curve Finance? I'm earning 25% AND protecting against a crash." *YouTube*, Whiteboard Crypto, 18 Aug 2021, y2u.be/MqRfurKVM1A; *see also* curve.fi.

108 *See* jup.ag.

109 *See* pancakeswap.finance

110 "What Is AAVE? (Animated) Crypto Borrowing and Lending Explained." *YouTube*, Whiteboard Crypto, 25 May 2021, y2u.be/dTCwssZ116A.

111 "Compound Finance DeFi Tutorial: How to Earn Interest on Your Crypto & $COMP Tokens." *Youtube*, Whiteboard Crypto, 20 June 2020, y2u.be/VYp9oiEI7GU.

simplicity of executing a DeFi transaction, especially compared to the onboarding process of centralized exchanges, which often requires personal information to comply with know-your-customer regulations.

The ease with which one can engage in DeFi transactions raises questions about how its protocols, essentially code without central oversight, should be regulated. Many DeFi activities would require government registration if offered by centralized entities. The question of whether developers or those providing access or infrastructure for these protocols should be liable for facilitating unregistered financial activities remains open.

The legal complexities surrounding DeFi are profound and the subject of ongoing debate. The supplemental section includes resources offering insights into the major regulatory discussions affecting decentralized financial applications. Most of these debates have yet to be resolved in court, with the few enforcement actions that have been brought having settled before judgment. Although not precedential on future cases, two differing regulatory approaches are discussed below.

In *Risley v. Universal Navigation Inc. d/b/a Uniswap Labs*, developers and financial backers of the Uniswap protocol were accused in a civil class action of liability for scam digital assets traded on the Uniswap DEX.[112] On August 29, 2023, Judge Katherine Polk Failla of the Southern District of New York dismissed the suit. She ruled that the developers and backers couldn't be held responsible for the actions of unrelated third parties who used Uniswap to launch and sell fraudulent tokens. The judge emphasized that the lack of identification of the scam token issuers did not justify proceeding with the claims against Uniswap and associated defendants, indicating that Congress, not the courts, should address any regulatory concerns.

Shortly after this decision, on September 7, 2023, the Commodity Futures Trading Commission initiated and settled enforcement actions against the developers of three DeFi projects for alleged

---

112 *Risley v. Universal Navigation Inc. et al.* No. 1:2022cv02780 - Document 90. *Southern District of New York*, 2023. Justia Law, shorturl.at/hiuGY.

legal violations, including offering leveraged digital assets without proper delivery and failing to comply with anti-money laundering obligations. These actions were taken despite the activities being conducted through third-party applications, not directly by the protocols themselves. CFTC Commissioner Summer Mersinger dissented from these enforcement actions, questioning the CFTC's jurisdiction and the approach of regulating DeFi through enforcement rather than engagement and guidance. She highlighted the need for the CFTC to work with market participants to develop clear rules and guidance for DeFi, rather than primarily pursuing enforcement.[113]

The *Risley* decision and CFTC settlements are some of the first data points we have on how regulators and courts may apply existing regulations to the developers of DeFi tools. Ultimately, as Judge Failla and Commissioner Mersinger both acknowledge, until Congress acts to address these novel questions directly, clarity will be elusive for the foreseeable future.

Decentralized Autonomous Organizations (DAOs)

DAOs are a subcategory of crypto projects that leverage a blockchain's infrastructure to create a governance model that allows it to operate without centralized management. A prominent example is "The DAO," an Ethereum-based project covered in Chapter 7. This project aimed to establish a decentralized venture capital fund where investment decisions were made by DAO token holders instead of a management team. Generally, DAOs aim to promote transparency and democratic governance by using smart contracts to automate decision-making and operational processes.

In their ideal form, DAOs operate without any centralized authority, relying on the collective decision-making of their members, typically token holders. However, the line between decentralized and centralized control can become blurred in practice. Often, especially in their early stages, DAOs can be significantly influenced by their

---

[113] Mersinger, Summer. "Dissenting Statement of Commissioner Summer K. Mersinger Regarding Enforcement Actions Against: 1) Opyn, Inc.; 2) Deridex, Inc.; and 3) ZeroEx, Inc." *Commodity Futures Trading Commission*, 7 Sept. 2023, rb.gy/im9txu.

founders or might depend on a centralized team for decisions with real-world implications, such as managing tangible assets or undertaking corporate actions like opening bank accounts. This reliance raises questions about the feasibility of DAOs in handling real-world interactions and whether the benefits of decentralized governance are undermined when activities extend beyond the digital realm.

Despite these challenges, DAOs have achieved considerable success within the decentralized finance sphere, with projects like MakerDAO, Compound, Uniswap, Aave, and Curve Finance forming key infrastructure components of the broader DeFi ecosystem. Much of the activity conducted through decentralized financial applications would be regulated and subject to registration and compliance requirements if offered through a centralized business. Putting aside the liability of developers of such services, a further question arises regarding the extent of liability members of a DAO have for its activities when management is offloaded to token holders, and whether there is a way to "wrap" a DAO in a legal banner to limit liability for its members.

These topics are explored in the Supplemental Resources. With respect to the first question, at least one court has held that members of a DAO are liable for its activities as general partners. In a decision involving Ooki DAO, discussed in Chapter 14, the CFTC alleged that as an unincorporated association its members could be held liable for its violations of the Commodity Exchange Act. Facing the challenge of enforcing actions against a non-legal entity like Ooki DAO, the CFTC secured court permission to serve DAO members through the DAO's online discussion forum. As a decentralized and loosely affiliated online organization, Ooki DAO did not mount a defense, resulting in a default judgment.

The potential for liability has led some to seek a corporate vehicle to protect DAO members. Some have attempted to "wrap" DAOs in existing limited liability structures, while others have advocated for DAO-specific legislation. For example, Wyoming became the first state to create a new form of business registration for DAOs and, in 2024, introduced another concept for registering DAOs as Decentralized Unincorporated Nonprofit Associations (DUNA).

Still, others have rejected the concept of registering DAOs altogether and have advocated for moving certain functions to "DAO adjacent" entities. I am unaware of a perfect solution and have provided information on the most popular proposals in the Supplemental Resources.

Ultimately, some questions do not have easy answers, and there might not be a way for every type of decentralized financial tool to operate or for every organization to adopt a decentralized governance model that shields its developers or members from liability in the same way existing corporate frameworks do. As discussed with respect to the Tornado Cash rulings in the next chapter, there are open questions regarding the liability stemming from creating code that enables engagement in activities that are traditionally conducted by a regulated centralized business.

In the coming chapters, we will see how regulators will instinctively try to apply existing concepts to new technologies. Although this approach is effective in many instances, certain innovations must prompt regulators to assess if these new capabilities warrant different considerations. Decentralized finance enables individuals worldwide to conduct complex financial transactions without the need for traditional gatekeepers such as banks, exchanges, or other institutions. As explored in the resources provided, this marks a significant shift in the delivery of financial services, one that does not neatly fit within our current regulatory framework, which is centered around intermediaries.

Supplemental Resources[114] - DeFi

- "The Block Presents: Defi and the Law." *YouTube*, The Block, 14 Oct. 2020, y2u.be/jBq2gdyvmwc. A good introductory discussion to DeFi and the law, featuring a who's who of digital asset attorneys.

- The SEC and Defi | Hester Peirce." *YouTube*, Bankless, 12 Apr. 2021, y2u.be/gd84ALWwpRQ. A

---

114 For ease of reference, all Supplemental Resources and footnote links are available at www.TheCryptoLegalHandbook.com/Resources.

conversation with SEC Commissioner Hester Peirce (@HesterPeirce) on the SEC's role in regulating decentralized finance.

- **"Miller Whitehouse-Levine, CEO of the DEFI Education Fund."** *YouTube,* **Pretty Good Policy, 3 Apr. 2023,** y2u.be/utatp0lK6s. A discussion with Miller Whitehouse-Levine of the DeFi Education Fund (@fund_defi) on the law and policy developing around decentralized finance.

- **"DeFi."** *YouTube,* **playlist by Whiteboard Crypto,** shorturl.at/iqQ19. Whiteboard Crypto creates accessible introductions for complex crypto topics. This is a playlist of DeFi-related videos covering the most common DeFi concepts and projects.

- **Lau, Darren, et al.** *How to Defi: Beginner.* **CoinGecko, 2021.** This is a physical book that provides a good introduction to decentralized finance that can be read through in a fairly short amount of time. CoinGecko also produces an "Advanced" edition that goes into more complex topics. DeFi moves so quickly that some of the information is already outdated, although it provides a good overview of several topics.

Supplemental Resources - DAOs

- **Wright, Aaron. "The Rise of Decentralized Autonomous Organizations: Opportunities and Challenges."** *Stanford Journal of Blockchain Law & Policy,* **30 June 2021,** stanford-jblp.pubpub.org/pub/rise-of-daos/release/1.

- **Delphi Labs. "Assimilating the Borg: A New Cryptolegal Framework for Dao-Adjacent Entities."** *Medium,* **Medium, 25 Oct. 2023,** delphilabs.medium.com/assimilating-the-borg-a-new-cryptolegal-framework-for-dao-adjacent-entities-569e54a43f83. As conceptualized in this article, a BORG is a complimentary entity that uses "autonomous technologies" like smart contracts and AI to assist DAOs in facilitating decentralized governance without the need to wrap the DAO itself in a corporate registration.

- **Jennings, Miles, and David Kerr. "The DUNA: An Oasis for DAOs."** *A16z Crypto*, **8 Mar. 2024,** a16zcrypto.com/posts/article/duna-for-daos. In 2024, Wyoming enacted the Decentralized Unincorporated Nonprofit Association Act which created a new type of corporate registration for DAOs that aims to allow DAOs to operate within a legal framework without having to sacrifice decentralized governance. This article goes into the background and details of the project.

- **Tan, Joshua Z., et al. "Open Problems in DAOs."** *arXiv.Org*, **29 Oct. 2023,** arxiv.org/abs/2310.19201.

CHAPTER 10

The Department of Treasury

The United States takes preventing the illicit use of funds very seriously. This commitment is reflected in extensive regulations that allow the government to monitor the financial system and enforce laws against those involved in prohibited activities. The Department of Treasury is at the forefront of this effort, primarily through its Financial Crimes Enforcement Network (FinCEN) and Office of Foreign Assets Control (OFAC). With the rise of digital assets, the Treasury Department has become an active regulator in this field. In 2013, it became the first federal agency to publish guidance on applying existing regulations to digital assets. Since then, the Department's focus on crypto has steadily intensified, particularly through the enforcement of anti-money laundering (AML) regulations and imposition of significant penalties for non-compliance.

A noteworthy example of such enforcement occurred in November 2023 when the Department of Treasury fined Binance, the world's largest digital asset exchange, a record $3.4 billion for failing to comply with the Bank Secrecy Act (BSA).[115] The fine was imposed because Binance allegedly enabled transactions for sanctioned entities and lacked a compliance program capable of preventing money laundering and terrorist financing. This action is among several targeting the digital asset industry.

This Chapter provides an overview of the Bank Secrecy Act and the Department of Treasury's guidelines on applying its rules to the digital asset industry. It also includes case studies of enforcement actions, highlighting the failure of some entities to establish comprehensive

---

115 "Binance and CEO Plead Guilty to Federal Charges in $4B Resolution." *United States Department of Justice*, 1 Dec. 2023, shorturl.at/arxJ6.

compliance programs to prevent illicit activities.

Many lawyers are well-versed in the theoretical aspects of the BSA but find it challenging to translate its requirements into actionable guidance. A compliance program's practical development and implementation typically fall under the purview of specially trained compliance professionals. These individuals navigate the intricacies of formulating and executing an effective compliance policy, which can be difficult for those lacking experience in the field.

Developing and sustaining a compliance program is intricate and differs across entities. No universal solution is suitable for all organizations, particularly those adapting to the sophisticated tactics used in illegal financial dealings with digital assets. To aid in understanding these complexities, the Supplemental Resources includes materials on designing and administering a compliance program. Nonetheless, this subject is complex, often requiring hands-on experience to fully comprehend. Establishing and overseeing a compliance program is more of an art than a science, demanding considerable resources and expertise for effective implementation at scale.

As we delve into the requirements of financial institutions to surveil and report on the transactions of Americans, I encourage you to reflect on the broader implications of extensive surveillance and reporting requirements on our privacy rights. We'll touch on the longstanding constitutional debates surrounding regulations that target financial intermediaries and will explore, in the Supplemental Resources, how extending these regulations to non-financial entities and digital asset technologies such as protocols, smart contracts, and wallets, may further implicate fundamental constitutional rights.

The Bank Secrecy Act

The Bank Secrecy Act, overseen by the Department of Treasury, was established to regulate the illicit use of the financial system. Enacted in 1970, it requires financial institutions to gather and retain information about their customers' financial activities and report this to the government. Initially, the BSA's definition of "financial institutions" was limited to insured banks, which were required to maintain customer information and file a Currency Transaction Report (CTR) with the Department of Treasury for any customer deposit, withdrawal, or transfer exceeding $10,000.

Since its inception, the Bank Secrecy Act has seen a significant expansion in its scope, though even its initial parameters sparked considerable controversy and debate. Critics contended that the BSA's obligatory record-keeping and reporting mandates violated the First, Fourth, and Fifth Amendment rights of banks and their clients. In *California Bankers Assn. v. Shultz*, 416 U.S. 21 (1974) and *United States v. Miller*, 425 US 435 (1976), the Supreme Court upheld the constitutionality of the BSA's record-keeping and reporting requirements. In those cases, the Court held that the BSA did not impose an undue burden on banks and that bank customers do not have an expectation of privacy in the commercial records of their activities with the bank, a concept known as the "Third-Party Doctrine."[116]

In the decades since the BSA was upheld, its reach has expanded significantly. The definition of "financial institution" now encompasses a wide array of businesses beyond just insured banks. This expanded list includes securities and commodities brokers or dealers, pre-paid card sellers, currency exchangers, travel agents, jewelry stores, money transmitters, telegraph companies, car dealers, realtors, casinos, the U.S. post office, and "any other business" engaged in activities similar to those of financial institutions. There are discussions about further expanding this definition to include service providers like accountants and lawyers, although many already voluntarily comply with the BSA.

The record-keeping and reporting requirements of the BSA have been considerably broadened by amendment. Since 1996, financial institutions have been required to file Suspicious Activity Reports (SARs) for transactions exceeding $5,000 for banks and $2,000

---

116 The Third-Party Doctrine posits that individuals forfeit their reasonable expectation of privacy when information is voluntarily given to third parties. Originating with bank records, its scope has been expanded to encompass data held by numerous other entities including phone and internet providers. In *United States v. Gratkowski*, 964 F.3d 307 (5th Cir. 2020), the Fifth Circuit held Bitcoin transaction data does not enjoy Fourth Amendment protections.

for non-bank financial institutions if they suspect the transaction involves illegal activities, aims to evade BSA regulations, or lacks a legitimate business or apparent lawful purpose. In the wake of the September 11th attacks, the PATRIOT Act further expanded the scope of the BSA by requiring additional customer identification procedures, enhanced due diligence policies, and increased civil and criminal penalties for non-compliance.

The BSA's scope has also increased over time due to inflation. When enacted in 1970, the reporting obligation to file CTRs applied to transactions of $10,000 or more. That threshold has never been increased, even though the equivalent spending power in 2024 is about $78,000. As a result, the Treasury Department now has broader oversight over financial transactions that are much smaller than the BSA initially contemplated.

The BSA is typically enforced by a business's principal federal regulator. For example, the Office of the Comptroller of the Currency regulates bank compliance, while the Financial Industry Regulatory Authority (FINRA), a self-regulatory organization under the supervision of the SEC, oversees securities broker-dealers for BSA compliance. In this Chapter, our focus will be on a broad category of business under the BSA known as "Money Services Businesses" (MSBs), which include "money transmitters" that accept and transmit value to another person or location. The Internal Revenue Service (IRS) conducts BSA compliance examinations of MSBs and other non-bank financial institutions, under delegated authority from FinCEN.

Since 1999, the Department of Treasury has mandated that MSBs register before commencing operations. In contrast to the money transmitter licenses overseen by various state regulators, which require discretionary approval before commencing operations, MSBs can register by submitting FinCEN Form 107. This form notifies the Treasury Department of the intent to operate as an MSB and is simpler than every state money transmitter application. It requires basic information about the business, its owners, and the individuals responsible for implementing and overseeing the company's BSA/AML program. While the registration process is relatively straightforward, MSBs must still invest time in developing a comprehensive compliance program as part of their obligations under the BSA. At the end of this chapter, I have included resources addressing the considerations necessary for a compliance program to meet BSA regulations and effectively monitor and report suspicious activities.

As the scope and requirements of the BSA have expanded, so too has the cost of compliance. For entities handling a significant volume of transactions, the expenses related to maintaining a compliance team of analysts and investigators and the requisite databases and technologies for large-scale automated transaction monitoring constitute a substantial portion of a financial institution's operational costs. However, the cost of non-compliance can be even greater. Entities found violating the BSA face hefty monetary penalties and individuals who willfully violate the BSA can incur fines and criminal penalties.

The Department of Justice (DOJ) is primarily responsible for pursuing enforcement actions in cases of criminal BSA violations, but it's worth noting that state regulators often also investigate adherence to the BSA during their examinations of regulated entities. Moreover, third-party entities like banks, insurers, bond issuers, and even technology partners like Google Play and the Apple App Stores reinforce compliance with the BSA by reviewing and sometimes requiring improvements to a company's compliance programs as a condition of their business relationship.

Virtual Currency Guidance

In March 2013, via FinCEN, the Department of Treasury became the first federal entity to articulate how existing federal regulations pertain to virtual currencies. In its memorandum, "Application of FinCEN's Regulations to Persons Administering, Exchanging, or Using Virtual Currencies," the Department clarified that those engaged in exchanging, accepting, or transmitting virtual currencies must comply with the Bank Secrecy Act, whereas users that use virtual currencies for personal consumption were exempt.[117]

---

117 "Fin-2013-G001: Application of FinCEN's Regulations to Persons Administering, Exchanging, or Using Virtual Currencies" *FinCEN*, 18 Mar. 2013, shorturl.at/gitPZ.

The 2013 guidance introduced the term "Convertible Virtual Currency" (CVC) to denote digital assets not tied to the value of "real" (fiat) currencies. It delineated three primary participants in the virtual currency sphere: administrators, exchangers, and users, defining their roles as follows:

- **Administrators:** Individuals or entities issuing a virtual currency and retaining the authority to withdraw it from circulation are engaged in MSB activities. This definition applies to centralized entities managing the issuance and redemption of stablecoins and digital asset issuers selling pre-mined digital assets.

- **Exchangers:** Individuals or entities operating a business that facilitates virtual currency exchange for real currency, funds, or other forms of virtual currency are regarded as engaging in MSB activities. The creators of decentralized virtual currencies can also fall under the BSA's scope when they sell their creations to a third party. In 2015, the Department of Treasury took its first enforcement action against virtual currency exchanger Ripple Labs and a related entity for failing to register as an MSB and adhere to the BSA's compliance requirements when it sold XRP to the public.[118]

- **Users:** Individuals obtaining or employing virtual currency solely for personal goods or service transactions are not considered to be engaged in MSB activities.

The six-page 2013 memo established that "administrators" and "exchangers" fall within the BSA's scope as MSBs, whereas mere "users" of virtual currencies do not.

In May 2019, FinCEN expanded its framework in a 30-page memorandum, "Application of FinCEN's Regulations to Certain Business Models Involving Convertible Virtual Currencies."[119] This

---

118 *In the Matter of Ripple Labs Inc.* Number 2015-05, Assessment of Civil Money Penalty. tinyurl.com/yd2d4vxt.

119 "FIN-2019-G001: Application of FinCEN's Regulations to Certain Business Models Involving Convertible Virtual Currencies." *FinCEN*, 19 May 2019, shorturl.at/dpBOY.

document provides insights into several business models in the virtual currency sector. FinCEN's classifications of virtual currency business models are briefly presented below. However, I recommend you read the 2013 and 2019 memoranda directly.

- **Virtual Currency Platforms:** Direct sales of virtual currency to users classify a platform as an MSB. However, platforms facilitating connections between buyers and sellers are not MSBs unless they act as transaction intermediaries.

- **Decentralized Exchanges:** Platforms enabling direct user-to-user connections without intermediate services are not categorized as MSBs. Similarly, developers of these platforms are not considered MSBs if their role is limited to software creation.

- **Peer-to-Peer Exchangers:** Individuals regularly involved in buying or selling virtual currency are MSBs. However, occasional transactions without profit motives fall outside the scope of an MSB.

- **Token Sellers:** Issuers selling tokens to third parties are deemed "administrators" if they retain the exclusive rights to issue and redeem the tokens at the time of sale.

- **Bitcoin ATM Machines:** These are classified as MSBs.

- **Miners and Mining Pools:** Individual miners are not MSBs, and mining pools also fall outside the MSB category unless they offer additional services like wallet hosting.

- **Mixers/Tumblers:** These services are categorized as MSBs due to their involvement in pooling and transferring funds. As discussed below, the Department of Justice prosecuted the creators of the virtual currency mixer "Tornado Cash" for failure to register as an MSB and violations of the BSA. Note that while the 2019 guidance provides that the developers of privacy-enhancing software without direct transaction involvement are not MSBs, Tornado Cash's developers have nevertheless been prosecuted for their role in developing a decentralized mixer.[120]

- **Virtual Currency Payment Processors:** Third-party entities that integrate with a merchant's point-of-sale system to facilitate virtual currency transactions are generally classified as MSBs that do not qualify for FinCEN's "payment processor" exception. Conversely, merchants who use their own digital asset wallets to accept virtual currencies as payment for goods or services are usually not considered MSBs.

- **Digital Wallet Providers:** FinCEN's guidance employs criteria focusing on value ownership, storage location, interaction with the payment system, and intermediary control to differentiate between "hosted" (custodial) wallets, which are MSBs, and "unhosted" (self-custodial) wallets, which are not.

Unhosted Wallets and the Funds Travel Rule

The Department of Treasury is considering a proposal to compel MSBs to gather identifying information for recipients of unhosted wallets involved in transactions exceeding $10,000. While this regulatory effort is still under consideration, most U.S. virtual currency platforms do not require users to provide details about digital asset transaction recipients. Although not a current mandate, there's a trend towards such data collection in other jurisdictions.

The initiative is intricately connected to the Bank Secrecy Act's "Funds Travel Rule," which compels financial institutions to collect and relay detailed information about the entities involved in transactions surpassing $3,000.[121] Yet, the rule's implementation presents notable challenges, as it is specifically tailored for transactions *between* financial institutions. Identifying a digital wallet as linked to a financial institution is not inherently evident

---

120 For an analysis regarding the potential contradictions between FinCEN's 2019 guidance and the prosecution of Tornado Cash's founders, *see* Gruenstein, Benjamin, et al. "Assessing the Tornado Cash Indictment against FinCEN's 2019 Guidance Applying Money Transmission Rules to Crypto Businesses." *NYU's Program on Corporate Compliance and Enforcement*, 26 Oct. 2023, tinyurl.com/3vfbkws4.

121 *See* 31 CFR § 1010.410 (Records to be made and retained by financial institutions), available at law.cornell.edu/cfr/text/31/1010.410.

from its address. Consequently, for an MSB to ensure compliance with the Funds Travel Rule in its present form, it would necessitate collecting information about all transactions processed through its platform, including those involving unhosted wallets.

Applying the Funds Travel Rule to cryptocurrency transactions remains an evolving issue. The consensus, for now, is that virtual currency platforms are not required to obtain detailed ownership information of digital wallets receiving funds. However, the Financial Action Task Force (FATF), an international organization responsible for setting global anti-money laundering standards, advocates that Virtual Asset Service Providers (VASPs)—a category encompassing crypto MSBs—collect information about all fund recipients. FATF's recommendations have not been adopted in the United States, and it faces criticism for misunderstanding how digital assets are transacted and for promoting mass surveillance measures that are fundamentally at odds with civil liberties across many jurisdictions.[122]

Despite concerns about the obligatory nature of recipient data collection, the industry has been proactive in complying with the Funds Travel Rule and parts of FATF's recommendations. One such effort is an industry-led consortium of VASPs called the "Travel Rule Universal Solution Technology" or "TRUST," which has developed a standardized platform for sharing encrypted customer information between VASPs.[123]

Sanctions and The Office of Foreign Assets Control

The Office of Foreign Assets Control (OFAC) was established in December 1950, succeeding the Office of Foreign Funds Control formed during World War II. Initially, OFAC's primary mission was to block enemy access to the U.S. financial system and manage the nation's foreign assets during wartime. As times evolved, so has OFAC's mandate. It now plays a critical role in implementing

---

122 For an analysis of the latest iteration of FATF's guidance, *see* Van Valkenburgh, Peter. "The Long-Awaited FATF Crypto Guidance Is Not as Bad as It Could Have Been, but Still Flawed." *Coin Center*, 28 Oct. 2021, shorturl.at/ahmH.

123 Information about the Coinbase-led initiative is available at coinbase.com/travelrule.

and enforcing economic and trade sanctions aligned with U.S. foreign policy and national security objectives. These sanctions are aimed at addressing threats from foreign nations, terrorist groups, international narcotics traffickers, and entities linked to the proliferation of weapons of mass destruction.

OFAC administers a comprehensive sanctions list of several countries, significantly restricting trade and financial transactions between these nations and U.S. persons. Currently, this list is comprised of Cuba, Iran, North Korea, Russia, Syria, and certain areas in Ukraine affected by conflict. In addition to country-specific sanctions, OFAC also curates a list of Specially Designated Nationals (SDN), which can include individuals, entities, or assets. U.S. persons and businesses are prohibited from conducting transactions with those listed as SDNs.

Being labeled an SDN requires financial institutions to freeze assets held on their platform and block attempted transactions. A robust compliance program will routinely screen customers and transactions to prevent the platform from being utilized to circumvent sanctions. Engaging in transactions with an SDN, whether by a U.S. person or business, irrespective of their global location, can result in civil and criminal penalties.

In recent developments, the Treasury Department has begun including digital wallet addresses of sanctioned individuals and entities in its SDN database. Recently, blockchain protocol addresses have been added to the list, sparking a novel legal debate: Can a smart contract's address be considered a person or property subject to OFAC's sanctioning authority?

A notable instance occurred in August 2022 when the Treasury Department listed the wallet addresses of Tornado Cash, an Ethereum-based DeFi mixing protocol, on the SDN list. Tornado Cash, developed by individual programmers and operated via a DAO, was implicated in illicit activities involving sanctioned entities such as North Korea and the Taliban, leading to its inclusion on the list.

This inclusion was legally contested in federal courts in Texas and

Florida, with the primary arguments questioning whether Tornado Cash, as a non-human entity, and its smart contract addresses, as non-tangible assets, could be sanctioned. Both courts upheld the Treasury Department's stance, affirming that Tornado Cash qualifies as a "person" and its smart contracts as "property" under OFAC's framework. Subsequently, the U.S. Attorney's Office for the Southern District of New York brought charges against Tornado Cash's founders for breaching U.S. sanctions and anti-money laundering regulations.

Coin Center, a digital currency think tank, challenged the Florida ruling and is currently appealing to the 11th Circuit. While initial judicial reviews have upheld the inclusion of smart contract addresses on the SDN list, the pending appeal raises profound questions about whether a protocol can be sanctioned and the broader implications for U.S. persons utilizing such platforms.[124]

Privacy and Financial Regulations

The desire for financial privacy is a fundamental human instinct, and numerous legitimate motivations exist for engaging in private financial transactions that are unrelated to money laundering or financing terrorism. Yet, since the introduction of the Bank Secrecy Act in 1970 and its intensification post-9/11, the U.S. government's surveillance of citizens' financial activities has markedly increased. In today's increasingly cashless society, conducting unmonitored financial transactions has become nearly impossible, especially online, where an intermediary is necessarily involved.

Significant reductions in financial privacy have primarily been accomplished through the stringent regulation of third parties, initially banks and subsequently a broader range of financial institutions, integral to participating fully in the global financial economy. However, the advent of Bitcoin and the ability to store and transmit value without intermediaries has challenged the government's capacity to monitor financial transactions through

---

[124] For a deeper dive into the arguments and the broader discourse on the necessity of tools that enhance financial privacy, see "OFAC's Tornado Cash Sanctions." *YouTube*, Coin Center, 15 Aug. 2022, y2u.be/KAKNz5rePho.

regulated intermediaries.

As the U.S. government adapts its laws to the emergence of different privately tradable assets, it seems increasingly inclined to extend regulation beyond financial institutions to the very tools and instruments used. While reviewing the Supplemental Resources, observe the developing Constitutional arguments that posit whether the use of digital assets and their supporting technologies implicates our fundamental rights. Since the BSA's earliest days, there has been a consistent tension between preventing illicit activities and respecting the privacy rights of Americans. As we move into a world less reliant on intermediaries, this tension has become more pronounced. Coin Center's Neeraj Agrawal (@NeerajKA) perfectly encapsulated the ongoing debate over increased financial surveillance of digital assets in a tweet:

> *"i'm sorry that your warrantless surveillance regime was built on the assumption that people would always need intermediaries to transact."*

Supplemental Resources[125]

- **Compliance Program Basics** – The intricacies of developing an adequate compliance program go beyond the scope of this book, and crafting and implementing a capable BSA/AML program requires someone with individual compliance training. For an accessible overview of the type of considerations and factors a compliance program should address, the FDIC has published a helpful overview of the BSA and the hallmarks of a compliance program. *See* "**Bank Secrecy Act.**" *YouTube,* **FDIC, 10 Dec. 2018,** y2u.be/7ld6YjfvgSI.

- For a slightly more in-depth undertaking, *see* "**How to Build a BSA/AML Compliance Program: Ebook.**" **Modern Treasury,** moderntreasury.com/

---

[125] For ease of reference, all Supplemental Resources and footnote links are available at www.TheCryptoLegalHandbook.com/Resources.

how-to-build-bsa-aml-compliance.

- **Coin Center Reports** — Below are three Coin Center reports that, taken together, provide an overview of the BSA's current and projected application to digital assets and their infrastructure. The first two reports scrutinize digital assets and the BSA within a constitutional framework, while the third offers a well-considered rebuttal to FinCEN's efforts to classify virtual currency mixing as a "Primary Money Laundering Concern."

    - Van Valkenburgh, Peter. "Electronic Cash, Decentralized Exchange, and the Constitution." *Coin Center*, March 2019, shorturl.at/hkBI6.

    - Van Valkenburgh, Peter. "Broad, Ambiguous, or Delegated: Constitutional Infirmities of the Bank Secrecy Act." *Coin Center*, Nov. 2023, shorturl.at/fxG34.

    - Van Valkenburgh, Peter. "Comments to the Financial Crimes Enforcement Network on 'Proposal of Special Measure Regarding Convertible Virtual Currency Mixing, as a Class of Transactions of Primary Money Laundering Concern.'" *Coin Center*, 22 Jan. 2024, shorturl.at/gkuAX.

- **DeFi and Compliance** - For an analysis of the unique compliance considerations inherent to DeFi:

    - Rettig, Rebecca, et al. "Genuine DeFi as Critical Infrastructure: A Conceptual Framework for Combating Illicit Finance Activity in Decentralized Finance." 29 Jan. 2024, SSRN, ssrn.com/abstract=4607332.

    - "How to Combat Illicit Finance without Killing Defi | Rebecca Rettig & Miller Whitehouse-Levine." *YouTube*, Empire, 17 Feb. 2024, y2u.be/LrpVhPnSn9g.

CHAPTER 11

The States

Except for the Bank Secrecy Act, which has been broadly overlayed across the financial system, a federal framework governing digital asset use, sale, or transmission does not exist. It has been 15 years since Bitcoin's creation, but no significant federal regulations have been enacted. Instead, federal agencies have issued piecemeal guidance or pursued individual enforcement actions to promote their view of how digital assets fit within existing laws. This approach has fueled a perception by some that crypto businesses are widely non-compliant with federal regulations, a view many believe is disingenuous since existing regulations often don't apply neatly to cryptocurrencies.

The lack of comprehensive regulation has left the industry dependent on a slowly evolving body of case law derived from isolated enforcement actions. These actions rarely offer clear guidelines for how the broader cryptocurrency industry should govern itself. Federal legislative efforts to establish comprehensive regulations, such as the *Lummis-Gillibrand Responsible Financial Innovation Act* and the *Financial Innovation and Technology for the 21st Century Act*, have been impeded by political gridlock and a lack of bipartisan support.[126]

In the absence of federal regulation, state governments have taken on the primary responsibility of regulating the industry, often within the framework of local money transmitter laws. Consequently, state agencies initially established to oversee entities like check-cashing services and currency exchangers have had to adapt their regulations to accommodate advanced financial technologies.

---

126 *See* Lummis-Gillibrand Responsible Financial Innovation Act, S. 2281, 118th Cong. (2023); Financial Innovation and Technology for the 21st Century Act, H.R. 4763, 118th Cong. (2023).

This state-level approach has led to inconsistencies in regulatory practices across the United States. Knowledge about digital assets and attitudes towards the industry vary greatly among state regulators and can change with local political shifts. As a result, the challenges of obtaining and maintaining licenses differ across states and evolve over time, posing operational hurdles and compliance risks for businesses seeking to offer a nationwide product.

Most books on digital asset law acknowledge the role of states in regulating the industry but offer little insight into the actual experience of being regulated. The narrative from federal regulators suggests that obtaining and maintaining state licensure is a straightforward process that allows companies to operate nationwide with minimal oversight.

But that is not the case.

Nearly every state exerts regulatory control over financial intermediaries. The extent of this control over digital assets is not uniform, and in practice, state regulators often adopt a broader view of their jurisdiction over digital asset businesses than their published guidance indicates. We will explore state regulations in some detail below, but the goal of this chapter is not to provide an exhaustive review of state law. Rather, I aim to present a practical overview of the experience of navigating and being regulated by several dozen authorities and to discuss the implications of this fragmented system on the industry.

Money Transmission Generally

Digital asset businesses are usually subject to state oversight to the degree that they act as a "money transmitter" that transfers value for their customers. As discussed in Chapter 10, business models that FinCEN does not classify as Money Services Businesses also typically find themselves outside of the scope of the definition of a money transmitter. Although the approach and scope of what constitutes "money transmission" vary from state to state, a representative definition of a "money transmitter" is one that "engages in the business of receiving money or monetary value for transmission or transmitting money or monetary value."[127]

The definition of "money" or "monetary value" differs among the states. All states with a money transmitter act regulate the transmission of fiat currency, but the inclusion of stablecoins or other digital assets in their definitions varies. There is a trend towards including digital assets within the definition of money, and subjecting digital asset transmitters to the state's existing money transmission rules, especially where fiat is also involved in the transmission.

Every state, except Montana, requires a money transmitter license to engage in money transmission as defined by that state. Applications are reviewed by a dedicated team within the state's Department of Banking or Finance, though the specific application requirements and the name of the department with regulatory authority vary. Once licensed, money transmitters must periodically submit documentation, including quarterly and annual call reports and audited financial statements, and keep their regulator apprised of business updates or material events. Licensed money transmitters are also subject to yearly examinations to ensure ongoing compliance with regulatory standards, financial solvency, and adherence to established anti-money laundering and consumer protection rules.

To regulate digital asset businesses, most states have amended their Money Transmitter Acts through guidance or legislation to encompass digital assets. Meanwhile, states like New York and Louisiana have introduced specific digital legislation, offering a more detailed regulatory framework for digital asset services. Known as a "BitLicense," this model is becoming more popular. California's BitLicense will be implemented in 2025, and other states will likely follow.

Unlike the Department of Treasury's notification requirement for Money Services Businesses, which involves informing the Department of the intent to operate as an MSB, obtaining state licensure as a

---

[127] The process of transmitting money on behalf of an individual inherently involves the custody of funds for some duration. There's an ongoing debate about when such custody, in anticipation of transmission, begins to intersect with regulations pertaining to trust companies.

money transmitter requires explicit approval. Depending on the state, the time it takes to secure a license can range from a few months to several years. Often, delays arise from deficiencies in the application. However, even applications prepared with meticulous attention to detail can face prolonged waits. These delays may be due to benign factors such as the novelty and complexity of the business plan or a backlog of pending applications alongside the regulatory department's limited resources.

However, at times, the root of state licensing delays lies in the regulatory authority's stance toward digital assets. After the collapse of the FTX Exchange, for example, several agencies informally imposed moratoriums on issuing new licenses for digital asset businesses. State regulators have considerable discretion in licensing and oversight decisions, and often there is no viable recourse for challenging a regulator's actions or inactivity. Initiating litigation or attempting to bypass one's current or future regulator is generally a strategy of last resort.

A money transmitter license application typically requires an applicant to submit a business plan, details about its direct and indirect owners, officers, and directors, the company's operational history, audited financial statements, a comprehensive compliance program, and evidence of financial stability, including meeting certain net worth or capital requirements. Most states also require a surety bond or other insurance coverage, copies of agreements with banks or business partners, and information about the applicant's cybersecurity policies and procedures.[128]

While a multi-state oversight process will necessarily be an expensive undertaking, there is a trend toward standardization. All states with a Money Transmitter Act, except Florida and New Jersey, use the Nationwide Multistate Licensing System & Registry (NMLS) for managing applications and ongoing submissions.[129] Several states

---

128 State Licensing, NMLS Resource Ctr., shorturl.at/zAJUW (checklists of application requirements for all states).

129 Originally named the "Nationwide Mortgage Licensing System," the platform was developed in 2008 by the Conference of State Bank Supervisors and the American Association of Residential Mortgage Regulators to establish uniformity among mortgage and

have also signaled support of a "One Company, One Exam" initiative, which would coordinate annual examination efforts between the states.[130]

The Supplemental Resources section provides additional details about NMLS. I have found that many lawyers lack hands-on experience with NMLS and depend on paralegals or licensing consultants to handle filings and ongoing communications with regulators. The NMLS platform has taken on a central role in managing ongoing licensing obligations and is primarily the venue through which quarterly and annual reports and other mandatory filings are submitted. Given this role, it is advisable for lawyers to become well-versed in the practical aspects of the platform.

State Specifics

Whether a license is required to conduct a digital asset business in a particular state is fact-specific and dependent on the business's relationship with its customers. Generally, a company providing some intermediary service requires a license. Sometimes, a business selling its own digital assets can trigger a licensing obligation, although in many states, that depends on whether it has sold the asset for fiat or exchanged it for a different cryptocurrency.

Below, I have categorized and provided an overview of each state's approach to regulating the sale and transmission of digital assets. When a state's stance on digital currency is explicitly stated in the statute, it's presented without comment; however, where the position arises from external guidance or information about a state's activities in digital asset regulation is material, such insights are included as notes.

---

non-bank financial institutions.

130 "State Regulators Roll Out One Company, One Exam for Nationwide Payments Firms." *Conference of State Bank Supervisors*, 15 Sept. 2020, csbs.org/regulators-announce-one-company-one-exam-for-payments-companies.

I. States That Regulate Transmissions of Virtual Currencies

State	Money Transmitter Act	Regulatory Authority
Alabama	Monetary Transmission Act - Code of Alabama, §§ 8-7a-1 to 8-7a-27	Alabama Securities Commission
Alaska	Uniform Money Services Act, Alaska Admin Code § 06.55.101 *et seq.*	Alaska Division of Banking and Securities
Arkansas	Uniform Money Services Act, Arkansas Code §§ 23-55-201 *et seq.*	Arkansas Securities Department
Connecticut	Money Transmission Act, Connecticut General Statutes Annotated, §§ 36a-595 to 36a-612	Connecticut Department of Banking
District of Columbia	Money Transmissions, Division V, Title 26, Chapter 10 (Money Transmissions), District of Columbia Code Annotated, §§ 26-1001 *et seq.*	D.C. Department of Insurance, Securities, and Banking

Notes: In *United States v. Harmon*, 474 F. Supp. 3d 76 (D.D.C. 2020), the United States District Court for the District of Columbia held that cryptocurrencies qualified as money under the District's Money Transmitter Act. In Bulletin 22-BB-001-08/04, D.C.'s financial regulator adopted the federal court's position but clarified that while receiving crypto for custody or transmission constitutes money transmission, direct sales from one's own inventory do not.[131]

Florida	Money Service Businesses, Florida Statutes, §§ 560.103 et seq.	Office of Financial Regulation

Notes: In May 2022, Florida updated its money transmitter law to clarify that while virtual currencies fall under the state's definition of money a license is not required unless a person serves as an intermediary to a transaction between other parties.

Georgia	Sale of Payment Instruments, Code of Georgia Annotated, §§ 7-1-680 et seq.	Department of Banking and Finance
Idaho	Money Transmitters Act, Idaho Code Annotated, §§ 26-2901 et seq.	Department of Finance

Notes: According to the Idaho Department of Finance's website, entities accepting legal tender to facilitate the purchase of virtual currency for a third party must obtain a money transmitter license.[132]

Maine	Money Transmitter Act, Maine Revised Statutes Annotated, § 6101 et seq.	Department of Professional and Financial Regulations, Bureau of Consumer Credit Protection

---

131 *Certain Bitcoin Activity Subject To District Of Columbia Money Transmission Laws.* 2022, disb.dc.gov/sites/default/files/dc/sites/disb/page_content/attachments/bulletin-disb-cryptocurrency-money-transmission-approved.pdf.

132 *Money Transmitters*, Idaho Dep't Fin., finance.idaho.gov/securities-bureau/money-transmitters.

| Maryland | Money Transmission Act, Annotated Code of Maryland, §§ 12-401 et seq. | Office of the Commissioner of Financial Regulation |

Notes: In 2021, the state amended its Money Transmission Act to expand its definition of monetary value to include "medium[s] of exchange whether or not redeemable in money." While this amendment did not explicitly reference virtual currencies, the Office of the Commissioner of Financial Regulation's website and NMLS checklist make clear that virtual currency transmission is licensable activity.[133]

| Nevada | Issuer of Instruments for Transmission or Payment of Money, Nevada Revised Statutes Annotated, §§ 671.020 et seq. | Department of Banking & Industry |

Notes: The Nevada Financial Institutions Division issued a statement regarding cryptocurrency regulation, advising digital asset industries to contact the Department of Banking & Industry to determine whether they require a license. The state's guidance mandates entities engaged in the business of receiving for transmission or transmitting money to obtain a license, and it is my understanding that the state includes digital asset transmission as a licensable activity. The state has also issued guidance that entities that serve as digital custodians may have to be regulated as trust companies.[134]

---

[133] "Regulated Financial Industries and Activities - Financial Regulation." *Maryland Department of Labor*, dllr.state.md.us/finance/industry/frregulatedind.shtml; "MD Money Transmitter License New Application Checklist (Company)." *NMLS Resource Center*, 2023, mortgage.nationwidelicensingsystem.org/slr/PublishedStateDocuments/MD-Money-Transmitter-New-App-Checklist.pdf.

[134] "Nevada Financial Institutions Division statement on regulation of cryptocurrency in Nevada," fid.nv.gov/uploadedFiles/fidnvgov/content/Home/features/FID%20Statement%20on%20Crypotcurrency.pdf.

New Mexico	*Uniform Money Services Act, New Mexico Statutes Annotated, §§ 58-32-101 et seq.*	Regulation & Licensing Department, Financial Institutions Division

Notes: According to a FAQ page on the New Mexico Regulation & Licensing Department's website, "it is the position of FID that any entity engaged in the business of providing the exchange of virtual currency for money or any other form of monetary value or stored value to persons located in the State of New Mexico must be licensed by the FID as a money transmitter."[135]

North Carolina	Money Transmitters Act, North Carolina General Statutes Annotated, §§ 53-208.41 *et seq.*	Office of Commissioner of Banks

Notes: North Carolina has advised that virtual currency transmission is regulated under its Money Transmitters Act.[136]

Ohio	Transmitters of Money, Ohio Revised Code Annotated, §§ 1315.01 *et seq.*	Department of Commerce, Division of Financial Institutions

Notes: The Division of Financial Institutions issued interpretive guidance for Ohio money transmitters indicating that the Division considers virtual currencies to be money or its equivalent.[137]

---

135 "General FAQs." *New Mexico Regulation & Licensing Department*, rld.nm.gov/financial-institutions/about-us/faqs.

136 "Money Transmitter Frequently Asked Questions," *NC Office of the Comm'r of Banks*, nccob.nc.gov/financial-institutions/money-transmitters/money-transmitter-frequently-asked-questions.

137 "DFI Interpretive Guidance for Ohio Money Transmitters," *Ohio Dep't of Com.*, Div. of Fin. Inst., com.ohio.gov/divisions-and-programs/financial-institutions/money-transmitters/guides-and-resources/dfi-interpretive-guidance-for-ohio-money-transmitters.

Oregon	Money Transmitters Act, Oregon Revised Statutes Annotated, §§ 717.200 *et seq.*	Department of Consumer and Business Services, Division of Financial Regulation

Notes: Oregon's Money Transmitters Act doesn't explicitly mention virtual currency. However, state-published guidance indicates that cryptocurrency transmissions should occur through a state-licensed digital currency exchange. Oregon mandates licensing for companies transferring digital currency between individuals, but not for those merely converting cash into digital currency.[138]

Rhode Island	Currency Transmissions, General Laws of Rhode Island Annotated, §§ 19-14-1 *et seq.* and §§ 19-14.3-1	Department of Business Regulation

Notes: In July 2019, Rhode Island enacted the Uniform Regulation of Virtual-Currency Businesses Act. This comprehensive legislation defines key terms related to virtual currency and stipulates that currency transmission activities require a state license. Simultaneously, the Uniform Supplemental Commercial Law for the Uniform Regulation of Virtual-Currency Businesses Act was also adopted, extending the Act's reach to nonresident users and transactions under certain conditions. The Department of Business Regulation has also issued guidance clarifying that activities involving control over virtual currency on behalf of others require a license, affirming that both cryptocurrency wallet businesses and cryptocurrency exchangers operating exchange platforms need a Rhode Island Currency Transmission License.[139]

---

138 *"Cryptocurrency,"* Or. Dep't of Consumer & Bus. Serv., Div. of Fin. Reg., dfr.oregon.gov/help/Documents/5342-cryptocurrency.pdf.

139 *"Rhode Island Currency Transmission Law Frequently Asked Questions."* R.I. Dep't of Bus. Reg., dbr.ri.gov/sites/g/files/xkgbur696/files/documents/rules/banking_securities/Currency_Transmission_FAQ_-_Frequently_Asked_Questions_NEW.pdf.

South Dakota	Money Transmission, South Dakota Codified Laws, §§ 51A-17-1 et seq.	Department of Labor & Regulation, Division of Banking

Notes: The Division of Banking released a memorandum in May 2019 stating that, according to the state's money transmitter law, virtual currencies are recognized as "monetary value," and as a result, entities receiving virtual currency for transmission are required to secure a license.[140]

Vermont	Money Services, Vermont Statutes Annotated, §§ 2500 et seq.	Department of Financial Regulation
Washington	Uniform Money Services Act, Washington Annotated, §§ 19.230.005 et seq.	Department of Financial Institutions

Notes: Washington updated its Uniform Money Services Act to include virtual currency as a form of money necessitating a license for transmitters. The Act mandates entities transmitting virtual currencies hold a volume of the currencies equivalent to the amount owed to consumers. It also specifies that storing virtual currency for others does not require a license if the custodian cannot independently transmit the stored value. Further guidance from the Department of Financial Institutions confirms that businesses involved in transmitting, buying, or selling virtual currencies in Washington must be licensed.[141]

---

140 "Memorandum Re: Virtual Currency Transmission in South Dakota.", S.D. Dep't of Labor & Reg., Div. of Banking, 25 May 2019, dlr.sd.gov/banking/legal/documents/11_002_virtual_currency_transmission_in_sd.pdf.

141 "Virtual Currency and Money Transmission Laws." Wash. Dep't of Fin. Inst, 13 May 2021, dfi.wa.gov/sites/default/files/virtual-currency-money-transmission-laws.pdf.

II. States That Do Not Regulate Transmissions of Virtual Currencies

California	Money Transmission Act, Annotated California Codes, Financial Code, Division 1.2, Chapter 1, §§ 2000 *et seq.*	Department of Financial Protection & Innovation, Money Transmitter Division

Notes: Since 2015, California's Department of Financial Protection and Innovation (DFPI) has not conclusively determined if cryptocurrencies are considered "money," leaving their status under the state's banking and money transmission laws undecided.[142] However, no-action letters from DFPI suggest that virtual currency businesses may not require a money transmission license to operate in the state.

Effective July 2025, California's new legislation will require businesses involved in "digital financial asset business activity" to secure a BitLicense issued by the state. This law mandates licensees to fulfill rigorous recordkeeping and disclosure requirements, grants the DFPI substantial enforcement powers, and imposes specific regulations on exchanges and stablecoin issuers. The law grants existing New York BitLicense holders reciprocity with California's BitLicense.[143]

Colorado	Money Transmitters Act, Colorado Revised Statutes Annotated, §§ 11-110-101 *et seq.*	Department of Regulatory Agencies, Division of Banking

Notes: Colorado does not categorize cryptocurrency as money

---

[142] "DBO Commissioner Owen Clarifies Coinbase Exchange's Regulatory Status in California." *Cal. Dep't of Fin. Protection & Innovation*, 27 Jan 2015, dfpi.ca.gov/wp-content/uploads/sites/337/2019/02/Statement_on_Coinbase_Exchange_Regulatory_Status_01-27-15.pdf.

[143] Cal. Digital Financial Assets Law, Cal. Fin. Code § 3101 *et seq.*

and does not require a license to directly transmit cryptocurrency between two consumers. A license may be required where fiat is used as part of the sale or transmission of a digital asset.[144]

| Hawaii | Money Transmitters Modernization Act, Hawaii Revised Statutes Annotated, §§ 489D-1 et seq. | Department of Commerce and Consumer Affairs, Division of Financial Institutions |

Notes: In 2016, Hawaii's Division of Financial Institutions issued an interpretation of the state's money transmitters act, finding that companies managing digital assets for clients must hold fiat reserves equal to the value of those assets. This unique and stringent requirement made it virtually impossible for digital asset businesses to become licensed. To address this, Hawaii created a temporary "Digital Currency Sandbox" to allow digital asset businesses to function while awaiting amendments to the state's money transmission regulations. However, efforts to revise the legislation did not succeed. Consequently, in January 2024, the Division of Finance abandoned its efforts, shut down its Digital Currency Sandbox, and issued guidance that "digital currency companies will no longer require a Hawaii-issued money transmitter license to conduct business within the state."[145]

| Illinois | Transmitters of Money Act, Illinois Compiled Statutes Annotated, 205 §§ 657/1 et seq. | Department of Financial and Professional Regulation |

Notes: The Illinois Department of Financial and Professional Regulation issued guidance stating that digital currency is not

---

144 "Interim Regulatory Guidance – Cryptocurrency and the Colorado Money Transmitters Act." *Colo. Dep't of Reg. Agencies, Div. of Banking* 20 Sept. 2018, drive.google.com/file/d/1MmpksD8aAPkmvdRdW0PztGe_eOceq4lk/view.

145 "Hawai'i Digital Currency Innovation Lab To Conclude." *Haw. Dep't of Com. & Consumer Affairs, Div. of Fin. Inst.*, 26 Jan 2024, governor.hawaii.gov/newsroom/dcca-release-hawaii-digital-currency-innovation-lab-to-conclude/.

"money" within the Illinois Transmitters of Money Act and that an entity engaged in transmitting solely digital currencies would not be required to obtain an MTL. But should the transmission of digital currencies involve money in a transaction, that transaction may be considered money transmission depending on how the transaction is organized.[146]

Indiana	Money Transmitters, Indiana Code, §§ 28-8-4-1, *et seq.*	Department of Financial Institutions

Notes: Indiana's money transmitter law does not directly mention virtual currencies. However, its NMLS licensing checklist clarifies that a money transmitter license is not required for fiat or virtual currency exchanges that restrict consumers from buying or selling without the ability to transfer fiat to others.[147]

Kansas	Kansas Money Transmitter Act, Kansas Statutes Annotated, §§ 9-508 to 9-513e	Office of the State Bank Commission

Notes: The State Bank Commissioner of Kansas has issued guidance stating that the Kansas Money Transmitter Act does not consider cryptocurrencies as "money" or "monetary value." As a result, the Act's regulations do not apply to them. Entities that only transmit decentralized cryptocurrencies do not need a license. Virtual and sovereign currency transactions could be considered money transmission, depending on how they are structured.[148]

---

146 "Digital Currency Regulatory Guidance." *Ill. Dep't of Fin. & Prof'l Reg.* 13 June 2017, idfprapps.illinois.gov/Forms/DFI/CCD/IDFPR%20-%20Digital%20Currency%20Regulatory%20Guidance.pdf.

147 "NMLS Resource Ctr., IN-DFI New Application Checklist." mortgage.nationwidelicensingsystem.org/slr/PublishedStateDocuments/IN-DFI-Money-Transmitter-Company-New-App-Checklist.pdf.

148 "Regulatory Treatment of Virtual Currencies Under the Kansas Money Transmitter Act." *Kan. Off. of the St. Bank Comm'r,* 18 May 2021, osbckansas.org/cml/mt_2014_01.pdf.

Massachusetts	Receipts of Deposits for Transmittal to Foreign Countries, Massachusetts General Laws Annotated, 169 §§ 1 et seq.	Executive Office of Economic Development, Division of Banks

Notes: Massachusetts does not have a law governing domestic money transmission. Therefore, transmitting virtual currencies is only subject to the state's money transmission laws if the virtual currencies are knowingly being sent to a specific location outside of the United States.[149]

Minnesota	Minnesota Money Transmitter Act, Minnesota Statutes Annotated, §§ 53B.27 et seq.	Department of Commerce, Financial Institutions Division

Notes: The Minnesota Department of Commerce has issued guidance that only fiat currencies are money under its Money Transmitter Act and that, therefore, a license is not required for activities involving only cryptocurrency. The guidance sets forth different scenarios where a license may be required, including intermediary virtual currency transactions involving fiat.[150]

Montana	Does Not Regulate Money Transmitters	Division of Banking and Financial Institutions

---

149 "Opinion 2021-009: Licensing requirements for digital currency trading and custody services and certain liquidity services." *Mass. Exec. Off. of Econ. Dev., Div. of Banks,* 2 Mar 2022, mass.gov/opinion/opinion-2021-009-licensing-requirements-for-digital-currency-trading-and-custody-services-and-certain-liquidity-services.

150 "Guidance on the Minnesota Money Transmitters Act and Virtual Currency." *Minn. Dep't of Com., Fin. Inst. Div.,* 20 Aug 2021, mn.gov/commerce-stat/pdfs/virtual-currency-guidance.pdf.

| New Hampshire | Licensing of Money Transmitters, Revised Statutes Annotated of the State of New Hampshire, §§ 399-G:1 et seq. | Department of Banking |

Notes: In 2017, New Hampshire enacted legislation exempting individuals involved in the sale, issuance, or transmission of virtual currency from its money transmitter regulations, subjecting them instead to the State's consumer protection regulations.[151]

| North Dakota | Money Transmitters Act, North Dakota Century Code Annotated, §§ 13-09.1-01 et seq. | Department of Financial Institutions |

Notes: The North Dakota Department of Financial Institutions has issued guidance stating that the control or transmission of virtual currency is not currently covered by the State's money transmitter law. However, companies that handle or transmit fiat currency in addition to virtual currency must obtain a money transmitter license.[152]

| Pennsylvania | Transmitting Money or Credit, Pennsylvania Statutes and Consolidated Statutes, §§ 6101 et seq. | Department of Banking and Securities |

Notes: The Pennsylvania Department of Banking and Securities has issued guidance that virtual currency does not meet the definition of "money" under its money transmitter law. Thus, platforms trading

---

151 N.H. Rev. Stat. § 399-G:3 (2022).

152 "Frequently Asked Questions – Non-Depository." *N.D. Dep't of Fin. Inst.,* nd.gov/dfi/about-dfi/non-depository/frequently-asked-questions-non-depository.

virtual currency for fiat currency without directly handling the fiat are not considered money transmitters. The guidance also specifies that virtual currency ATMs and kiosks do not qualify as money transmitters, as they only exchange fiat for virtual currency without transferring funds to third parties.[153]

| South Carolina | South Carolina, Code of Laws of South Carolina Annotated, §§ 35-11-100 et seq. | Office of the Attorney General, Money Services Division |

Notes: The South Carolina Attorney General's website clarifies that virtual currency is not regarded as a medium of exchange under the Act and, therefore, does not constitute monetary value. However, virtual currency transactions that involve fiat currency may require regulation under the Act's money transmission provisions.[154]

| Tennessee | Money Transmitter Act of 1994, Tennessee Code Annotated, §§ 45-7-101 et seq. | Department of Financial Institutions |

Notes: The Tennessee Department of Financial Institutions has stated that it does not regulate virtual currency, and its Money Transmitter License does not extend to virtual currency transmission. However, companies that exchange, administer, or maintain virtual currencies for sovereign currency may still be subject to state and federal regulations and licensing requirements.[155]

---

153 "Guidance for Virtual Currency Businesses." *Pa. Dep't of Banking & Sec.*, dobs.pa.gov/Documents/Securities%20Resources/MTA%20Guidance%20for%20Virtual%20Currency%20Businesses.pdf.

154 "Money Services FAQs." *S.C. Off. of the Att'y Gen., Money Serv. Div.*, scag.gov/inside-the-office/legal-services-division/money-services/money-services-faqs.

155 "Virtual Currency Statement of Policy." *Tenn. Dep't of Fin. Inst.*, tn.gov/tdfi/mortgage-consumer-lending/money-transmitter.html.

| Utah | Money Transmitters Act, Utah Code Annotated, §§ 7-25-101 et seq. | Department of Financial Institutions |

Notes: In 2019, Utah amended its Money Transmitter Act to clarify that transactions involving "blockchain tokens" do not qualify as money transmissions.

| Virginia | Money Order Sellers and Money Transmitters, Annotated Code of Virginia, §§ 6.2-1900 et seq. | State Corporation Commission |

Notes: The Virginia Bureau of Financial Institutions said it does not regulate virtual currencies. Transactions involving virtual currencies that also include the transfer of fiat currency may fall under the regulatory scope of money transmitters statute.[156]

| Wisconsin | Seller of Checks Law, Wisconsin Statutes Annotated, §§ 217.01 et seq. | Department of Financial Institutions |

Notes: The Department of Financial Institutions advises that it does not oversee companies dealing only in virtual currency. Transactions that handle both virtual and sovereign currency may require a license, dependent on the structure of the transaction.[157]

---

156 The notice has been removed from the Virginia Corporation Commission's website but found archived at web.archive.org/web/20231001223433/ scc.virginia.gov/getattachment/1bb52b42-9a10-45a2-ba48-b352e48b6d2e/VirCur.pdf. There is no indication that the removal of this notice signals a shift in the State's position.

157 "Seller of Checks." *Wis. Dep't of Fin. Inst.*, dfi.wi.gov/Pages/FinancialServices/LicensedFinancial/SellerofChecks.aspx.

| Wyoming | Money Transmitters Act, Wyoming Statutes Annotated, §§ 40-22-101 et seq. | Division of Banking |

Notes: Wyoming has positioned itself as the favorite state of the cryptocurrency industry and has adopted a range of laws to promote blockchain and cryptocurrency operations. Specifically, the State has introduced exemptions in its money transmitters act for key virtual currency activities, including buying, selling, issuing, taking custody, and transmitting virtual currency within Wyoming and across its borders.

Among the State's many legislative measures, it has enacted exemptions for "consumptive purpose" utility tokens from its state securities regulations, property tax breaks for virtual currencies, provisions for DAOs to acquire legal status, and the authorization to create a state-backed stablecoin.[158] Moreover, Wyoming has also introduced the Special-Purpose Depository Institution (SPDI), a chartered trust tailored to be a regulated custodian for cryptocurrency assets.[159]

While Wyoming's pioneering laws have been lauded, their practical impact remains uncertain, especially outside of the sparsely populated state. For instance, state-level exemptions do not address the more complex federal securities regulations affecting the industry. The State's specific rules for DAO registration have faced criticism for potentially causing more confusion than clarity and offering no significant advantages over traditional LLC structures.[160] Furthermore, the landmark SPDI legislation has yet to see much

---

158 "Decentralized Autonomous Organization (DAO): Frequently Asked Questions." *Wyo. Sec. of St., Bus. Div.*, sos.wyo.gov/Business/Docs/DAOs_FAQs.pdf; *see also* Jennings, Miles, and David Kerr. "The Duna: An Oasis for Daos." *A16z Crypto*, 8 Mar. 2024, a16zcrypto.com/posts/article/duna-for-daos.

159 "Special Purpose Depository Institutions." *Wyo. Div. of Banking,* wyomingbankingdivision.wyo.gov/banks-and-trust-companies/special-purpose-depository-institutions.

160 *See* Shapiro, Gabriel, and Sydney Abualy. "Wyoming's Legal DAO-Saster." 9 Apr. 2021, lexnode.substack.com/p/wyomings-legal-dao-saster.

practical application by its intended users for numerous reasons, including a refusal by the Federal Reserve to grant them a master account to the Federal Reserve's payment system.[161] These points suggest that while groundbreaking on paper, Wyoming's legislative advancements face significant hurdles in practical application and broader legal integration.

III. States That Have Not Issued Clear Guidance

| Arizona | Monetary Transmission Act, Arizona Revised Statutes, §§ 6-1201 to 6-1242. | Department of Insurance and Financial Institutions |

Notes: Arizona's money transmitter statute does not explicitly address virtual currency. However, the NMLS Arizona Money Transmitter License New Application Checklist ambiguously lists "virtual currency exchanging and trading services" as an activity permitted under the license.[162]

| Delaware | The Sale of Checks Act, Delaware Code Annotated, 5 Del. C. §§ 2301 *et seq*. | Office of the State Bank Commissioner |

Notes: While Delaware has not provided explicit guidance on virtual currency, the NMLS New Application Checklist for a Check

---

161 On March 29, 2024, a Wyoming SPDI lost a suit brought against the Federal Reserve for denying it access to a Federal Reserve master account. De, Nikhilesh. "Custodia Bank Loses Lawsuit Challenging Fed Rejection of Master Account Application," *CoinDesk*, 29 Mar. 2024, shorturl.at/oxK45. While the specifics of acquiring a master account are beyond our scope, the suit underscores the digital asset sector's challenge in integrating with traditional finance. *See also*, Schwartz, Leo. "Custodia is leading a one-bank crypto crusade against the Fed and reviving claims of Operation Chokepoint 2.0." *Fortune Mag.* 17 Jan. 2024, fortune.com/crypto/2024/01/17/custodia-operation-chokepoint-caitlin-long-federal-reserve-crypto-banking.

162 "NMLS Resource Ctr., AZ New Application Checklist." mortgage.nationwidelicensingsystem.org/slr/PublishedStateDocuments/AZ_Money_Transmitter_License-Company-New-App-Checklist.pdf.

Seller/Money Transmitter License suggests that the state allows "virtual currency exchanging and trading services" under its money transmitter license, despite elsewhere acknowledging that the state does not regulate the trading of virtual currency.[163]

| Iowa | Uniform Money Transmission Modernization Act, Iowa Code Annotated, §§ 533C.101 et seq. | Department of Insurance and Financial Services, Division of Banking |

Notes: Iowa has not issued direct public guidance.

| Kentucky | Kentucky Money Transmitter Act of 2006, Kentucky Revised Statutes Annotated, §§ 286.11-001 et seq. | Department of Financial Institutions |

Notes: Kentucky has not held itself out as regulating cryptocurrency actively, even though its legal framework could allow for such oversight. The definition of "money transmission" under the Kentucky Money Transmitters Act of 2006 includes the notion of "monetary value," which is broadly described as a "medium of exchange," whether redeemable in money or not. Despite this inclusive language, the state has not explicitly positioned itself as a cryptocurrency regulator.

| Michigan | Money Transmission Services Act, Michigan Compiled Laws Annotated, §§ 487.1001 et seq. | Department of Insurance and Financial Services |

---

163 "NMLS Resource Ctr., DE Check Seller, New Application Checklist." https://mortgage.nationwidelicensingsystem.org/slr/PublishedStateDocuments/DE_Check_Seller_Money_Transmitter_License_Company-New_App-Checklist.pdf.

Notes: In 2019, the Michigan Department of Insurance and Financial Services published a bulletin announcing the development of an approach to virtual currencies, but it has not published any additional guidelines since then.[164]

Missouri	Sale of Checks Law, Annotated Missouri Statutes, §§ 361.700 to 361.727	Division of Finance

Notes: Missouri has not clarified whether cryptocurrencies fall under its money transmission laws. The state has amended its definition of money laundering to categorize cryptocurrency as a "monetary instrument," but the implication of this change is unclear.

Mississippi	Money Transmitters Act, Mississippi Code Annotated, §§ 75-15-1 et seq.	Department of Banking and Consumer Finance

Notes: Mississippi has not issued direct public guidance.

Nebraska	Money Transmitters Act, Revised Statutes of Nebraska Annotated, §§ 8-2701 to 8-2747	Department of Banking and Finance

Notes: Nebraska has not provided direct guidance on whether virtual currency transmissions are regulated under its Money Transmitters Act. However, the State's "monetary value" definition is broad and includes a medium of exchange "whether or not redeemable in value."

---

164 "Virtual Currency: What Consumers Need to Know." *Mich. Dep't of Ins. & Fin. Serv.*, michigan.gov/-/media/Project/Websites/difs/Publication/Financial/FIS-PUB_5200.pdf?rev=645dbb7140074630953609a18897be53.

In 2021, Nebraska authorized the establishment of specialized cryptocurrency depository entities. This initiative enables the creation of new digital asset depositories and allows existing state-chartered banks to form digital asset divisions. The legislation outlines detailed guidelines for forming, operating, and regulating these depositories, including incorporation processes, supervision by the Nebraska Department of Banking and Finance, and a requirement for the main operational and executive offices to be situated in Nebraska. The State has yet to issue a Digital Asset Depository Institution charter.[165]

New Jersey	Money Transmitters Act, New Jersey Statutes Annotated, §§ 17:15C-1, et seq.	Department of Banking & Insurance

Notes: New Jersey has not provided guidance on applying its money transmitter regulations to the sale or transmission of virtual currencies, but there is pending legislation that, if enacted, requires virtual currency money transmitters and related businesses to obtain a newly developed Bit License from the state.[166]

Oklahoma	Financial Transaction Reporting Act, Oklahoma Statutes Annotated, §§ 1511 to 1515	Banking Department

Notes: In 2014, Oklahoma's legislature appended a comment to its statute on money transfers, highlighting the ambiguous legal standing and regulatory approach toward digital currencies. Since then, no further clarification or guidance has been issued on the matter.[167]

---

165 "Digital Assets." *Neb. Dep't of Banking & Fin.*, ndbf.nebraska.gov/industries/digital-assets.

166 New Jersey Digital Asset and Blockchain Technology Act, S. 1756/A. 2371 (2022).

167 The legislature's comment on the ambiguous status of virtual currency under Okla-

Texas	Money Services Modernization Act, Texas Statutes and Codes Annotated, §§ 152.001 et seq.	Department of Banking

Notes: In 2019, the Texas Department of Banking clarified through a supervisory memorandum that cryptocurrency transactions, including those between virtual and sovereign currencies, were not subject to the state's financial regulations since cryptocurrencies were not classified as money.[168] However, the guidance noted that stablecoins fell under the purview of the state's Money Services Act.

Shifting its approach in 2023, Texas expanded its regulatory scope with Chapter 160 of the Texas Finance Code, thereby placing digital assets under the Texas Department of Banking's jurisdiction. This new legislation sets forth stringent requirements for digital asset service providers, mandating the segregation of customer funds, the maintenance of adequate reserves, and the periodic filing of "proof-of-reserves" audits conducted by independent auditors.[169] Chapter 160 seems to increase the Department of Banking's authority over virtual currencies, creating uncertainty about whether the 2019 guidance—stating that transactions involving non-stablecoin virtual currencies don't require a license—still stands. Consequently, industry participants are looking to Texas for clear directions on which activities will necessitate a license.

---

homa's financial regulations is documented in the Oklahoma Bar Journal. The comment no longer appears in the current Oklahoma statutes, reinforcing the uncertainty about the legal standing of virtual currency in the state. See Tankersley, Kaimee. "Legal and Regulatory Developments Arising From the Growth of Cryptocurrency." *Okla. Bar Journal,* Dec. 2018, okbar.org/barjournal/may2018/obj8913tankersleydavisahloy/#:~:text=As%20of%20mid%202014%2C%20the,for%20goods%20or%20services%20sold.

168 "Supervisory Memorandum – 1037, Regulatory Treatment of Virtual Currencies Under the Texas Money Services Act." *Tex. Dep't of Banking* 1 Apr. 2019, dob.texas.gov/sites/default/files/files/consumer-information/sm1037.pdf.

169 Tex. Fin. Code § 160.001 et seq.

| West Virginia | Checks and Money Order Sales, Money Transmission Services, Transportation and Currency Exchange, Annotated Code of West Virginia, §§ 32A-2-1 et seq. | Division of Financial Institutions |

Notes: West Virginia has yet to provide specific guidance on whether virtual currency falls under its money transmission regulations. Although the state broadly defines currency and money transmission in a way that could encompass cryptocurrency and has even included cryptocurrency in its definition of monetary instruments within its money laundering statute, clarity regarding the regulation of virtual currency in the context of money transmission is still pending.

IV. States That Have Bespoke Virtual Currency Regulations

| Louisiana | Virtual Currency Business Act, Louisiana Statutes Annotated, §§ 1381 et seq. | Office of Financial Institutions |

Notes: Louisiana requires entities conducting various virtual currency activities, such as exchanging, storing, or administering virtual currency, to secure a Virtual Currency Business Activity (VCBA) license. Like New York's BitLicense, the VCBA license targets a broad spectrum of virtual currency operations and necessitates compliance with stringent regulatory standards, including anti-money laundering protocols and cybersecurity measures.

| New York | Virtual Currency Businesses, New York Codes, Rules and Regulations, 200 et seq. | Department of Financial Services |

Notes: In June 2015, the New York Department of Financial Services (NYDFS) introduced its BitLicense, a pioneering regulatory framework for virtual currency businesses operating in or serving customers in New York. The BitLicense is fundamentally a money transmitter's license tailored for virtual currency transmissions. However, licensees wishing to conduct traditional money transmission must still obtain a separate money transmitter license. New York also offers a Limited Purpose Trust Company (LPTC) charter, designed for virtual currency businesses, which operates similarly to other state-chartered trusts. LPTCs offer greater flexibility than a BitLicense, permitting entities to engage in a broader range of activities, including fiduciary services and issuing stablecoins. LPTCs are not required to obtain a separate money transmitter license to engage in fiat services.

The BitLicense rightfully has a reputation for being particularly difficult to obtain, not because its requirements are inherently tougher than those in other jurisdictions, but due to the regulator overseeing them. The NYDFS seems disinclined to approve new BitLicenses and LPTCs, a stance that appears at least partially ideologically motivated. The NYDFS granted only two BitLicenses in 2023 and has chartered only one LPTC since 2021. This inaction results in applicants who have paid the NYDFS application fees and incurred the substantial cost of applying experiencing years-long delays.

Simultaneously, the NYDFS has engaged in severe enforcement actions against existing licensees. This includes hefty fines imposed on major entities like Coinbase ($100M) and Robinhood ($30M) and the revocation of Genesis Global Trading's license over compliance failures.[170] Moreover, the NYDFS has worked to limit the types

---

170 "Superintendent Adrienne A. Harris Announces $100 Million Settlement with Coinbase, Inc. after DFS Investigation Finds Significant Failings in the Company's Compliance Program." *N.Y. Dep't of Fin. Serv.* 4 Jan. 2023, dfs.ny.gov/reports_and_publications/press_releases/pr202301041; "DFS Superintendent Harris Announces $30 Million Penalty on Robinhood Crypto for Significant Anti-Money Laundering, Cybersecurity & Consumer Protection Violations." *N.Y. Dep't of Fin. Serv.,* 2 Aug. 2022, dfs.ny.gov/reports_and_publications/press_releases/pr202208021; "Superintendent Harris Announces $8 Million Penalty Against Genesis Global Trading, Inc. After DFS Investigation Finds Significant Failings in Anti-Money Laundering and Cybersecurity Programs." *N.Y. Dep't of Fin. Serv.,* 12 Jan. 2024, dfs.ny.gov/reports_and_publications/press_releases/pr2024011224.

of cryptocurrencies accessible to New York residents, removing popular cryptocurrencies like Dogecoin, Bitcoin Cash, Litecoin, and XRP from its "green list" of tokens companies can offer customers without prior approval. Only Bitcoin, Ether, and six stablecoins are now presumed safe for customers, and the NYDFS has proposed additional regulations that would make it more difficult for licensees to offer other assets.

The apparent distrust of the NYDFS towards the digital asset industry goes beyond its hesitance to approve new applications. Some, including former Congressman Barney Frank, have accused the NYDFS of placing New York chartered Signature Bank into receivership due to the bank's crypto-friendly reputation. Congressman Frank suggested that Signature Bank was targeted to send an "anti-crypto message."[171] Although the NYDFS has denied these claims, the prevailing sentiment is that the world's self-proclaimed financial capital may not be so open to the future of finance.

New York's skeptical approach toward the digital asset industry is not limited to the NYDFS. A rivalry has emerged between the NYDFS and the Attorney General's Office over who can be tougher on crypto. Determined to "rein in the cryptocurrency industry," the Attorney General has proposed a far-reaching bill called the "Crypto Regulation, Protection Transparency and Oversight Act," which would create an additional layer of regulations for digital asset businesses beyond what the NYDFS demands, including regulations that would require existing BitLicensees to fundamentally restructure the way in which they do business.[172] The bill is unlikely to become law.

The Attorney General has also brought her focus to the crypto industry through what might be termed experimental enforcement actions. This includes utilizing an obscure clause in NY's Martin Act

---

171 Mulvihill, Geoff. "Barney Frank coauthored the Dodd-Frank 'too big to fail' law. Now he says his bank's failure was a message about 'dealing with crypto.'" *Fortune Mag.*, 13 Mar 2023, fortune.com/2023/03/13/signature-bank-seized-to-send-a-message-crypto-barney-frank/.

172 "Attorney General James Proposes Nation-Leading Regulations on Cryptocurrency Industry." *N.Y. St. Att'y Gen.*, 5 May 2023, shorturl.at/awGI6.

that mandates commodities brokers to register with the Attorney General to assert that even those with a BitLicense have an additional reporting requirement.[173] In a particularly novel argument, the Attorney General's office claimed in a case against the crypto trading platform KuCoin that ether—one of the few digital assets still on the NYDFS's green list—is a security. Regrettably, this position, which exceeds even the SEC's boldest theories, was not tested due to a settlement with KuCoin.[174]

Managing Differing Approaches

Navigating the regulatory landscape for digital assets across so many states poses a complex challenge, due to the substantial lack of uniformity. Many states still haven't issued definitive guidance, complicating the planning process for companies aiming to launch a product across multiple jurisdictions. However, unlike federal regulators, who often hesitate to provide informal guidance, most state financial regulators are surprisingly open to offering non-binding, informal advice to prospective applicants about their business models and licensing needs. These "no-name" inquiries, typically made anonymously and not legally binding, are invaluable for understanding the extent of a state's money transmitter regulations. As a practical exercise, consider contacting a few state regulators to inquire whether a hypothetical digital asset business would require a license under their regulations.

For those managing regulatory relationships across multiple states, it's important to note that state regulators have a wide scope of authority to inquire about and request information about activities that are not directly under their purview. Many digital asset companies depend on fiat payment systems or some form of fiat transmission, potentially requiring a money transmitter license regardless of a state's official stance on digital assets. Regulators often extend their oversight to digital asset activities involving licensed entities, irrespective of the

---

[173] "Industry Alert: Registration of Commodity Brokers-Dealers, Salespersons, and Investment Advisors Doing Business Relating to Virtual or "Crypto" Currency." *N.Y. St. Att'y Gen.*, shorturl.at/kqrMV.

[174] "Attorney General James Secures More Than $22 Million from Cryptocurrency Platform for Operating Illegally." *N.Y. St. Att'y Gen.* 12 Dec. 2023, shorturl.at/dgnyU.

specific legislative framework.

While this chapter primarily focused on money transmitter regulations, the involvement of other state regulatory entities—such as state securities regulators, consumer protection departments, and attorney general's offices—in digital asset oversight cannot be overlooked. This multi-layered regulatory engagement frequently results in overlapping jurisdictions within states, further complicating the operational landscape for digital asset businesses operating in multiple jurisdictions.

The fragmented nature of state regulatory oversight has led many to call for federal intervention to establish a unified registration and oversight framework. The *Lummis-Gillibrand Responsible Financial Innovation Act*, proposed in 2022, was a comprehensive legislative attempt that aimed to, among other things, standardize state licensing requirements.[175] Nonetheless, harmonizing the disparate approaches of states like Wyoming and New York into a unified standard seems unfeasible due to their radically different approaches to the industry.[176] Considering the longstanding tradition of state-level regulation in this area, the idea of completely federalizing the money transmitter license and supplanting state financial regulators seems politically impractical.

A federal effort to simplify the state-by-state regulatory framework might inadvertently introduce new complexities such as the creation of an additional federal licensing requirement overlayed on top of the existing state infrastructure. The most effective path forward remains a subject of ongoing debate, but given the dysfunction in Congress, for better or worse, we appear destined to operate within the existing piecemeal system for the foreseeable future.

---

[175] Lummis-Gillibrand Responsible Financial Innovation Act, S. 2281, 118th Cong. (2023); Financial Innovation and Technology for the 21st Century Act, H.R. 4763, 118th Cong. (2023).

[176] Although Senator Lummis is from Wyoming and Senator Gillibrand is from New York, so maybe I'm being cynical.

Supplemental Resources[177]

- **Benson, Carol Coye, et al. *Payments Systems in the U.S.: A Guide for the Payments Professional.* Glenbrook Press, 2017.** We have centered our discussion on the regulatory aspects of money transmission as applied to virtual currency transactions. However, many businesses in this crypto space also engage with fiat services and traditional payment systems that are themselves subject to money transmission regulations. Payments Systems in the U.S. comprehensively explore how conventional payment networks and instruments—including ACH, wires, checks, cards, and cash—are processed and settled. A comprehension of traditional payment systems will enrich your understanding of the regulations applicable to crypto payments and is crucial for those operating in the field.

---

177 For ease of reference, all Supplemental Resources and footnote links are available at www.TheCryptoLegalHandbook.com/Resources.

CHAPTER 12

The Commodity Futures Trading Commission

The role of the Securities and Exchange Commission and Commodity Futures Trading Commission as financial market regulators is often misunderstood. Each is responsible for enforcing compliance and market integrity, but neither has general oversight over investments nor is tasked with evaluating the quality of investments for the public. The freedom to make investment decisions, good or bad, is a hallmark of the American financial market.

Discussions about the role these agencies should play in overseeing the crypto industry have become ubiquitous in the space. Consequently, newcomers are frequently introduced to complex debates about the intricacies of the *Howey* test or whether the CFTC or SEC is better equipped to be appointed the primary regulator of digital assets before learning about the history and authority vested in these agencies in the first place. Before examining the SEC and CFTC's involvement in regulating digital assets, it's essential to understand the actual scope of each agency's responsibilities within our financial system.

This chapter will focus on the history and mandate of the Commodity Futures Trading Commission and analyze its stance on cryptocurrency. We will examine the CFTC's origins, its congressional mandate to regulate certain specific financial products, and the application of this framework to the crypto industry. Understanding the CFTC's role is vital, especially amidst discussions about the classification of digital assets and opinions that the CFTC should take on a more proactive role in regulating digital assets.

Commodity Futures

The U.S. government has regulated commodity futures trading since the 1920s. The Commodity Futures Trading Commission, established in 1974, initially focused on regulating futures contracts for agricultural commodities, but its mandate has broadened over time to encompass a wider range of derivative products and leveraged transactions. The term "derivative" merely refers to the fact that the value of these regulated contracts is derived from the value of its underlying asset.

The CFTC has never regulated cash sales of commodities. This is evident in its name, which reflects that the CFTC was created to regulate the trading of specific derivative financial contracts called "*commodity futures.*" The U.S. government's interest in regulating these products stems from their importance to agricultural markets and the risk management they provide to those whose livelihoods are affected by the market price of different commodities.

Futures contracts were created as a way for those relying on crop harvests to manage the risk of a poor harvest by locking in prices ahead of time. The practice originated in 16th century England and was exported to markets across the globe. The first exchange market for futures contracts dates back to 17th century Japan and was created to stabilize the price of rice at a time when it was used as a form of payment. The most traded natural commodity futures in the U.S. are oil, gold, natural gas, soybeans, corn, sugar, silver, and wheat, although many other commodity futures, including financial commodities like treasuries or Eurodollars, are traded in the U.S. and abroad.

Understanding the role of commodity futures in the stability of agricultural markets is necessary to understand why the U.S. government created a specific agency to oversee this financial product.

Consider a wheat farmer facing uncertainty about the future price of wheat due to potential changes in market demand or unpredictable weather conditions. A futures contract allows the farmer to sell a specified amount of wheat to a buyer at a predetermined price at a future date. If the market price of wheat falls by that future date, the farmer is protected from the price drop because the futures contract has locked in the sale price. If the market price rises, a manufacturer incorporating wheat into their product benefits from securing a lower price in advance. In this way, both parties can hedge against price volatility, with the farmer ensuring a guaranteed income for the crop and the buyer securing a stable supply at a known price. Most futures contracts are not settled by physical commodity delivery but through cash settlement. In this process, the difference between the contract price and the market price at expiration is paid in cash, eliminating the need to physically handle the commodity.

The complexities of futures contracts go beyond the scope of this book, but for a thorough overview, I encourage you to watch an hour-long lecture by Yale's Robert Schiller titled "Forward and Futures Markets," linked in the Supplemental Resources. I also suggest you watch "Trading Places," a 1980s comedy whose climax centers around the trading of frozen orange juice futures that is every commodity lawyer's favorite movie.[178]

The United States started regulating commodity futures in 1922 with the introduction of the Grain Futures Act, created in response to the chaotic market conditions and extensive price manipulation in the grain markets following World War I. This period saw rampant speculation, extreme price volatility, and trading practices that destabilized grain prices and threatened the country's economic stability. The Grain Futures Act marked the first major step towards comprehensive federal regulation of commodity futures markets in the United States and was instrumental in restoring order and confidence in the grain markets.

The Grain Futures Act was replaced in 1936 by the Commodity Exchange Act (CEA), which, among other things, requires futures contracts for agriculture or other commodities to be traded on registered exchanges. These exchanges, called Designated Contract Markets (DCM), must meet specific criteria and adhere to CFTC

---

[178] Trading Places is so popular among those in the commodities industry that a 2010 reform prohibiting trading commodity futures based on nonpublic or misappropriated government information is informally known as the "Eddie Murphy Rule" after the movie's star.

regulations that ensure transparent trading practices. The Chicago Mercantile Exchange and the New York Mercantile Exchange are examples of DCMs. The CEA requires transactions made through a DCM to be cleared or settled through a separate entity called a Derivatives Clearing Organization (DCO) and requires brokers that facilitate commodity futures and other derivative or leveraged transactions, called Futures Commission Merchants (FCM) or Introducing Brokers (IB), to register with the CFTC.

The Commodity Exchange Act defines a "commodity" to include nearly every product, good, or service imaginable. The sole, determinative factor of whether something is a "commodity" under the CEA is whether it is feasible to write a futures contract on the asset's price.[179] Accordingly, a commodity includes not just natural commodities like the agricultural products discussed above, but intangible commodities such as financial indexes and other man-made or commercial assets. This broad definition has been deemed to include virtual currencies as well as assets that are deemed "securities" under federal law.

The **only** lawful goods or services of which futures are categorically not permitted are onions[180] and motion picture box office receipts.[181]

The CFTC's Expanding Role

The CFTC was created as a stand-alone agency to enforce the CEA in 1974. Before its creation, oversight rested with the U.S. Department of Agriculture's Commodity Exchange Authority. Although the CFTC is no longer under the Department of Agriculture and

---

179 See 7 U.S. Code § 1a(9). "The term "commodity" means…all services, rights, and interests…in which contracts for future delivery are presently or in the future dealt in."

180 This exemption resulted from the Onion Futures Act of 1958. The act was introduced after traders manipulated the onion futures market which lead to significant losses for farmers and public outcry. For an entertaining overview of the event, see "Why Trading Onions on Financial Markets Is Illegal." YouTube, Half as Interesting, 27 Oct. 2020, y2u. be/u2hVK24UPWQ.

181 Box office receipts were exempted from being treated as commodities under the CEA as part of the 2008 Dodd-Frank Act. This exemption came about after lobbying by the entertainment industry over concerns about insider trading and the manipulation of revenue predictions.

regulates many non-agricultural financial products, the Senate Agriculture, Nutrition, and Forestry Committee and the House Agricultural Committee still retain oversight over the agency. The Chair of the CFTC is currently a Democrat named Rostin Behnam, who was appointed by the President and confirmed by the Senate. He oversees a five-person bipartisan commission of which no more than three Commissioners from a single political party may serve at a time.

The Dodd-Frank Wall Street Reform and Consumer Protection Act of 2010 broadened the CFTC's scope by granting it extended powers to combat fraud and manipulation in commodity markets, including spot markets. A spot market is a venue where a commodity can be bought or sold for immediate delivery. While this enhanced oversight of the spot market doesn't introduce new registration obligations for marketplaces, it empowers the CFTC to probe and address fraudulent or manipulative actions in the spot sale of commodities.

The CFTC's jurisdiction now extends to the regulation of non-security commodity options, swaps, and transactions involving margin or leverage:

Options - An options contract grants the holder the right, but not the obligation, to buy (in a call option) or sell (in a put option) an underlying asset at a predetermined price within a specific time frame. This contrasts with a futures contract, where both parties must complete the transaction on the set date. The flexibility of an options contract allows the holder to decide whether to execute based on market conditions, acting as a form of insurance against price volatility. The holder pays a premium for this right, and the total they stand to lose is limited to this amount. This contrasts with a futures contract, which exposes both parties to unlimited risk and reward. Options for non-security commodities may be traded on Designated Contract Markets or Swap Execution Facilities.[182]

Swaps – The Dodd-Frank Act of 2010 expanded the CFTC's jurisdiction to include the swaps market. Swaps enable two parties to

---

182 "Options | Introduction to Derivatives." *YouTube*, Corporate Finance Institute, 10 June 2020, y2u.be/7pVWvXSUcPM.

exchange cash flows or other financial instruments over a specified period, commonly for hedging or speculating on market fluctuations. Unlike a futures contract, which culminates in a single settlement, swaps entail a series of cash flow exchanges. Traditionally, swaps are traded OTC. However, Dodd-Frank introduced the concept of a centralized marketplace for certain swaps called a Swap Execution Facility (SEF). The CFTC oversees most swap transactions, but the SEC regulates "security-based" swaps tied to single securities and certain indices.[183]

Margined and Leveraged Transactions – The Dodd-Frank Act gave the CFTC primary regulation over retail commodity transactions that are structured as margined, leveraged, or financed transactions. The CEA subjects transactions offered to non-eligible contract participants or entities (non-ECP/ECE) to oversight akin to commodity futures, including mandating that such transactions are conducted on DCMs, SEFs, or foreign boards of trade. An ECP is an individual with $10 million in discretionary investments or $5 million if the individual enters into the transaction to manage risks associated with an asset or liability already or likely to be owned. An ECE is a corporation with $10 million in assets or a net worth of $1 million that enters into the transaction to manage the risk associated with business activity likely to occur.

All Virtual Currencies Are "Commodities" Under the CEA

The CFTC has made clear its view that "bitcoin and other virtual currencies are encompassed in the definition and properly defined as commodities."[184] You'll recall that the test for determining whether something is a commodity is whether a futures market for the asset can be feasibly developed. In 2017, the CFTC became the first major regulator to approve a crypto financial product when it permitted various designated contract markets to self-certify and offer bitcoin futures to their customers.[185] In the years since, the CFTC has allowed

---

183 "Swap Contracts | Introduction to Derivatives." *YouTube*, Corporate Finance Institute, 24 June 2020, y2u.be/lt_csUMbw7E.

184 *In re BFXNA INC. d/b/a BITFINEX, CFTC Docket* No. 16-19. 2 June 2016, shorturl.at/oGHN2.

185 *See* "Release Number 7654-17: CFTC Statement on Self-Certification of Bitcoin

several other digital asset futures products to come to market.[186]

The CFTC has recognized a broad spectrum of digital assets as commodities under the CEA. This includes not only mainstream assets like bitcoin and ether, but assets with smaller market caps like dogecoin and litecoin, as well as stablecoins like USDT, USDC, and BUSD. Even lesser-known, niche assets, including those fraudulently sold to investors as part of an ICO, have been characterized as a commodity.[187] The CFTC's approach to defining virtual currencies as commodities thus encompasses a wide range of digital assets regardless of their market cap or the nature of their initial offering.

The CFTC's conclusion that virtual currencies are commodities was first tested in *CFTC v. McDonnell*. In that case, the Eastern District of New York concluded that bitcoin fit the CEA's definition because of the potential for a futures market in the asset to develop. The Court also found that bitcoin satisfied a more general definition of a commodity as it is a good whose quality and value were uniform in markets throughout the world.

The *McDonnell* ruling is among the first explorations into whether virtual currencies qualify as commodities under the CEA. While the court correctly found bitcoin was a commodity, it further noted that bitcoin's functionality as a currency or store of value were traits typically associated with other commodities. While this conclusion

---

Products by CME, CFE and Cantor Exchange." CFTC, 1 Dec. 2017, shorturl.at/hxR56. The success of bitcoin futures has been instrumental in creating a mature and liquid bitcoin market that is largely free of fraud. Its success has laid the groundwork for other crypto financial products to reach the market, including bitcoin futures and spot-market exchange-traded funds (ETF), which have been approved by the SEC. More about the approval of bitcoin ETFs is available in Chapter 15.

186 The CFTC allows certain regulated entities, including DCMs, to self-certify products they list. The CFTC is often active in the pre-certification process and has stated it subjects crypto certifications to a "heightened review." In the years since bitcoin futures have come to market, several other crypto futures products, including ether, litecoin, bitcoin cash, and doge futures, have been self-certified without objection by the CFTC. For an overview of the process of self-certifying crypto futures, *see* "Written Testimony of Chairman J. Christopher Giancarlo before the Senate Banking Committee." *CFTC*, 8 Feb. 2018, shorturl.at/rAIX0.

187 "Release Number 7820-18 - Court Denies Defendants' Motion to Dismiss in Commodity Fraud Case Involving the Virtual Currency My Big Coin." *CFTC*, www.cftc.gov/PressRoom/PressReleases/7820-18.

is accurate, the discourse perpetuates an incorrect notion that an asset must possess some intrinsic utility to meet the definition of a commodity. It does not.

The inaccurate belief that an asset's classification as a commodity depends on its inherent utility has created a false dichotomy, misleading many into thinking that if a token possesses qualities analogous to commodities like oil, dollars, or gold, it cannot be classified as a security. It is similarly incorrect that every asset is either a commodity or a security or that classifying an asset as a commodity will preclude a finding that it meets the definition of a security. The determination of whether an asset is a commodity under the Commodity Exchange Act or a security under federal securities laws requires two distinct evaluations that are independent of each other.

Securities *Are* Commodities

The CEA stipulates that a "commodity" is defined only by the potential to write a futures contract based on the underlying asset's price. Securities are often the subject of futures contracts.[188] Accordingly, securities are commodities.

Some reading this may be taken aback, given the widespread view that classifying an asset as a commodity or security is mutually exclusive. However, the CEA itself categorizes securities as a subset of commodities, called "excluded commodities," which Congress carved out of the CEA and granted the SEC jurisdiction over their sales.[189] Thus, an asset's classification as a security doesn't negate its alignment with the CEA's definition of a commodity. It necessitates it.

Some might see this distinction as pedantic, considering that an asset being deemed a security nevertheless results in the SEC having

---

188 The Commodity Futures Modernization Act of 2000 lifted the ban on the trading of futures on single securities and narrow-based security indices. Security futures are regulated as securities and future contracts and must be traded on trading facilities and through intermediaries registered with the SEC and CFTC.

189 7 U.S. Code § 1a(19)." *Legal Information Institute, Cornell Law School,* law.cornell.edu/uscode/text/7/1a.

jurisdiction over it. However, many in the digital asset space have fallen victim to the incorrect view that the way to challenge the SEC's jurisdiction over a digital asset is to assert that it has been, or should be, classified as a commodity by the CFTC. As explained, the consideration is not whether a digital asset is a commodity—it almost certainly is—but whether that commodity meets the definition of a security under the Securities Acts.

CFTC Enforcement Actions

Although the CEA's definition of a commodity is broad, Congress's grant of authority to the CFTC is limited to regulations on the sales of commodity futures, non-securities options and swaps, offerings of margin or leverage for retail commodity transactions, and the authority to bring enforcement actions related to fraud or manipulation in the market. This narrow mandate is reflected in the CFTC's enforcement actions.

Below is a sample of CFTC enforcement actions. When some see a list of cases dumped toward the end of a chapter, they tend to skip over it, so rather than providing a comprehensive list of cases, I want to highlight a few that represent the CFTC's approach to the industry. For a more thorough list of actions, see the litigation tracker referenced in the Supplemental Resources.

The enforcement actions brought by the CFTC have primarily been against centralized actors that offered regulated products or services to customers without registering their business with the CFTC. Of the actions brought against crypto companies, most involve allegations that margin or leverage had been offered to non-eligible retail customers, but the CFTC has also brought cases for brokering futures, options, and swaps on unregistered platforms. A few notable cases against digital asset trading platforms:

- ***In re BFNXA Inc., d/b/a Bitfinex*** – Bitfinex allowed users to borrow funds from other users in order to trade bitcoin on margin. Bitfinex entered into a consent order for engaging in illegal leveraged commodity transactions and failing to register as an FCM. In 2016, Bitfinex agreed to pay a $75,000 fine to settle the case.¹⁹⁰ In 2021, the CFTC alleged Bitfinex had continued to offer margin to ineligible retail customers and settled a subsequent action against Bitfinex for another $1.5M.¹⁹¹

- ***In re Payward Ventures, Inc. d/b/a Kraken*** – Kraken is a digital asset platform that offered margin retail commodity transactions to U.S. customers. In 2021, the Company settled charges that it offered illegal retail commodity transactions and acted as an unregistered FCM. They were fined $1.25 million.¹⁹²

- ***CFTC v. Changpeng Zhao, Binance Holdings Ltd, et. al.*** – In 2023, Binance, the largest cryptocurrency exchange, entered into a $2.7 billion settlement agreement with the CFTC to settle multiple CEA violations, including the unregistered offering of futures, options, swaps, and leveraged retail commodity transactions, as well as evasion of the CFTC's swaps rules. Binance's owner, Changpeng (CZ) Zhao, also consented to a $150 million penalty against him individually.¹⁹³

The CFTC has also prioritized actions against those who conduct fraud or manipulation in the spot market. Such actions typically involve allegations of fraudulent marketing, or "pump and dump" schemes, designed to manipulate the market of a virtual currency.

I encourage you to explore the details of the CFTC's fraud actions, which can be found in the litigation tracker below. One thing you'll notice is that they tend to involve fairly low-tech fraudulent schemes.

---

190 In *re BFXNA INC. d/b/a BITFINEX*, CFTC Docket No. 16-19 2 June 2016, shorturl.at/oGHN2.

191 "Release Number 8450-21: CFTC Orders Tether and Bitfinex to Pay Fines Totaling $42.5 Million." *CFTC*, 15 Oct. 2021, cftc.gov/PressRoom/PressReleases/8450-21.

192 "Release Number 8433-21: CFTC Imposes A $1.25 Million Penalty against Kraken for Offering Illegal Off-Exchange Digital Asset Trading and Failing to Register as Required." *CFTC*, 28 Sept. 2021, cftc.gov/PressRoom/PressReleases/8433-21.

193 "Release Number 8825-23: Binance and Its CEO, Changpeng Zhao, Agree to Pay $2.85 Billion for Willfully Evading U.S. Law, Illegally Operating a Digital Asset Derivatives Exchange, and Other Violations." *CFTC*, 21 Nov. 2023, cftc.gov/PressRoom/PressReleases/8825-23.

This is common throughout crypto, where much of the fraud in the industry is not a function of new technology but age-old scams cloaked in the veneer of blockchain.

For example, *In re Tether Holdings*, in which the CFTC alleged that the issuer of the USDT stablecoin fraudulently represented that USDT was backed 100% by fiat reserves. The CFTC found that contrary to public statements made by Tether there were periods of time when the asset was not fully backed and that Tether had misled the public about its reserves being audited, the makeup of its reserves, and that its reserves were segregated from its parent company's funds. The CFTC and Tether Holdings entered into a consent order requiring Tether to pay a $41 million fine.[194] While that case centered around the reserves of a stablecoin, the case is not dissimilar to thousands of other fraud cases brought by the CFTC or other agencies that come down to a centralized business misleading the public about the sufficiency of its finances.

Similarly, in *CFTC v. Eisenberg*, the CFTC brought its first fraud action based on "oracle manipulation," a scheme taking advantage of the infrastructure of digital assets to perpetrate a classic form of asset manipulation. The case alleged that Eisenberg exploited over $110 million from Mango Markets, a decentralized crypto exchange, by manipulating its oracle system. An oracle is a data feed that provides real-world information to blockchain networks, which in this case, was used to determine prices of different token pairs.[195] Eisenberg set up fake accounts to place large bets on Mango Markets' token to artificially increase its price on other exchanges. This manipulation inflated the value of his bets through the oracle's price feed resulting in him taking a huge profit. Eisenberg has been charged criminally and is awaiting trial.[196]

---

194 "Release Number 8450-21: CFTC Orders Tether and Bitfinex to Pay Fines Totaling $42.5 Million." *CFTC*, 15 Oct. 2021, cftc.gov/PressRoom/PressReleases/8450-21.

195 An "oracle" is a bridge that provides external data to smart contracts, enabling them to execute transactions based on real-world information. Oracles are essential for the functionality of smart contracts that depend on data from outside their blockchain. See "What Are Oracles in Crypto? (Animated)." *YouTube*, Whiteboard Crypto, 22 Sept. 2021, y2u.be/uycQ7ReSt_c.

196 For an interesting discussion with Eisenberg regarding the ethics of the Mango exploit, see "The Mango Markets Attacker on Whether His 'Trade' Was Ethical or Not - EP.

A Focus on DeFi

The CFTC's focus in recent years has shifted to creators of blockchain protocols or software that can be used to engage in decentralized financial transactions that, were they conducted on a centralized platform, would require registration under the CEA. For example:

- ***In re Blockratize, Inc. d/b/a Polymarket.com*** - Polymarket, operated by Blockratize, Inc., is an online platform that offered event-based binary options contracts to U.S. persons without the required registration. These contracts allowed users to bet on outcomes of various events, such as cryptocurrency price movements, COVID-19 case numbers, or election results. The CFTC imposed a $1.4 million fine and ordered the company to cease its unregistered operations, as it lacked the necessary DCM or SEF registrations.[197]

- ***In re Opyn Inc.*** – Opyn Inc. introduced a protocol and website for trading a leveraged token named oSQTH, which was linked to the price of Ethereum. The CFTC determined these tokens were swaps and found that Opyn did not have the proper SEF or DCM registration, offered margin products to ineligible customers, and acted as an unlicensed FCM. Opyn agreed to a consent order and paid $250,000 to settle the matter.[198]

- ***In re Deridex, Inc.*** - Deridex, Inc. developed a decentralized platform that let users speculate on the future prices of digital currencies using leverage. The CFTC charged Deridex with not registering as an SEF or DCM, offering margin products to ineligible customers, and functioning as an unlicensed FCM. Deridex settled for $100,000.

413." *YouTube*, Unchained, 28 Oct. 2022, y2u.be/e-y4WmrndQ4.

197 "Release Number 8478-22: CFTC Orders Event-Based Binary Options Markets Operator to Pay $1.4 Million Penalty." *CFTC*, 3 Jan. 2022, cftc.gov/PressRoom/PressReleases/8478-22.

198 "Release Number 8478-22: CFTC Issues Orders Against Operators of Three DeFi Protocols for Offering Illegal Digital Asset Derivatives Trading." *CFTC*, 7 Sept. 2023, cftc.gov/PressRoom/PressReleases/8774-23

- ***In re ZeroEx, Inc.*** – ZeroEx, Inc., developed the 0x Protocol, a DeFi protocol allowing users, including those in the United States, to trade digital assets peer-to-peer across various blockchains with a user interface called "Matcha." The CFTC charged ZeroEx for offering leveraged digital asset transactions to retail customers without the required actual delivery within 28 days, a violation under the CEA. It's important to note that the allegations suggest that neither ZeroEx, the 0x protocol, nor Matcha directly facilitated these transactions. Instead, it seems that a third party utilized the protocol to create leveraged digital assets accessible through Matcha, using smart contracts to borrow stablecoins from third-party lending platforms for automated trading on other decentralized exchanges, not directly involving 0x.

In response to the ZeroEx action, which settled for $200,000, CFTC Commissioner Summer Mersinger raised concerns regarding the CFTC's approach of regulating DeFi through enforcement. Mersinger highlighted concerns over the CFTC's jurisdiction and the efficacy of enforcement actions as a primary regulatory strategy. She advocated for collaboration between the CFTC and DeFi market participants to develop clear, constructive rules or guidance for the burgeoning DeFi sector, aiming to foster innovation while ensuring compliance with regulatory standards. This perspective underscores a significant debate within the regulatory community about the most effective methods to oversee and support the evolution of decentralized financial technologies.[199]

As Commissioner Mersinger recognized in her dissent, an essential question to the development of decentralized finance is the extent of responsibility that creators of decentralized tools, such as exchanges and protocols, hold for the actions taken on their platforms. Often, decentralized protocols rely on centralized entities for their operation, prompting regulators to target these companies and alleging direct responsibility for activities conducted through their technology. The cases mentioned above illustrate this point, with each involving a

---

199 Mersinger, Summer. "Dissenting Statement of Commissioner Summer K. Mersinger Regarding Enforcement Actions Against: 1) Opyn, Inc.; 2) Deridex, Inc.; and 3) ZeroEx, Inc." *Commodity Futures Trading Commission*, 7 Sept. 2023, rb.gy/im9txu.

centralized organization that developed the technology and played a role in managing the protocol's operations.

A notable action by the CFTC involved bZeroX LLC and its founders, who developed, marketed, and operated a decentralized trading platform known as the bZx protocol. This platform facilitated margined and leveraged retail commodity transactions. The CFTC charged bZeroX with functioning as an unlicensed FCM by offering margin products to ineligible customers. The CFTC and bZeroX settled the case for $250,000.

The bZeroX case is intriguing because the entity handed over control of the bZx protocol to a decentralized autonomous organization called "Ooki DAO," which changed the protocol's name to Ooki Protocol and continued to support its functions. In *In re Ooki DAO*, the CFTC alleged that transferring bZx's operations to Ooki DAO was an attempt to evade enforcement. The founders of bZx were said to be actively involved in Ooki DAO.

The CFTC determined that Ooki DAO, being an unincorporated association, meant its members could be held liable for its violations of the CEA. Facing the challenge of how to enforce actions against a non-legal entity like Ooki DAO, the CFTC secured court permission to serve DAO members through the DAO's online discussion forum. Ooki DAO, as a loosely affiliated online organization, did not mount a defense, resulting in a default judgment against the DAO.

All the DeFi actions by the CFTC, except for Ooki DAO which concluded with a default judgment, have settled without a court ruling on whether creators of protocols for trading futures, options, swaps, or leveraged products are regulatorily the same as centralized actors offering such products directly. These outcomes leave unresolved questions about the liability of DAO members and if creators of decentralized platforms have ongoing liability, even without active involvement in the protocol's operations. These cases are further analyzed in the Supplemental Resources, and the unique legal challenges faced by developers in the decentralized finance space are explored in Chapter 9.

The Role of the CFTC

No federal agency has been granted authority to regulate the spot sales of commodities that are not themselves securities. The Commodity Futures Trading Commission, despite its expanded role, is still limited to targeting manipulation and fraud in commodity sales, and the CEA requires registration for only certain derivative or leveraged transactions. State governments are the main regulators of spot digital asset sales. However, there is an emerging view among some that a federal entity, possibly the CFTC, should take on the primary regulatory role for these markets. Yet, there is no detailed plan for how the CFTC would manage oversight of all digital asset transactions, and expanding its regulatory reach in this manner is unlikely in the near term.

In the following chapters, we will explore the Securities and Exchange Commission's complex relationship with the digital asset industry. While some argue that the CFTC would be a more suitable regulator given the SEC's seemingly hostile approach to digital assets, this perspective overlooks the possibility of future CFTC leadership also adopting a negative stance towards the industry. After all, the SEC's current chair, Gary Gensler, previously served as Chairman of the CFTC. Political dynamics aside, given that the orientation of federal agencies can shift with changing administrations, the fundamental issue is not about choosing between the CFTC and SEC for oversight of spot digital asset transactions. Instead, the critical question is whether the role of the federal government should be expanded for the first time in our country's history to grant federal oversight of spot commodities markets.

Supplemental Resources[200]

- **The Commodity Exchange Act and Other Regulations,** cftc.gov/LawRegulation/CommodityExchangeAct/index.htm.
- **Litigation Tracker** - The Morrison Cohen law firm

---

[200] For ease of reference, all Supplemental Resources and footnote links are available at www.TheCryptoLegalHandbook.com/Resources.

publishes a litigation tracker quarterly that collects civil and criminal cases in the industry, including CFTC and other agency actions. You can find the latest version of the tracker at morrisoncohen.com/insights/the-morrison-cohen-cryptocurrency-litigation-tracker. I encourage you to follow Jason Gottleib (@ohaiom) from the firm as he usually pushes out updates.

- **"Forward and Futures Markets."** *YouTube*, **Yale Courses, 5 Apr. 2012,** y2u.be/rxHu93YzHpc. Robert Schiller is a Nobel Prize-winning economist and Yale professor. His entire "Financial Markets" course is available on YouTube and provides a thorough overview of traditional financial markets. The linked video provides his overview of forward and futures markets and will provide a good overview of what to expect in the broader course.

- **Giancarlo, J. Christopher.** *CryptoDad: The Fight for the Future of Money.* **Wiley, 2022.** Chris Giancarlo (@GiancarloMKTS) is a former CFTC Commissioner and, since leaving the government, has become a vocal advocate for digital assets. This book provides a fascinating look into the policy debate and politics influencing the future of digital asset regulations. For a video overview, *see* **"The Fight for the Future of Money | CryptoDad Chris Giancarlo."** *YouTube*, **Bankless, 15 Nov. 2021,** y2u.be/NeQrSWa_qy8.

- *CFTC's Digital Assets and Blockchain Technology Subcommittee Release of Decentralized Finance Report*, **CFTC, 8 Jan. 2024,** shorturl.at/bfgUZ. This is a report published by the CFTC on DeFi risks and opportunities that was created to inform the public policy debate over regulations of decentralized financial technologies. For a presentation of the Report's findings, *see* **"Commissioner Goldsmith Romero Announces January 8, 2024 Technology Advisory Committee Meeting."** *YouTube*, **CFTC, 2024,** y2u.be/RAwq1m0PVFE&t=9349s.

CHAPTER 13

A Primer on Federal Securities Law

The application of federal securities regulations to digital assets is a hotly contested topic. This debate has been captured in thousands of articles, podcasts, and videos of "thought leaders" pontificating about how digital assets align with existing securities frameworks. The issue's complexity has been exacerbated by the government's reluctance to introduce new regulations or amend existing laws for a clear standard of when a digital asset should be considered a security. In the absence of regulations designed specifically to address the application of federal securities rules to digital assets, the industry has been forced to wait for guidance on the results of sporadic enforcement actions by the SEC.

The complexities of securities laws are significant, and this book does not attempt to provide a comprehensive scope of all federal securities regulations. Rather, my goal is to offer context and a perspective on the essential concepts and regulations that have informed the debate over how to determine whether digital assets should be classified as securities.

Securities ≠ Investments

"Security" is a term of art originating from the late Middle Ages, initially referring to an asset pledged as collateral to secure a debt. This usage is similar to the modern concept of a "security deposit," where an asset guarantees a financial obligation. Over time, the term expanded beyond the pledged asset to include the document or note enforcing the debt. These documents, embodying the right to collect interest and repayment, were traded and collectively termed "securities." By the 17th century, the definition had widened to encompass not only documents related to debt but also certificates of company ownership. When shares of the Dutch East India Company became the first publicly traded stocks on the Amsterdam Stock Exchange in 1602, they were called securities.

The term "security" has evolved to denote a range of financial instruments that represent a promise of value for the benefit of its holder. It has never been just another word for "investment."

Early Securities Regulations

The trading of securities such as stocks and debt instruments in the United States predates the nation's founding. The first stock exchanges appeared in Philadelphia and New York in the 1790s. Initially, these exchanges operated with self-imposed rules, lacking external oversight.

By the late 19th century, the necessity for formal securities regulation became evident, particularly in Western states. Investors in these regions often felt disadvantaged by dubious investments orchestrated by Eastern financiers. In response, Kansas enacted the first comprehensive securities law in 1911, requiring both securities and their salespeople to register with the state. This law aimed to protect investors from fraudulent schemes, like the sale of shares in non-existent gold mines, by ensuring that securities were backed by real assets and not just mere promises as empty as the "blue sky." The Kansas statute thus became known as a "blue sky law," a term still used to describe state securities regulations.

Kansas's securities law implemented a "merit review" system, evaluating the fairness and potential profitability of investments before allowing the public to invest. Following Kansas's lead, other states adopted blue sky regulations, leading to a patchwork of laws across the nation. It was only after the 1929 stock market crash and subsequent depression demonstrated the limitations of state-level oversight that a unified approach to securities regulation gained traction.

This period of financial turmoil revealed weaknesses in the existing regulatory framework and highlighted the necessity for federal intervention in securities markets. The crisis prompted President Franklin D. Roosevelt to champion the implementation of "Truth in

Securities" laws as a cornerstone of his "New Deal," aiming to rebuild investor trust in U.S. capital markets.

The Securities Acts

President Roosevelt's "Truth in Securities" laws manifested in two landmark regulations: the Securities Act of 1933 (the "Securities Act" or the "'33 Act") and the Securities Exchange Act of 1934 (the "Exchange Act" or the "'34 Act"). Although distinct laws, they are frequently mentioned together as the "Securities Acts," reflecting their complementary roles in establishing a comprehensive framework for the sales of securities in the United States. As part of this framework, Congress created the Securities and Exchange Commission to enforce federal securities regulations.

The Securities Act defines "security" as the following financial instruments.

> The term "security" means any note, stock, treasury stock, security future, security-based swap, bond, debenture, evidence of indebtedness, certificate of interest or participation in any profit-sharing agreement, collateral-trust certificate, preorganization certificate or subscription, transferable share, investment contract, voting-trust certificate, certificate of deposit for a security, fractional undivided interest in oil, gas, or other mineral rights, any put, call, straddle, option, or privilege on any security, certificate of deposit, or group or index of securities (including any interest therein or based on the value thereof), or any put, call, straddle, option, or privilege entered into on a national securities exchange relating to foreign currency, or, in general, any interest or instrument commonly known as a "security", or any certificate of interest or participation in, temporary or interim certificate for, receipt for, guarantee of, or warrant or right to subscribe to or purchase, any of the foregoing.

Note that among the listed financial instruments is an undefined category known as an "investment contract." How to apply this term to digital assets is one of the central points of debate within the crypto industry. In the next chapter, we will examine the criteria for defining an "investment contract" in detail.

The Securities Act of 1933: Regulating the Initial Sale of Securities

The Securities Act of 1933 regulates the initial offering and sale of securities to the public. Unlike some early state blue sky laws, the Securities Act does not undertake a review of the "merit" of an investment. Instead, federal securities regulations have adopted a "disclosure" based approach that requires issuers to register securities with the SEC and provide material information about the investment to the public so they can assess its merit for themselves.

Under Section 5 of the Securities Act, it is unlawful to offer or sell a non-exempt security without registering it with the SEC. Most people typically associate registered securities with the initial public offering (IPO) of a company's shares, but the registration requirement applies equally to other categories of securities. Each necessitates the submission of a designated registration form that caters to its specific characteristics and requires issuers to provide detailed disclosures that include the nature of the investment or business, associated risk factors, information about the management or ownership, and audited financial statements.[201]

The process of registering public offerings is costly, often requiring millions of dollars in legal and accounting fees.[202] While these expenses can be a worthwhile investment for those wishing to tap into the United States' robust capital markets, the cost of conducting a registered offering to raise funds is impractical for most businesses.

---

[201] The most commonly recognized registration form is "Form S-1," used for a company's initial public offering of stock. Additional form types are available for review at sec.gov/forms. All these forms, along with mandatory reporting requirements and submissions, can be filed with the SEC via its "EDGAR," (Electronic Data Gathering, Analysis, and Retrieval) System.

[202] Reg CF and Reg A+ are alternative fundraising options that offer a simplified registration process for offerings up to $5 and $75 million. For more information. *See* "Understanding Reg A, Reg CF, and Reg D in Syndication." *YouTube*, Moschetti Syndication Law, 23 June 2023, y2u.be/N_dl9SwYaCU.

The Securities Act exempts a variety of offerings[203] from its registration requirement, including:

- **Regulation D Exemption (Reg D)** encompasses a set of rules that permit companies to raise capital without the need for a formal registration of the offering with the SEC. To utilize this exemption effectively, companies must file "Form D" with the SEC no later than 15 days after the first sale of securities. This exemption primarily targets sales to "accredited investors" which are individuals characterized by an annual income exceeding $200,000 or a net worth greater than $1 million.[204]

    - **Rule 504** allows companies to raise up to $10 million from accredited or non-accredited investors within a 12-month period without registering the offering.

    - **Rule 506(b)** enables companies to raise unlimited funds from accredited investors and up to 35 non-accredited investors. It prohibits general solicitation or advertising of the offering.

    - **Rule 506(c)** allows companies to raise unlimited funds but restricts participation exclusively to accredited investors. Unlike Rule 506(b), it allows for general solicitation and advertising of the offer.

- **Regulation S Exemption (Reg S)** permits issuers to offer and sell securities outside the United States without registering the offering with the SEC. Unlike the Reg D exemption, there is no requirement to file a specific form with the SEC to utilize Reg S. However, securities sold under Reg S generally cannot be resold into the United States for a period of one year, imposing a restriction designed to prevent immediate re-entry of these securities into the U.S. markets.

---

203 For a full list of exempt offerings, *see* sec.gov/education/capitalraising/exemptofferings.

204 For a full set of requirements, *see* sec.gov/education/capitalraising/building-blocks/accredited-investor

- **Private Placement Exemption (Section 4(a)(2))** exempts securities offered to a potential investor individually, as opposed to a public solicitation, from registration. In practice, this exemption is typically used by companies to raise funds from accredited investors, though it doesn't strictly limit sales to this group.

The Securities Act also contains several anti-fraud provisions that subject issuers to civil penalties, including fines, damages, and recission for sales of securities involving fraud or misrepresentation. For example, Section 11 creates a private right of action for issuers and other signatories of the registration statement for material misstatements or omissions. Section 12 outlines liabilities for selling unregistered securities or misstatements made in the initial sale of securities. Section 17 prohibits fraudulent practices in the offer or sale of securities.

The Securities Exchange Act of 1934: Regulating Secondary Markets

The Securities Exchange Act of 1934 expanded federal oversight into the secondary securities markets, building upon the initial public offering and sale framework established by the Securities Act. This legislation introduced regulations for the post-initial offering trading of securities, targeting the exchanges, broker-dealers, and other entities that facilitate these transactions.

The Exchange Act also established the Securities and Exchange Commission as an independent federal agency tasked with enforcing federal securities laws. The SEC is overseen by the Senate Committee on Banking, Housing, and Urban Affairs and the House Committee on Financial Services. The current Chair of the SEC, Democrat Gary Gensler, leads a five-member bipartisan commission. Commissioners are appointed to 5-year terms by the President and are confirmed by the Senate.

The Exchange Act primarily regulates the venues through which securities can be resold and the disclosures that must be provided to the public. The Exchange Act requires the following exchanges and brokers of securities to register with the SEC:

- **National Securities Exchanges:** Formal marketplaces for the buying and selling of securities that must comply with strict rules designed to ensure fair and orderly markets. Examples include the New York Stock Exchange and NASDAQ.

- **Alternative Trading Systems (ATS):** An ATS is a trading venue that matches buyers and sellers of securities. Although ATSs must register with the SEC, the applicable regulation (called Reg-ATS) allows ATSs to operate with more flexibility than a National Securities Exchange. ATSs typically cater to institutions seeking to execute large transactions discreetly, unlike National Securities Exchanges, which act as central marketplaces for securities.

- **Broker-Dealers (BDs):** Individuals or firms that buy and sell securities either on behalf of their clients (as brokers) or for their own accounts (as dealers). BDs are required to register with both the SEC and the Financial Industry Regulatory Authority (FINRA), a non-governmental self-regulatory authority responsible for overseeing the securities industry.[205] Broker-dealers can operate an ATS, provided they have the appropriate registration, allowing them to offer alternative trading platforms in addition to their brokerage services.

Like the '33 Act, the '34 Act contains provisions against fraudulent and manipulative practices in securities trading, including Section 10b-5, which prohibits insider trading of securities based on material, non-public information. The Exchange Act also requires public companies to file periodic reports with the SEC to ensure continued transparency for investors.

Other Federal Regulations and Considerations

Since the enactment of the Securities Acts, the SEC has seen its oversight role expanded. Other notable federal regulations include:

---

[205] FINRA oversees the operations and compliance of brokerage firms with its rules and federal securities laws, including the registration, education, and testing of brokers. For more information about FINRA's scope, *see* finra.org/about.

- **Investment Company Act of 1940:** Regulates the organization and activities of investment companies and mutual funds, focusing on the protection of investors through disclosure requirements and restrictions on activities to minimize conflicts of interest.

- **Investment Advisers Act of 1940:** Requires investment advisers to register with the SEC and adhere to regulations designed to protect investors, including fiduciary duties and disclosure obligations.

- **Dodd-Frank Wall Street Reform and Consumer Protection Act of 2010:** A comprehensive financial reform that broadened the oversight powers of the SEC and CFTC. Among the many reforms initiated through this legislation are regulations and mandatory registration requirements for clearing agencies that transfer and settle transactions for securities.[206]

The SEC also has extensive authority to issue guidance that influences the securities markets. For instance, in 2022, the SEC released Staff Accounting Bulletin No. 121 (SAB 121), stipulating that public companies holding digital assets on behalf of clients must reflect these holdings on their balance sheets. SAB 121 creates significant challenges for public banks interested in holding digital assets, as it would, at scale, lead to increased capital requirements. Lawmakers are pushing for the SEC to retract this guidance, which, despite being directly applicable only to public companies, has had a profound indirect impact on private entities within the industry. SAB 121 exemplifies the discretionary power federal regulators like the SEC wield to influence the securities industry and broader markets beyond the formal rulemaking process.[207]

---

206 For a digestible overview of settling securities transactions, *see* "Securities Trading Market Infrastructure." *YouTube*, asymilate, 9 July 2012, y2ube/mEnCKNIb0Bs.

207 "Staff Accounting Bulletin 121." *SEC*, 24 Mar. 2022, sec.gov/oca/staff-accounting-bulletin-121; *see* also, Hamilton, Jesse. *U.S. Lawmakers Seek to Overturn SEC's Crypto Accounting Policy*, CoinDesk, 8 Mar. 2024, shorturl.at/fhoW8.

Consequences of Being Categorized as a Security

The disclosures required to register a security with the SEC contemplate the existence of a centralized issuer whose efforts are material to the potential success of the venture. Because securities have involved a centralized issuer since the Middle Ages, it makes sense that the SEC's registration has developed to require information about the issuer of the security. Accordingly, to register a security, the issuer of that security must provide financial audits and material information about their business and operations.

Chair Gensler has asserted that he believes every digital asset except bitcoin is a security and has implored the industry to "come in and register." Assuming for the sake of argument that he is correct in concluding that all non-BTC digital assets are securities, the current registration documents do not contemplate decentralized digital assets and the SEC has declined to provide guidance on how such assets could practically be registered.

The type of disclosure regime that focuses on a centralized issuer is incompatible with many digital asset projects, and there is no framework for a digital asset whose underlying blockchain is maintained by a global network to register with the SEC.

Consider the digital assets SOL and ADA, both of which have been alleged by the SEC in enforcement actions to be securities. A finding confirming the SEC's theory would not just prevent those wishing to purchase these assets as investments from being able to easily obtain them. It would also make it impossible for many who seek to purchase these assets in order to develop or interact with smart contracts on the Solana and Cardano networks to do so. Under the SEC's current framing, a platform that sells bitcoin to users wishing to mint NFTs on the Bitcoin network is unregulated by federal securities law, but the same company wishing to sell users SOL to mint NFTs on the Solana network would be S.O.L. (shit out of luck).

The practical effect of such disparate treatment is that all public blockchains except Bitcoin cannot be freely accessed by U.S. persons.

The impossibility of registering most digital assets as securities is analyzed in Paradigm's article "SEC's Path to Registration."[208] Paradigm points out the lack of a clear path for digital asset networks to file registration statements due to their fundamentally different nature from traditional securities. For example, there is no clear path for how a decentralized network can provide the audited financial statements or quarterly reports required for registration with the SEC.

Because digital assets cannot, in most cases, register with the SEC, a national securities exchange or broker-dealer that wished to sell a digital asset could not do so because they generally only deal in registered securities. This creates a dilemma where the inability to register a digital asset means registered digital asset platforms have nothing to list, which in turn makes it unviable for entrepreneurs to incur the expense of creating trading venues for digital asset securities in the first place. As Paradigm explains, the handful of centralized digital assets that have been able to register their tokens with the SEC failed because there is no marketplace to list these tokens.

If the SEC does not clarify its guidelines or revise the registration process for digital assets, its enforcement stance—that most digital assets are securities—would doom the digital asset market in the United States absent court intervention. This potential collapse would stem not from an explicit judicial or legislative decision but from the SEC's reluctance to adapt its registration process so that a publicly maintained digital asset can be feasibly registered.

In the upcoming chapters, we will examine the SEC's activity in the digital asset space, including enforcement actions against token issuers and digital asset platforms for allegedly selling unregistered securities. As we explore these actions, keep in mind that because there is no viable registration opportunity for decentralized digital assets to register, the consequence of the SEC's position is that nearly all digital assets, as well as their underlying networks, will become inaccessible in the United States. This result suggests that the SEC has strayed from its role as a disclosure-based regulator to seemingly determine that digital assets are without merit and, therefore,

---

[208] "Due to SEC Inaction, Registration Is Not a Viable Path for Crypto Projects." *Paradigm Policy*, policy.paradigm.xyz/writing/secs-path-to-registration-part-i.

unsuitable for the American public.

Supplemental Resources[209]

- **The Securities Act of 1933,** govinfo.gov/content/pkg/COMPS-1884/pdf/COMPS-1884.pdf
- **The Securities Exchange Act of 1934,** govinfo.gov/content/pkg/COMPS-1885/pdf/COMPS-1885.pdf
- **List To Other Statutes Governing Securities,** sec.gov/about/about-securities-laws.
- **"Due to SEC Inaction, Registration Is Not a Viable Path for Crypto Projects."** *Paradigm Policy*, policy.paradigm.xyz/writing/secs-path-to-registration-part-i.

---

[209] For ease of reference, all Supplemental Resources and footnote links are available at www.TheCryptoLegalHandbook.com/Resources.

CHAPTER 14

Investment Contracts

Federal law defines a "security" as any one of the 17 financial instruments listed in the Securities Acts. While each category has itself been the subject of regulatory and judicial guidance to determine its bounds, we will focus specifically on defining the term "investment contract" as the application of its framework to digital assets has emerged as the central regulatory question facing the industry.[210]

The term "investment contract" is undefined in the Securities Acts.[211] As with the word "security" itself, the term "investment contract' was never used to mean just an "investment." It has always referred to an investment that relied on the promise of another for it to reach its potential. There is an instinct by some to read out the term "contract" from the phrase, but while an investment contract may not require a formal written agreement, the term has always required some relationship between the issuer and investor.

The modern articulation of how to define an investment contract comes from the Supreme Court's 1946 *SEC v. W.J. Howey Co.* decision. The *Howey* case has become so ubiquitous among discussions about digital assets that I have found, ironically, many in the space have

---

210 As different financial products are "tokenized," it is likely that many digital assets will intersect with other categories of securities in the future. While most types of securities are beyond our scope, I want to flag the category of promissory "notes" as the SEC has suggested some digital assets may fit into this category. I recommend familiarizing yourself with *Reves v. Ernst & Young*, 494 U.S. 56 (1990) and its "family resemblance" test for determining under what circumstances a note is a security. For a broader discussion, see Davis, Peter. "The Limits of Applying Reves v. Ernst & Young to Defi and the Perils of Regulating Web3 by Enforcement." *JD Supra*, 26 Jan. 2022, shorturl.at/bdnpE.

211 For an interesting background on the pre-Securities Act history of the term, I encourage you to read a brief submitted by a group of securities law scholars in the *SEC v. Coinbase* case, linked in the Supplemental Resources.

absorbed the case's facts and holding through a sort of legal osmosis but have not studied the case itself. The opinion is only seven pages, so read it if you haven't already.[212]

SEC v. W.J. Howey Co.

The Howey Company bought 500 acres of citrus groves in Florida. It kept half the land and offered the remainder for sale to prospective investors, many of whom were tourists at a hotel resort also owned by the company. The land was marketed as an investment promising double-digit profit percentages. Buyers were deeded the land through a warranty deed and owned the land outright, but because the buyers were mostly tourists with no farming experience, the Howey Company encouraged purchasers to enter into a separate services agreement with a company they also owned called Howey-in-the-Hills Service, Inc. to manage the land and sell the crops.

The vast majority of buyers entered into the services agreement with Howey-in-the-Hills. As part of the services agreement, Howey-in-the-Hills was granted a 10-year leasehold that gave them complete control over the land and full discretion on all agricultural and business decisions. The services agreement gave the landowners no right to the fruit grown on their land and allowed Howey-in-the-Hills to pool and sell their crops together with fruit from other tracts. In return, landowners were promised an allocation of the net profits of the pooled harvest.

The SEC brought claims against the Howey Company and Howey-in-the-Hills for offering an unregistered investment contract, arguing that the land sale agreement and services agreement should be analyzed together as a single offering. The lower courts ruled against the SEC, analyzing the two agreements independently and finding that neither constituted a security as defined by the Securities Act.

The Supreme Court disagreed, holding that by coupling the offer to sell land with a services agreement to cultivate the crops and distribute the proceeds, the Howey defendants had made an integrated offer to investors that fit within the meaning of "investment contract"

---

212 *SEC v. W.J. Howey Co.*, 328 U.S. 293 (1946), available at shorturl.at/qUY56.

under the Securities Act. In its holding, the Court recognized that the concept of "investment contract" was included in the Securities Act to embody "a flexible rather than a static principle, one that is capable of adaptation to meet the countless and variable schemes devised by those who seek the use of the money of others on the promise of profits."

In siding with the SEC, the Supreme Court established the following test:

> An investment contract is a contract, transaction, or scheme whereby a person invests his money in a common enterprise and is led to expect profits solely from the efforts of the promoter or a third party.

The *Howey* Test

The *Howey* test imposes a four-factor analysis for determining whether a "contract, transaction, or scheme" fits the definition of an investment contract. Subsequent case law has slightly reformulated the test such that it is now understood that an investment contract exists if there is:

1. An **investment of money**;
2. in a **common enterprise**;
3. with an **expectation of profits**;
4. based on the **efforts of others**.

Each factor of the *Howey* test must be present for an investment contract to be found. The test requires courts to analyze the specific facts of an investment to determine whether it satisfies the *Howey* criteria. This fact-specific inquiry makes it difficult to transpose case holdings directly from one investment scheme to another.

There have been relatively few investment contract cases taken up by the Supreme Court since *Howey*, so the task of interpreting its test has fallen mostly to lower trial and appellate courts. This has led to a patchwork of inconsistent rulings on what constitutes an investment contract or how to apply *Howey* to a particular set of facts and circumstances.[213] As opinions on the application of *Howey* to digital assets emerge, we are likely to see inconsistent approaches develop until either Congress or the Supreme Court establishes a national standard.

I. Investment of Money

Whether an "investment of money" in an enterprise has occurred is typically straightforward and rarely disputed. This element is satisfied when an investor commits any resource to an enterprise. This includes not just "money" but any benefit provided by the investor, including non-cash assets like crypto and services provided to the venture.

An often cited case in the digital asset space used to demonstrate the breadth of the investment of money prong is *In the Matter of Tomahawk Exploration LLC and David Thompson Laurence*. There, a token project earmarked tokens for the public as part of a "bounty program" to incentivize supporters of the project to provide services for the issuer. The tokens were sent to the service providers through an "airdrop," and the SEC alleged that services provided in exchange for the tokens met the "investment of money" test under *Howey*.[214]

Although the *Tomahawk* case was settled before it could be judicially tested, the rationale is consistent with other courts who have considered services provided to an issuer as an investment of money.[215] *Tomahawk* is sometimes cited incorrectly for the

---

213 The U.S. has a dual court system of state and federal courts. Federal trial courts, or District Courts, are in every state, sometimes divided by region (e.g., Southern District of New York). Circuit Courts of Appeals hear appeals from these courts, with each overseeing multiple states. Appeals can be made to the U.S. Supreme Court, which has discretion as to what cases it hears. A Supreme Court ruling sets the law nationwide, but until then, Circuit Court decisions are binding only within their jurisdiction. For a map of the Circuits, *see* shorturl.at/acBGK.

214 An "airdrop" is the distribution of a cryptocurrency into digital wallets without the recipient taking any affirmative steps to claim the distribution. Airdrops are sometimes provided to users whose wallet addresses have met activity thresholds to distribute tokens to active crypto users. For more information on airdrops generally, *see* "What Is an Airdrop? How to Find Free Crypto & Why It's Given." *YouTube*, Whiteboard Crypto, 2 July 2021, y2u.be/oW3Cp4JDhI4.

215 But *see*, *SEC v. Ripple Labs*, which held on summary judgment that certain crypto

proposition that a project that provides even gratuitous airdrops can satisfy the "investment of money" prong, but there has not yet been any judicial support for this proposition.[216]

II. Common Enterprise

An investment contract requires an investor to enter into a "common enterprise" in which its interests and fortunes are tied to the interests and fortunes of others. The Supreme Court has not provided guidance as to who those "others" are or how to assess if a common enterprise exists. This has left the Circuit Courts to decide for themselves what constitutes a common enterprise, leading to different approaches among the Circuits as to how to satisfy this prong. The debate comes down to whether the relevant common interest is between similarly situated investors (horizontal commonality) or between the investor and the promotor of the investment (vertical commonality).

Consider the *Howey* case as an example: Was the relevant common enterprise the relationship between investors who bought land and pooled the fruit together for shared profits, or was it between each landowner and Howey-in-the-Hills, both of whom profited from the successful management of the land? The Supreme Court did not specify which relationship satisfied the common enterprise factor. This has led to confusion among the Circuit Courts on which type of relationship fulfills this criterion.

The Circuit Courts have adopted the following differing approaches:

- **Horizontal Commonality** focuses on the pooling of investors' assets and the sharing of profits and risks among them. This form of commonality is seen as a group-centric approach, where the fortunes of individual investors are directly linked to one another. The First, Sixth, and Seventh

---

allocations provided in exchange for services did not satisfy the "investment of money" prong. *SEC v. Ripple Labs Inc.*, No. 1:20-cv-10832, Order on Motion for Summary Judgment, Doc 874. SDNY. 13 Jul. 2023. CourtListener, shorturl.at/aqJR5. This case is discussed further in Chapter 15 and this holding will likely be a focus on appeal.

216 In *re Tomahawk Exploration LLC*. File No. 3-18641. Order Instituting Administrative and Cease and Desist Proceedings, 14 Aug. 2018, sec.gov/files/litigation/admin/2018/33-10530.pdf.

Circuits strictly adhere to this interpretation, requiring clear evidence of pooled assets and shared outcomes among similarly situated investors.[217] The Second, Third, Fourth, and D.C. Circuits also recognize horizontal commonality but have not ruled on whether a vertical commonality standard could also apply.[218]

- **Vertical Commonality** is divided into two subtypes: strict vertical and broad vertical commonality. This approach looks at the relationship between the investors and the promoter, emphasizing the dependency of investors' fortunes on the efforts or success of the promoter. The Eighth and Tenth Circuits appear to have adopted vertical commonality but have not specified whether they favor a strict or broad approach.[219]

  - **Strict Vertical Commonality** requires the fortunes of the investor and the promoter to be closely intertwined, rising and falling together based on the promoter's efforts. This form of commonality suggests a direct correlation between the promoter's success and the investors' returns. The 9th Circuit accepts both horizontal and strict vertical commonality to support a common enterprise.[220]

  - **Broad Vertical Commonality** is the easiest to satisfy and the only one that does not require an investor to have a common financial interest with another party. Instead, it only requires the investors' fortunes to be tied to the promoter's *efforts*, regardless of the direct financial link between them. The Fifth and Eleventh

---

217 *SEC v. SG Ltd.*, 265 F.3d 42 (1st Cir. 2001); Curran v. Merrill Lynch, 622 F.2d 216, 222 (6th Cir. 1980); *Milnarik v. M-S Commodities, Inc.*, 457 F.2d 274 (7th Cir. 1972).

218 *Revak v. SEC Realty Corp.*, 18 F.3d 81 (2d Cir. 1994); *Salcer v. Merrill Lynch*, 682 F.2d 459 (3d Cir. 1982); *Teague v. Bakker*, 35 F.3d 978 (4th Cir. 1994); *SEC. v. Life Partners*, 102 F.3d 587 (D.C. Circ).

219 *Miller v. Cent. Chinchilla Grp.*, 494 F.2d 414, 416 (8th Cir. 1974); *McGill v. Am. Land & Exploration Co.*, 776 F.2d 923, 925 (10th Cir. 1985).

220 *Hocking v. Dubois*, 839 F.2d 560, 567 (9th Cir. 1988).

Circuits have adopted this approach.[221]

III. Expectation of Profits

The Supreme Court has defined "profit" as a financial return on an investment. The expectation of profit is determined primarily by whether the transaction was made for a financial return or for personal consumption. Two Supreme Court cases, *SEC v. C.M. Joiner Leasing Corp.*, 320 U.S. 344 (1943) and *United Housing Foundation v. Forman*, 421 U.S. 837 (1975), illustrate this distinction.

In *Joiner*, the Supreme Court concluded that the sale of lease assignments for land by an oil-drilling outfit was a security. Central to the Court's analysis was whether investors purchased the lease assignments because of an expectation of profits or for an interest in the land itself. Based on the promotional materials that highlighted its economic potential and the fact that the purchasers had no expertise in oil drilling, the Court found purchases were primarily made in anticipation of profits from the venture.

The *Forman* case also involved the purchase of a real estate interest, shares in a New York City building that required residents to own shares of the entire building as a condition of their residence. Unlike *Joiner*, those who purchased shares did so in order to secure a New York City apartment and not for financial gain. The promotional materials focused on the benefits of living in the building and not the potential for economic returns. Indeed, the promotional materials warned purchasers that they would be required to sell their shares back for the purchase price if they moved out. Under those facts, the Court concluded the housing shares were not investment contracts under *Howey*.

The difference between *Joiner and Forman* lies in the motivations for purchasing the real estate interest. The *Joiner* purchasers were motivated by a potential financial return from oil drilling. In *Forman*, the motivation was to obtain housing with no expectation of profit,

---

221 *SEC v. Koscot Interplanetary, Inc.*, 497 F.2d 473 (5th Cir. 1974); *Bonner v. City of Prichard*, 661 F.2d 1206 (11th Cir. 1981) (holding decisions of the 5th Circuit before September 30, 1981 are binding on the newly formed 11th Circuit).

resulting in a finding that it was not an investment contract.

There are many open questions regarding how to apply the expectation of profits prong that are relevant to the sale of digital assets, especially those made on secondary markets in which the initial issuer of a digital asset is not a party to the transaction. For example, how does one treat an asset purchased for both consumptive and financial motives and what is the relevance of promotional materials made by the issuer of a digital asset for sales conducted on secondary markets?

IV. Efforts of Others

For a venture to be considered an investment contract, the anticipated profits must come from the "efforts of others." The Supreme Court initially set the standard as being "solely" from the efforts of others, but the test has broadened over time to require only a significant or material effort that represents a dominant influence in the venture's success.

The critical aspect of this analysis is control. The determination hinges on who holds meaningful control over the success of the venture. If the control lies predominantly with the promoters rather than the investors, then the venture likely meets the *Howey* test's requirement of depending on the efforts of others for profits. If investors retain significant control, if general market conditions cause the success of the project, or because the managerial efforts of an investment have become distributed such that its issuer's efforts no longer drive the venture's success, it may not be an investment contract.

Control is based on the "economic reality" of the venture, which considers the practical operation of the scheme beyond what's stipulated in written agreements or promotional materials. If investors are granted control on paper but can't exercise it in practice, such control is deemed "illusory." An illustrative case is the Fourth Circuit's *Bailey v. JWK Properties*, 904 F.2d 918 (4th Cir. 1990) decision, where a cattle breeding program promised profits from selling superior cattle. Despite agreements suggesting investor control over selecting embryos and managing cattle, investors lacked the expertise and practical ability to do so, relegating actual control to the promoters. This demonstrated that the venture's success was dependent materially on the promoters' efforts, satisfying *Howey*'s fourth prong.

The "efforts of others" criterion presents numerous questions of first impression when attempting to apply this factor to digital assets whose underlying networks are supported by publicly maintained software and a distributed community of supporters. Many digital assets have the capacity to become less reliant on their initial creators over time. This distribution of control and effort, where a global community plays an increasingly significant role in the asset's development and success, makes it difficult to apply traditional case law assumptions that focus on the issuer or promoter's efforts.

"Sufficiently Decentralized"

SEC Chair Gary Gensler has stated on several occasions that the reason Bitcoin is not a security under *Howey* is that there is no centralized group in control of the asset's success. The SEC's former Head of Enforcement, William Hinman, similarly stated in a 2018 speech that, in his opinion, ether also did not satisfy the *Howey* test because, as of the time of the speech, it was no longer reliant on the efforts of its founders for its success. As Mr. Hinman explained:

> If the network on which the token or coin is to function is sufficiently decentralized – where purchasers would no longer reasonably expect a person or group to carry out essential managerial or entrepreneurial efforts – the assets may not represent an investment contract. Moreover, when the efforts of the third party are no longer a key factor for determining the enterprise's success, material information asymmetries recede. As a network becomes truly decentralized, the ability to identify an issuer or promoter to make the requisite disclosures becomes difficult, and less meaningful.[222]

While courts have not adopted Mr. Hinman's language, it seems he used the phrase "sufficiently decentralized" as a stand-in for "efforts

---

222 Hinman, William, Director, Division of Corporation Finance, SEC. "Digital Asset Transactions: When Howey Met Gary (Plastic)." 14 June 2018, bit.ly/2l8t5dB.

of others." Digital assets differ from traditional securities in that the "control" of a digital asset can diminish over time. As Mr. Hinman recognized, this dynamic nature likely influences how *Howey* applies to digital assets.

Every digital asset, including bitcoin and ether, began with a founder or founding team whose efforts were crucial to its success. Digital assets are unique in that they allow outsiders to contribute to the development of underlying network infrastructure and allow the public to take over the management and control of a project over time. Unfortunately, neither regulators nor courts have specified what metric to use to assess whether public contributions to a project have reduced a founding team's control to such an extent that the asset's success cannot be attributed to its creators' efforts.

Are the Oranges Securities?

Now that we have familiarized ourselves with the *Howey* test, it is important to take a step back to consider what the test analyzes in the first place. In an investment contract, an investor devotes funds to a money-making venture managed by someone else. The business could use the investor's funds to try to make money in any number of ways; it could manufacture widgets, mine gold, or grow oranges. The investor is not investing in the widgets, gold, or oranges, but the business created to bring those products to market.

There are plenty of cases providing examples of courts finding the existence of an investment contract in businesses involving the production or sale of ordinary commodities. The Minnesota Supreme Court once found that the sale of muskrats was an investment contract because they were sold with the commitment of a fur trader to raise the critters and sell their pelts for profit.[223] In another often-cited case, the Second Circuit held that the sale of receipts for whiskey barrels was an investment contract because it was coupled with a promise by a distiller to store and sell the liquor once it was aged.[224] In these cases, as in *Howey*, an asset was produced

---

[223] *State v. Robbins*, 240 N.W. 456 (Minn. 1932) (muskrats); *Cont'l Mktg. Corp. v. SEC*, 387 F.2d 466 (10th Cir. 1967) (beavers).

[224] *Glen-Arden Commodities, Inc. v. Costantino*, 493 F.2d 1027 (2d Cir.1974).

by a business that had raised money through an investment contract. The asset it produced was not itself the security.

Every security requires the presence of a promise made by an issuer that places that person in a trusted position. It is the reliance that an investor has on an issuer to act honestly that creates a unique type of risk for investors of a security that is not present for someone just buying an item that the company produced. This is true for items purchased both for one's consumption and for investment purposes. For instance, the sale of shares in a gold mine is considered a security that must be registered and sold on regulated platforms, given that the gold mining venture has obligations to its shareholders. However, the gold produced by the mine, even if bought with the expectation of profit, does not carry any obligation from the business that extracted it. Consequently, the sale of gold, as well as other items commonly bought in the hope that their value will increase, like baseball cards, sneakers, or art, is not subject to securities sale regulations.[225]

It is the reliance on another to make good use of an investor's funds that first caused Kansas to create its blue sky law and President Roosevelt to call on Congress to pass "Truth in Securities" regulations. For cases involving fruit, furs, whiskey, or gold produced by a business that raised money through an investment contract, the conclusion that the products of the investment are just ordinary commodities and not securities is uncontroversial. That's because after the orange is picked, there is no longer reliance on the part of its purchaser on the business that grew it. A finding to the contrary, that the oranges are securities, would necessitate supermarkets to register with the SEC before they could sell them. That result would be absurd, but that is essentially the SEC's theory when it comes to crypto.

As we'll read in the next chapter, the SEC has advanced a position that, for every digital asset except Bitcoin, the figurative oranges are the securities, and no matter how many miles away they are from the farm, they always will be. Unfortunately, the SEC has not provided a framework for registering digital assets and their exchanges anymore than it has for oranges and fruit stands.

---

225 *See, e.g., SEC v. Belmont-Reid*, 794 F.2d 1388 (9th Cir. 1986) (arrangement to pre-sell gold to investors did not qualify as an "investment contract.").

Supplemental Resources[226]

- **Cohen, Lewis, et al. "The Ineluctable Modality of Securities Law: Why Fungible Crypto Assets Are not Securities." 10 Nov. 2022. SSRN,** shorturl.at/aBCDL Over 90 years of case law have interpreted *Howey*, and more than a decade of discourse has been held on its application to digital assets. This chapter barely scratches the surface of the debate. Fortunately, Lewis Cohen (@NYcryptolawyer) and DLx Law's 2022 article offers an in-depth analysis of the history of *Howey*, as well as a review of federal cases interpreting its holding, and a nuanced discussion as to how to apply its factors to digital assets. The article has been incredibly influential within the crypto legal community and is a must-read. For a video of Lewis Cohen explaining the paper's thesis, *see* **"Lewis Cohen - Ineluctable Modality of Securities Law."** *YouTube*, **Porkopolis Economics, 4 Apr. 2023,** y2u.be/wuG8OWcZbxI.

- **"*SEC v. Coinbase Inc.* Brief of Securities Law Scholars as Amici Curiae in Support of Coinbase's Motion for Judgment on the Pleadings." SDNY, Case No. 23 Civ. 4738, Doc 159, 11 Aug. 2023,** shorturl.at/dqCFX. This brief was authored by a group of law professors in support of Coinbase in its defense against the SEC. The brief traces the history of the term "investment contract" and provides a good introduction to the development of U.S. securities rules.

---

226 For ease of reference, all Supplemental Resources and footnote links are available at www.TheCryptoLegalHandbook.com/Resources.

CHAPTER 15

The Securities and Exchange Commission

The Securities and Exchange Commission has initiated an aggressive enforcement agenda against digital asset platforms and token issuers for selling what they have termed unregistered "crypto asset securities." In this Chapter, we'll examine the SEC's history of enforcement in the digital asset space.

Navigating the state of digital asset securities law is challenging. First, we're still very early; appellate courts have yet to fully address securities law as it pertains to digital assets, and critical cases are still in their briefing stages. Second, the SEC has launched almost 200 enforcement actions related to digital assets, most ending in non-precedential settlements that offer, at best, an anecdotal understanding of the SEC's position rather than a reliable legal framework for the industry at large.[227] The political landscape complicates the issue further. The SEC has refused to establish new rules, and Congress has failed to pass legislation to clarify the regulatory status of digital assets.

Without formal rulemaking, the industry is left to decipher the law from isolated enforcement actions as they proceed through the legal system. Before we explore these pending cases, it's critical to examine the Commission's historical actions and statements to understand the backdrop against which the current enforcement agenda is set.

The SEC's History of Digital Asset Activity

The Securities and Exchange Commission was relatively late among federal regulators in addressing crypto. Although the agency prosecuted its first case involving digital assets in 2013—a Ponzi

---

[227] For a list of actions, *see* sec.gov/spotlight/cybersecurity-enforcement-actions.

scheme where investments were made in bitcoin—it remained silent on how federal securities law might apply to digital assets generally.[228] Other regulators were more proactive. In 2013, the Department of Treasury issued guidance on applying the Bank Secrecy Act to digital assets, and in 2015, the CFTC stated its view that digital assets were commodities under the Commodity Exchange Act.

It was not until 2017, when the SEC published its Report of Investigation Regarding the DAO (the "DAO Report"), that it first provided an indication of how digital assets fit into the existing securities framework.

The DAO Report

The DAO Report was a reaction to an exploit of a decentralized autonomous organization that used smart contracts built on Ethereum's blockchain to create a community-run investment fund known as "The DAO." The DAO allowed investors to contribute ether that would be deployed to fund investments based on a vote of DAO members. In exchange for their investment of ether, investors received DAO Tokens that entitled its holder to vote on how to deploy the funds collected by The DAO and a share of any profits made by the fund.

The DAO Report's conclusion that DAO Tokens were securities was fairly uncontroversial at the time. I encourage you to read it if you haven't, but as described, DAO Tokens served a similar function to shares of a traditional investment fund in that they were tradeable representations of an interest in The DAO that granted its holder a right to a share of its profits. DAO Tokens were determined to be securities because they carried with them promises made to their holders by their issuer to receive a portion of The DAO's profits.

Given the unique characteristics of DAO Tokens, the practical effect of the DAO Report was not to put the crypto industry on widespread notice that all digital assets would be treated as securities, but that securities that take the form of digital assets would not avoid regulation just because they are wrapped in a digital form.

---

228 *SEC v. Shavers*, No. 4:13-CV-416 (E.D. Tex. 2013).

The ICO Bubble

The SEC published the DAO Report at the height of the "ICO Bubble," a period between 2016 and 2019 in which thousands of businesses raised billions through "Initial Coin Offerings." As discussed in Chapter 7, the ICO Bubble attracted all types of people into the crypto space eager to sell tokens to the public in order to raise funds. Some of the projects that sold tokens to the public did so to attract participants to a network they intended to build. Others saw ICOs as a tool to defraud investors and make a quick profit.

In 2017, approximately $6 billion in funds were raised through ICOs. Mainstream news outlets started to document huge sums being raised through the sale of tokens by projects that had sometimes produced no more than a short white paper promising their tokens would grow in value. With this high volume of fundraising in the background, the SEC turned its attention to the digital asset industry.

The first actions brought by the SEC following the DAO Report addressed fraud that had been perpetrated on investors during token sales. A representative example is *US v. Zaslavskiy*, in which tokens were sold to the public in an ICO under the false promise that the tokens were backed by real estate and diamonds. As the SEC acknowledged in that case, and as is true in many other fraud cases involving digital assets, the fraud conducted by token issuers was simply "old-fashioned fraud dressed in a new-fashioned label."

The *Munchee* Settlement

By the end of 2017, the SEC had broadened the scope of its enforcement actions to include not only cases involving fraud but also non-fraudulent token sales under the theory that the initial sales constituted unregistered securities offerings. In December 2017, the SEC settled its first crypto enforcement action against Munchee Inc. for selling $60,000 in MUN tokens to 40 people. The tokens were intended to be used by holders on a restaurant review platform that would be developed with the proceeds from the sale. There were no allegations of fraud.

Confronted with the possibility of litigation, and having raised only

$60,000, Munchee agreed to cease operations and settle the SEC's claims. The *Munchee* consent order, though not setting a legal precedent, is noteworthy as the SEC views it as a warning to the crypto industry that issuing a token and selling it to the public may be viewed by the SEC as the sale of an investment contract.[229]

The order refuted Munchee's argument that MUN tokens were not securities, but "utility" tokens meant to have a functional role within the yet-to-be-built Munchee ecosystem. The SEC rejected this differentiation, determining that the economic reality of the token sale indicated they were sold as investment contracts. Since Munchee settled the charges, the SEC's conclusion that MUN tokens were securities was not judicially reviewed.

SAFTs

In 2018, global token sales reached $7.5 billion. The surge in volume led the SEC to increase its oversight of digital assets, targeting fraudulent activities as well as legitimate token offerings. The SEC also started bringing enforcement actions against celebrities like DJ Khaled and Floyd Mayweather for endorsing ICOs to their followers.[230] The increased attention on the industry by the SEC caused many to view offering ICOs to U.S. persons as too risky.

As a workaround, blockchain startups began selling tokens to accredited investors through SAFTs (Simple Agreements for Future Tokens). Under the SAFT's terms, token distribution to investors would be delayed until the network became operational. This strategy was intended to take advantage of the Securities Act's Regulation D exemption, dividing the process into an exempt securities offering (the SAFT), and the subsequent distribution of what they hoped would be classified as non-security tokens.[231]

---

229 In *re Munchee Inc.* File No. 3-18304. *Order Instituting Cease-and-Desist Proceedings*, 11 Dec. 2017, sec.gov/files/litigation/admin/2017/33-10445.pdf.

230 "Two Celebrities Charged with Unlawfully Touting Coin Offerings." *SEC*, 29 Nov. 2018, sec.gov/news/press-release/2018-268.

231 SAFTs were designed to mirror a fundraising mechanism called a SAFE (Simple Agreement for Future Equity), in which an investor would receive a future right to a equity in a business. You can read more about the theory behind SAFTs at saft-project.org.

The prevalence of SAFTs in the crypto industry between 2017 and 2019 was widespread, and its growth can likely be attributed to the adoption of SAFTs as the preferred fundraising tool of venture capitalists eager to prepurchase tokens at deep discounts ahead of a public sale. In recent years, the use of SAFTs has waned, largely due to a decline in demand for new tokens and successful enforcement actions against projects that utilized SAFTs for fundraising. Despite SAFTs having largely fallen out of use, the premise behind the strategy—that the tokens to be delivered in the future may not themselves be securities—has not been fully adjudicated.

Telegram and _Kik_

In 2019, the SEC successfully pursued legal actions against two companies, Kik Interactive Inc. and Telegram Group Inc., for selling unregistered securities. In both instances, the companies used SAFTs to raise funds from accredited investors. These cases are two of the SEC's most notable successes in the digital asset space and are credited with the SAFTs decline in popularity. Although impactful, the legal implications of these cases on future decisions are limited.

First, the cases should not be read to imply that SAFTs are inherently impermissible. Both decisions were based on the specific facts of each case that resulted in a finding that the particular SAFTs were non-exempt from registration, not that SAFTs are universally impermissible. Moreover, neither case determined that digital assets are inherently securities. Instead, the courts adopted the approach that the sales of digital assets required an assessment of the facts and circumstances under _Howey_ to determine whether, at the time of the sale, the tokens were sold as an investment contract.

Second, since both cases were settled soon after the trial court's decisions, they were not subject to an appellate review that might have set broader legal precedents. Still, despite these limitations, both cases are frequently referenced and familiarity with each case is recommended.

SEC v. Kik Interactive Inc. – Kik developed plans for a digital currency named KIN, an ERC-20 token on the Ethereum blockchain. The token was intended for use across a range of digital services. To finance the project, Kik aimed to raise $100 million via public and private token sales.

In the private phase of fundraising, Kik raised about $50 million from accredited investors using SAFTs, which promised KIN tokens at a future date and at a reduced rate compared to the public sale. Shortly after, Kik held a public token sale, garnering an additional $50 million from approximately 10,000 participants.

The SEC filed a lawsuit against Kik for executing an unregistered securities offering. The court ruled in favor of the SEC, determining that the public sale of KIN constituted an unregistered securities offering under *Howey*. The court also found that the private sale of KIN, occurring soon after and with the proceeds going towards Kik's operations, was part of a unified fundraising effort. Thus, the court concluded that the SAFTs sold to accredited investors did not qualify for an exemption under Reg D since the court regarded the private and public sales as a single unregistered offering.[232] Following summary judgment, Kik settled with the SEC for a $5 million penalty. The settlement foreclosed the possibility of the order being appealed.[233]

SEC v. Telegram Group Inc. - Telegram, a popular messaging service platform, planned to create a cryptocurrency known as Grams, which would be integrated into a proposed blockchain network. The company sold more than $1 billion in SAFTs to accredited investors who would take possession of the tokens upon the release of Telegram's blockchain. Once distributed, the investors would be able to sell Grams in the open market.

The SEC filed a lawsuit against Telegram before its blockchain network could launch, alleging that the scheme constituted an unregistered securities offering. Agreeing with the SEC, the district

---

232 *SEC v. Kik Interactive Inc.*, No. 1:2019-cv-05244, Opinion and Order on Motions For Summary Judgment, Doc 88. SDNY. 30 Sept. 2020. Justia, shorturl.at/fnuR4; *see also* Miller, David. "Another Significant Cryptocurrency Decision: *SEC v. Kik Interactive Inc.* and Token Offerings under the Securities Laws: Insights: Greenberg Traurig LLP." Greenberg Traurig, 6 Oct. 2020, shorturl.at/mtxPS.

233 "SEC Obtains Final Judgment Against Kik Interactive for Unregistered Offering." *SEC*, 21 Oct. 2020, sec.gov/news/press-release/2020-262.

court issued a preliminary injunction, finding the SEC would likely prove at trial that the SAFTs and the intended public sale of Grams violated the Securities Act.

The court noted that the SAFTs were not exempt under Reg D and found that Telegram sold the SAFTs not just for the investors' personal use, but with the understanding that the investors would distribute Grams to the public market. The court found that this intent to distribute the tokens in the future made the investors statutory underwriters who did not qualify for a Reg D exemption.[234] Following the decision, the parties entered a settlement in which Telegram agreed to return the money it had raised and pay an $18.5 million fine.

A Framework for Investment Contracts

In April 2019, the SEC published a *"Framework for 'Investment Contract' Analysis of Digital Assets,"* which was targeted at those considering raising funds through an ICO.[235] The framework identifies several factors the SEC deemed as relevant to applying *Howey* to the initial sale of digital assets. Some examples include statements made to prospective token buyers, the operational status of the digital network, whether the tokens could be used immediately, and the involvement of "active participants" in the sale, such as a promoter, sponsor, or other third parties, to support the network's development or to help establish secondary markets for the tokens.

The SEC's framework addressed only the initial sale of tokens, suggesting that both initial and subsequent sales—whether directly from the issuer or on secondary markets—should be periodically re-evaluated to determine if changes in the network's functionality or the conduct of parties altered the security status of the tokens. This perspective indicates that the SEC believed that tokens distributed during an ICO were not inherently securities and that as the

---

234 *SEC v. Telegram Group Inc.*, No. 1:2019-cv-09439, Opinion and Order on Emergency Motion for Temporary Restraining Order, Doc 227. SDNY. 24 Mar. 2020. Justia, shorturl. at/fglou; *see* also Miller, David. "SEC v. Telegram: A Groundbreaking Decision in Cryptocurrency Enforcement?" *Greenberg Traurig*, 1 Apr. 2020, shorturl.at/pzAWZ.

235 sec.gov/corpfin/framework-investment-contract-analysis-digital-assets#_ednref9

circumstances of the token offering evolve, the same tokens might later be traded as non-security transactions. This interpretation aligns with remarks from senior SEC officials at the time, including William Hinman, then Director of the Division of Corporate Finance, who noted in a speech that a token previously sold as part of a securities offering could eventually be sold in a manner that does not constitute a securities transaction.[236]

A Change of Administration

During this time, the SEC was chaired by Republican appointee Jay Clayton. When Joe Biden took office in January 2021, he appointed Gary Gensler as Chair of the SEC. Gensler had previously served as Chair of the CFTC and had taught a course on digital assets at MIT before taking office. When he was first appointed, those in the digital asset space were optimistic that, given Mr. Gensler's background, he would help to bring clarity to the industry.

When Chair Gensler took office, he appeared to have a view similar to Chair Clayton that the sale of tokens to investors likely implicates securities regulations, but that, in general, tokens were not themselves inherently securities and that the SEC lacked jurisdiction to regulate digital assets, including secondary market sales, more broadly.

In May 2021, Chair Gensler testified that Congress would need to act for the SEC or the CFTC to take a greater role in regulating secondary sales of digital assets, stating: "Right now these exchanges do not have a regulatory framework at the SEC or at our sister agency, the Commodity Futures Trading Commission…Right now, there's not a market regulator around these crypto exchanges."

As we'll see through several cases brought against digital asset exchanges below, Chair Gensler's view of the SEC's authority to regulate secondary sales of digital assets has since evolved.[237]

---

236 Hinman, William, Director, Division of Corporation Finance, SEC. "Digital Asset Transactions: When Howey Met Gary (Plastic)." 14 June 2018, bit.ly/2l8t5dB.

237 Wilkins, Joseph. "SEC's Gary Gensler Is Waging War against Crypto. Here's a Look at How His Views on the Industry Have Evolved over the Years." *Business Insider*, 3 Sept. 2023, shorturl.at/equDV.

SEC v. Ripple Labs

In the final days of Chair Clayton's administration, the SEC filed a lawsuit against Ripple Labs and its executives alleging that XRP sales in several categories to investors and the public were unregistered securities offerings. This action was seen as particularly significant, given XRP's prominence as one of the most traded digital assets behind bitcoin since its release in 2012. The lawsuit, filed in December 2020, raised concerns across the U.S. digital asset industry due to its implications for secondary market sales, with many viewing it as an existential risk to the digital asset industry in the United States.

The *Ripple Labs* case questioned whether direct sales of tokens from an issuer to a purchaser, including "institutional sales" and "other distributions" of XRP, as well as "programmatic sales" on exchanges, constituted unregistered securities offerings. This was notable because the programmatic sales were made on digital asset exchanges where buyers did not know they were purchasing XRP directly from Ripple Labs. In this regard, the programmatic sales resembled typical secondary market transactions made on a digital asset exchange.

In July 2023, Judge Analisa Torres issued a split decision in the case. She granted summary judgment in favor of the SEC regarding the institutional sales but ruled in favor of Ripple Labs on the argument that the programmatic sales and other distributions did not constitute unregistered securities offerings. Below is a brief overview of the major holdings from Judge Torres' order, although anyone in the space should read the entire opinion.[238]

- **Institutional Sales:** Judge Torres applied the *Howey* test to sales of XRP made to institutional investors. After finding an investment of money, she held that commonality was present between institutional investors because all were given fungible XRP tokens, effectively aligning their fortunes

---

[238] *SEC v. Ripple Labs Inc.*, No. 1:20-cv-10832, Order on Motion for Summary Judgment, Doc 874. SDNY. 13 Jul. 2023. CourtListener, shorturl.at/aqJR5; Miller, David. "SEC v. Ripple Labs, Inc.: A Turning Point in Cryptocurrency Jurisprudence?" *Greenberg Traurig*, 17 July 2023, shorturl.at/dfxTX.

with Ripple Labs. Judge Torres also found that institutional investors reasonably expected profits based on Ripple Labs' efforts, citing several examples of statements made directly to the investors by Ripple Labs linking their efforts to potential increases in XRP's value.

- **Programmatic Sales:** The court determined these sales did not meet the *Howey* test's criteria for an investment contract since buyers could not have known they were purchasing from Ripple and did not base their profit expectations on Ripple's efforts. The "blind" nature of the programmatic transactions highlighted a fundamental difference between the programmatic sales and the institutional sales that involved statements made directly by Ripple Labs to investors.

- **Other Distributions:** The court ruled in favor of Ripple that distributions made to employees or other service providers were not investment contracts because there was no "investment of money" as required under *Howey*. This portion of the ruling appears to take a narrower view of *Howey*'s first prong than other courts, which have analyzed whether the provision of services could satisfy the investment of money requirement.

Judge Torres's decision emphasized the importance of evaluating the totality of circumstances surrounding each transaction under *Howey*. This aligns with other district court decisions, including *Kik and Telegram*, that suggested that digital assets are not inherently securities, although they may be sold as part of an investment contract depending on the facts of the sale.

In so holding, Judge Torres rejected a request by Ripple Labs to find that the XRP were not investment contracts because they lacked the "essential ingredients" of one: (1) a contract establishing investor rights, (2) post-sale obligations on the promoter for the investor's benefit, and (3) a right for the investor to share in profits from the promoter's efforts. The court refused to adopt a new "essential ingredients" test, finding that the second and third factors did not align with the Supreme Court's focus on the expectation of profits from the efforts of others. The court recognized that *Howey* had developed to embody a flexible test and not formal post-sale obligations on a promoter to provide an explicit grant to an investor or a right to share in profits. Notably, the court did not assess the necessity of an underlying contract for an investment contract under *Howey*, stating it was unnecessary for this case since a contract existed in every instance that the court found XRP was offered or sold as an investment contract.

Both the SEC and Ripple Labs said they would appeal the unfavorable parts of the decision to the Second Circuit.

SEC v. Terraform Labs

In February 2023, the SEC filed charges against Terraform Labs, accusing the company of selling unregistered securities. This legal action followed the failure of Terra's native token, LUNA, and the UST stablecoin, which were integral parts of Terra blockchain's ecosystem. These events had a widespread impact in the crypto industry and led to the failure of several businesses in the space, as well as criminal charges against Terraform's founder, Do Kwon, for securities, commodities, and wire fraud.[239]

Terraform launched its blockchain in 2019. Similar to Ethereum's blockchain, it supported the development of smart contracts and protocols. LUNA was the native token necessary for building or utilizing these smart contracts on Terra. Terraform issued LUNA and also introduced its wrapped equivalent, wLUNA, which allowed users to transfer LUNA across different blockchain networks. LUNA was marketed as an investment into the Terra ecosystem, with promises by Terraform to enhance its value and create trading opportunities.

Concurrently, Terraform launched an algorithmic stablecoin called Terra USD (UST) on the Terra blockchain. Its price was set to remain equivalent to one US dollar, linked to the value of LUNA and adjusted algorithmically. Additionally, Terraform created the Anchor Protocol, a smart contract platform offering UST-based

---

[239] *See* Sandor, Krisztian. "The Fall of Terra: A Timeline of the Meteoric Rise and Crash of UST and Luna." *CoinDesk*, 22 Dec. 2022, coindesk.com/learn/the-fall-of-terra-a-time-line-of-the-meteoric-rise-and-crash-of-ust-and-luna.

loans. UST holders were enticed to deposit their tokens in return for an advertised interest rate of up to 20% per year. Most UST was held in this protocol.

In 2020, Terraform released the Mirror Protocol which enabled users to create "mirrored assets" or "mAssets" that reflected the prices of real-world assets, such as stocks. To mint mAssets, users had to provide collateral exceeding the value of the asset by 50%. These mAssets allowed users to benefit from price changes without direct ownership. If the real asset's value increased, users were required to add more collateral. The Mirror Protocol featured the MIR token, which granted governance rights and the potential to obtain trading fees derived from the protocol's activity to its holders. MIR was initially offered to select investors through a SAFT.

In December 2023, Judge Jed Rakoff ruled in the SEC's favor, finding UST, LUNA, wLUNA, and MIR were securities under *Howey*. The court determined that despite its design as a "stablecoin" that would not rise in value, UST was nevertheless sold as an investment contract because there was an expectation by UST holders to earn profits by depositing funds through the Anchor Protocol, which was dependent on Terraform's efforts.

The Court analyzed UST, as well as LUNA and MIR, not as individual assets, but as components within the larger Terra ecosystem designed and promoted by Terraform. For LUNA, the court found that Terraform's representations of investing in LUNA as akin to buying equity into Terra blockchain were significant and that buyers' expectations of profit were based on the company's promises to further develop the Terra ecosystem and improve the tokens' marketability. The court also noted that purchasers of MIR anticipated gains from Terraform's commitment to grow the Mirror Protocol, expecting MIR's value to increase with the protocol's success.[240] Consistent with *Telegram*, the Court also found that sales of tokens made via SAFTs to institutional investors were not exempt

---

240 The SEC did not allege mAssets were securities, but securities-based swaps. The Court disagreed, finding mAssets were not swaps because they did not shift a risk since those who minted mAssets were required to increase their deposit as the underlying asset price went up.

under Reg D because they were sold with the intent that purchasers would distribute the tokens to secondary markets.

Judge Rakoff's decision aligns with other legal findings that digital assets are not inherently securities; however, it diverges significantly from *Ripple Labs* by holding that direct sales to institutional investors and sales on secondary markets should be viewed equally regarding the issuer's promises of enhancing an investment's value. He was explicit on this point, stating, "A secondary resale transaction has no impact on whether a reasonable individual would objectively view the defendants' actions and statements as evincing a promise of profits based on their efforts."

On April 5, 2024, a jury found Terraform liable for civil fraud related to the sale of digital asset securities. It is unclear whether they will appeal the ruling.

Centralized "Staking" and FTX's Collapse

The collapse of the Terra ecosystem in May of 2022 brought about a chain of high-profile business failures in the crypto industry and coincided, and potentially contributed, to the dramatic collapse of the FTX exchange and the prosecution of its founder, Sam Bankman-Fried, for financial misconduct.[241] The impact of these failures on U.S. regulatory attitudes toward the industry was profound, especially following the collapse of FTX in November 2022, which, for many, underscored the need for greater oversight of centralized digital asset trading platforms and exchanges.[242]

---

241 The SEC charged Sam Bankman-Fried and several others for their role in FTX's collapse. The charges centered mainly on fraud committed against FTX's investors and the unauthorized use of customer funds. In March 2024, Sam Bankman-Fried was sentenced to 25 years in prison for his crimes. *See* "SEC Charges Samuel Bankman-Fried with Defrauding Investors in Crypto Asset Trading Platform FTX." *SEC*, 13 Dec. 2022, sec.gov/news/press-release/2022-219.

242 The details of FTX's rise and fall are fascinating, and you should be familiar with the fraud and its fallout. Ultimately, what caused FTX's demise was its founder's hubris and deceit. Like many bad acts in the space, the underlying crime was not unique to crypto, although the collapse of FTX certainly caused a shift in how regulators and the public viewed digital assets. For an overview of the sage, *see* Faux, Zeke. Number Go Up: Inside Crypto's Wild Rise and Staggering Fall. Currency, 2023.

Among the high-profile businesses that failed during this period were several that offered to pay customers interest on their deposits to yield-generating lending programs. These companies, including BlockFi and Celsius, generally described the act of depositing funds with them as "staking," although it is important to note that this term was not used to describe *network* staking, such as with a Proof of Stake protocol, where the network pays rewards to users who validate transactions. Instead, the companies would take a user's funds and loan it out to others at a high-interest rate and would pay the depositor a percentage of the rate the lending platform charged to borrowers. When UST and the Terra ecosystem failed, many of these companies were unable to recover customer deposits, which had been lent out to traders who lost everything when UST collapsed.

The SEC had already brought several actions against lending programs before Terra collapsed, alleging that the offer to pay interest on customer deposits were investment contracts under the *Howey* test because the customers invested money into a shared enterprise and were promised rewards based on the lender's ability to utilize the invested funds to make loans and collect interest. The SEC settled its charges with BlockFi for $100 million and obtained a final judgment against Celsius.[243] Notably, the settlement with BlockFi included $50 million to settle parallel charges by 32 state securities regulators for offering unregistered securities in their states.[244] A prominent case against digital asset platform Gemini for its lending program is pending.

Exchange-Traded Drama

An exchange-traded fund (ETF) is a type of investment fund that trades on exchanges similar to stocks. ETFs can contain stocks, bonds, or commodities like gold. Regardless of the assets they hold, ETFs are securities that require approval from the SEC. As noted in Chapter 12, the CFTC approved a bitcoin futures product in 2017. In 2021, the SEC approved a bitcoin futures ETF that allowed

---

[243] *SEC v. Celsius Network Ltd.*, No. 1:23-cv-06005, Judgment, Doc 18. SDNY. 1 Nov. 2023. CourtListener, shorturl.at/sEVX7.

[244] "BlockFi Agrees to Pay $100 Million in Penalties and Pursue Registration of Its Crypto Lending Product." *SEC*, 14 Feb. 2022, sec.gov/news/press-release/2022-26.

investors to gain exposure to funds holding bitcoin futures contracts. However, the SEC declined to approve a spot-market bitcoin ETF, which would allow exposure to funds directly invested in bitcoin.

This refusal led to a lawsuit against the SEC by an applicant whose spot ETF application was rejected. In August 2023, the D.C. Circuit Court of Appeals ruled that the SEC's rejection of a spot bitcoin ETF was arbitrary and capricious because the SEC had already approved a bitcoin futures ETF.[245] Consequently, the SEC was compelled to approve several spot bitcoin ETF applications, including those submitted by major asset managers like Blackrock and Fidelity. In January 2024, several spot bitcoin ETFs launched, becoming popular investment vehicles, and attracting billions in investments. The success of the spot bitcoin ETFs suggests that there may be a similar demand for other spot crypto ETFs. At the time of this writing, spot ether ETF applications are pending. Although the SEC has already approved ETFs on ether futures, it remains uncertain if the Commission will approve spot ether ETFs absent another judicial intervention.[246]

A Focus on Digital Asset Platforms

In the aftermath of FTX's collapse, the SEC's enforcement agenda shifted beyond actions against direct token issuers to the platforms and intermediaries that allowed its users to purchase and sell digital assets on secondary markets. During this period, Chair Gensler's assessment that the SEC lacked authority to regulate secondary market sales of cryptocurrencies appeared to shift. In May 2021, he testified before Congress that there was no regulatory framework for digital asset exchanges and that Congress would need to act to create one. At some point, that public position changed to a conviction that the SEC did not need new rules to regulate secondary sales of digital assets. In February 2023, Gensler stated that, in his view, "everything other than bitcoin" was a security and that "the law is clear" that businesses facilitating secondary market sales of securities must

---

245 *Grayscale Investments, LLC v. SEC.*, No. 22-1142, (D.C. Cir. 2023), shorturl.at/fNP04.

246 For an in-depth discussion on the history of bitcoin ETFs, *see* "Unraveling Bitcoin's Record-Breaking Spot ETFs with Eric Balchunas." *YouTube*, Thinking Crypto, 28 Feb. 2024, y2u.be/QK4NyoT8yqU.

register with the SEC.²⁴⁷ This change in perspective has manifested itself in several ways.

First, it has resulted in a reluctance by the SEC to engage with the industry in rulemaking that might bring clarity to the space. As discussed in Chapter 13, even beyond the question of how to determine whether a digital asset is a security, there are open questions regarding how an entity wishing to bring a "crypto asset security" to market could practically do so. The SEC has refused to engage in a rulemaking process, going so far as to deny an official petition for rulemaking, reiterating in its denial that "existing laws and regulations already apply to the crypto securities markets."²⁴⁸ Second, with the view that the law is settled and that all digital assets except bitcoin are securities, the SEC has started to bring actions against non-issuers of tokens for selling unregistered crypto asset securities.

In *SEC v. Wahi*, the SEC brought insider trading charges against a former Coinbase employee and two associates for violating Section 10b-5 of the Exchange Act. The case is notable as it represents a shift in focus to non-issuers and a strategy to assert that digital assets are securities in cases in which the digital asset's issuer is not a party. It is worth noting that the Department of Justice separately charged the Wahi defendants with wire fraud but not for criminal violations of the Exchange Act. The SEC settled its claims with the *Wahi* defendants before its theories could be tested in court.²⁴⁹

---

247 Sigalos, MacKenzie. "SEC's Gensler Says, 'the Law Is Clear' for Crypto Exchanges and That They Must Comply with Regulators." *CNBC*, CNBC, 27 Apr. 2023, shorturl.at/eDMO4; Khardori, Ankush. *Gary Gensler on Meeting with SBF and His Crypto Crackdown*, New York Magazine, 23 Feb. 2023, shorturl.at/bGSU9.

248 "Statement on the Denial of a Rulemaking Petition Submitted on Behalf of Coinbase Global, Inc." *SEC*, 15 Dec. 2023, sec.gov/news/statement/gensler-coinbase-petition-121523.

249 "Former Coinbase Manager and His Brother Agree to Settle Insider Trading Charges Relating to Crypto Asset Securities." *SEC*, 30 May 2023, sec.gov/news/press-release/2023-98. On March 1, 2023, the SEC obtained a default judgment against a third defendant. In its Order, the Court agreed the assets in question were securities, although because the defendant had not mounted a defense and the allegations in the complaint were accepted as true the impact of this decision is minimal. See *SEC v. Wahi*, No. 2:22-cv-01009, Order on Motion for Default Judgment, Doc 119. District Court, W.D. Wash. 1 Mar. 2024. CourtListener, shorturl.at/egpMU.

In June 2023, the SEC brought actions against platforms Binance and Coinbase, alleging that by facilitating the purchase, custody, and sale of digital assets on their platforms they had acted as unregistered exchanges, broker-dealers, and clearing agencies.[250] In November 2023, it brought a similar action against the digital asset platform Kraken. Each case is premised on the allegation that non-bitcoin digital assets are securities, and, therefore, services that facilitate sales of those assets must be registered. Although the SEC has taken a broad position that nearly all digital assets are securities, it did not allege that every digital asset except bitcoin listed on these platforms are securities. With the exception of BUSD and BNB in its Binance suit, there are no allegations that the platforms they sued had issued the named digital assets.

Pending Digital Asset Platform Cases And Links To Dockets

The defense of the pending cases against Coinbase, Binance, and Kraken is anchored on two principles:

First, the assets identified by the SEC are not securities, and therefore, the second-order liabilities for facilitating unregistered transactions in them must fail. Each defendant argues that the identified tokens cannot fulfill the *Howey* test's criteria for an investment contract at the time of sale because of the lack of a direct relationship between the token issuers and the platforms' customers. The platforms point to previous case law which found that while digital assets may be the subject of an investment contract, they are not inherently securities. The SEC has asked the court to interpret the *Howey* test more broadly, in line with its application in *Terraform*. This interpretation would consider the efforts of a token's issuer to develop the token's network, even when assessing the resale of the token by parties who have no direct relationship with the issuer.

Second, each case sees the defendants urging the courts to consider the broader regulatory and political debates surrounding the

---

250 In April 2023, the SEC filed a similar complaint against digital asset exchange Bittrex. By the time of the suit, Bittrex had planned to cease U.S. operations due to regulatory uncertainty. They settled the charges for $24 million. "Crypto Asset Trading Platform Bittrex and Former CEO to Settle SEC Charges for Operating an Unregistered Exchange, Broker, and Clearing Agency." *SEC*, 10 Aug. 2023, sec.gov/news/press-release/2023-150.

regulation of digital assets. They argue for the dismissal of the actions under the "Major Questions Doctrine," a principle of statutory interpretation in administrative law that mandates that "when an agency asserts 'extraordinary' power, it 'must point to clear congressional authorization for the power it claims.' And when an agency 'claim[s] to discover in a long-extant statute an unheralded power' representing a 'transformative expansion in its regulatory authority,' courts apply heightened skepticism" *W. Va. v. EPA*, 597 U.S. 697, 723 (2022).

A summary of the status of the pending digital asset platform cases at the time of this writing is provided below:

SEC v. Coinbase, 1:23-cv-04738, Southern District of New York Docket[251]

The SEC alleges that Coinbase acted as an unregistered securities exchange, broker, and clearing agency by facilitating the sale and settlement of 13 identified digital assets on its platform. The lawsuit also alleges that Coinbase's "staking-as-a-service" product, which provides technology that allows customers to stake assets on public blockchains for network rewards, is itself a securities offering. The SEC alleges the following assets are "crypto asset securities": ADA, AXS, CHZ, DASH, FIL, FLOW, ICP, MATIC, NEAR, NEXO, SAND, SOL, and VGX.

On March 27, 2024, Judge Failla issued an order on Coinbase's Motion for Judgment on the Pleadings that largely ruled in favor of the SEC and allowed claims that Coinbase operated as an unlicensed broker, exchange, and clearing agency to proceed to discovery. I encourage you to read the Court's order, which is linked in the footnotes.[252]

The Court took an expansive view of *Howey*'s common enterprise and expectation of profits requirements, clearly influenced by Judge Rakoff's analysis in *Teraform*. Judge Failla rejected Coinbase's argument that an investment contract necessarily requires a contract

---

251 *SEC v. Coinbase Inc.* docket available at shorturl.at/lZ145

252 *SEC v. Coinbase Inc.* No. 1:23-cv-04738, Order on Motion for Judgment on the Pleadings, Doc 105. District Court, S.D.N.Y., 27 Mar. 2024. CourtListener, shorturl.at/hxBL0.

or a direct relationship between the original issuer and purchaser, holding that because the prices of the assets were allegedly influenced by the issuers' efforts to build the tokens' networks or ecosystems, the SEC could proceed to discovery on its claims based on secondary market digital asset sales. She also held that, as alleged, administrative activities Coinbase performed in furtherance of its staking service were sufficient for the SEC's claims that it constituted a securities offering to proceed. Judge Failla rejected Coinbase's argument that the major questions doctrine was implicated, finding that the digital asset industry was not one of "vast economic and political significance."

While Coinbase largely lost its motion, the Court ruled in its favor and dismissed claims that it acted as an unregistered broker as related to its non-custodial digital wallet product. This portion of the ruling has been seen as a major victory for self-custody service providers.

It is important to note that because this was a preliminary motion seeking dismissal of the claims, Judge Failla was required to accept the SEC's allegations as true. It is unclear how the arguments and factual allegations will develop as the cases move forward to discovery. Given the scope of the SEC's claims, it is likely that discovery will not be concluded until late 2024 or early 2025, and a ruling on summary judgment is unlikely until at least late 2025.

SEC v. Binance Holdings Ltd., 1:23-cv-015990, District Court for the District of Columbia Docket[253]

This case involves similar allegations to the Coinbase action, including claims that Binance acted as an unlicensed exchange, broker-dealer, and clearing agency when it facilitated the sales of 12 listed "crypto asset securities." The case also alleged that Binance acted as an unlicensed securities issuer with respect to the BNB token and BUSD stablecoin, as well as its staking-as-a-service program. The case also claims that Binance misled investors, manipulated the market, and failed to restrict U.S. persons from accessing its global platform. The SEC alleges the following assets as securities: ADA, ALGO, ATOM, AXS, BNB, BUSD, COTI, FIL, MANA, MATIC, SAND, and SOL.

---

253 *SEC v. Binance Holdings Ltd.* docket available at shorturl.at/arQW4.

SEC v. Payward Inc. d/b/a Kraken, 3:23-cv-06004, Northern District of California Docket[254]

This case likewise accuses Kraken of operating as an unlicensed exchange, broker-dealer, and clearing agency. Note that there are no allegations regarding Kraken's staking service which had been shuttered in the United States prior to this action as a result of a $30 million settlement with the SEC that occurred in February 2023.[255] The SEC alleges the following assets as "crypto asset securities": ADA, ALGO, ATOM, AXS, CHZ, COTI, DASH, FIL, FLOW, ICP, MANA, MATIC, NEAR, OMG, SAND, and SOL.

Supplemental Resources

- It is likely additional enforcement actions have been pursued after the publication of this book. The SEC maintains a list of pending enforcement actions at sec.gov/spotlight/cybersecurity-enforcement-actions.

- "Why the SEC's Case against Coinbase Is so Significant for Crypto - EP. 597." *YouTube*, Unchained, 2024, y2u.be/udQjDmTmGfc.

- "Video Library: Did the SEC Give Fair Notice to XRP Holders?" *CryptoLaw*, crypto-law.us/video-library. This is an outline of information prepared in response to the SEC's case against Ripple Labs regarding whether the SEC provided "fair notice" to the public that XRP would be deemed a security. While Judge Torres rejected the defendant's fair notice argument, this timeline presents an informative view into how the SEC's statements over digital assets have evolved.

  - "Document Library." *CryptoLaw*. crypto-law.us/document-library. CryptoLaw was founded by a

---

254 *SEC v. Payward Ventures d/b/a Kraken* docket available at shorturl.at/biqLU.

255 "Kraken to Discontinue Unregistered Offer and Sale of Crypto Asset Staking-As-A-Service Program and Pay $30 Million to Settle SEC Charges." *SEC*, 9 Feb. 2023, sec.gov/news/press-release/2023-25.

lawyer named John Deaton (@JohnDeaton1), who is most well-known for representing XRP holders as amicus counsel in the *SEC v. Ripple Labs* case. He maintains a document library from different SEC actions against digital asset companies that I encourage you to bookmark.

- **Litigation Tracker** - The Morrison Cohen law firm publishes a litigation tracker quarterly that collects civil and criminal cases in the industry, including SEC and other agency actions. You can find the latest version of the tracker at morrisoncohen.com/insights/the-morrison-cohen-cryptocurrency-litigation-tracker. I encourage you to follow Jason Gottleib (@ohaiom) from the firm as he usually pushes out updates.

- **Statements by Hester Peirce.** SEC Commissioner Peirce has emerged as a prominent dissenter to the Commission's focus on enforcement actions over rulemaking. Her criticisms, often shared through interviews, written dissents, and speeches, highlight concerns with the SEC's approach. You can find the collection at shorturl.at/ajST3.

CHAPTER 16

NFTs and Web3

I saved a discussion on non-fungible tokens (NFTs) for near the end because I think they are, in many ways, a step removed from the type of financial applications that are the current focus of most "crypto lawyers" and part of a broader category of digital assets and interactive applications that some classify as "Web3."

It is hard to define the line between crypto and Web3 or to reach a consensus on whether there is even a line at all. While I don't think there is an agreed-upon definition, I think of Web3 as the application layer of blockchain, whether financial or non-financial, that allows users to interact with a protocol directly without reliance on a centralized intermediary. In the same way that decentralized finance represents a shift in banking by getting rid of the need for financial intermediaries, a Web3 ecosystem strives to do the same across numerous types of internet applications that are popular under our current "Web2" model which is hyper-reliant on large tech companies to function. Web3 aims to give users greater control over their data, identities, and transactions.

This book and the laws we've discussed have focused specifically on crypto, which plays a crucial role in maintaining the public blockchains that Web3 could be built upon. However, if the vision of Web3 comes to fruition, its scope will be far beyond "crypto" and have the potential to be as vast as the Internet itself.

Chris Dixon (@cdixon), a venture capitalist with Andreessen Horowitz, published a book called "Read, Write, Own: Building The Next Era of the Internet" that presents an accessible vision of what Web3 is currently and what it could be. I encourage you to read the book if you are interested in the potential of blockchain beyond finance. I have also included a link to an interview with Chris Dixon sharing his thesis in the Supplemental Resources section.

NFTs And Tokenization

NFTs are cryptographic assets minted through a smart contract, with their ownership tracked on the underlying blockchain's ledger. The idea of using a blockchain to record transfers of unique digital identifiers originated from a concept on the Bitcoin network of "coloring" small fractions of bitcoin with additional information that would tie the bitcoin to the ownership records of an external property. These "Colored Coins" could then, in theory, be used to easily transfer ownership of the underlying asset through a simple transfer of the colored bitcoin.

One of the limitations of Colored Coins, and a reason why they never really took off, was a reliance on third parties to transfer the real-world assets tracked on the Bitcoin ledger.[256] For example, if I wanted to designate 1 satoshi of a bitcoin as a representation of the ownership of my car, I would need to associate the bitcoin with my car's title on some database. This requirement to reference an external source of truth diminishes the value of utilizing Bitcoin's blockchain, which was designed for decentralized consensus without needing outside verification. Since possession of the Colored Coin does not actually effectuate ownership of the car, its use is just a way for private parties to track records with one another. It does not convey the type of ownership interest a bearer asset like bitcoin conveys in its native form.

The creation of Ethereum and other networks allowed users to write smart contracts that could be used to create digital assets whose ownership could be traded on the network's ledger. As discussed in Chapter 7, soon after Ethereum's launch, people began to use smart contracts to create new cryptocurrencies. The adoption of a technical standard for token contracts, called ERC-20, made it very simple for developers to create new tokens that could be easily sold to the public. New token projects were designed so each individual token was fungible, or interchangeable, with one another just as

---

[256] "Bitcoin Q&A: What Are Colored Coins?" *YouTube*, Aantonop, 2 Oct. 2019, y2u.be/r2FaaLS9vqE.

every dollar or bitcoin is interchangeable with each other.

Developers also began creating smart contracts that produced digital assets that possessed unique characteristics that made them dissimilar, or non-fungible, with other assets. An early example is a 2017 project called "CryptoPunks," which consists of 10,000 unique computer-generated pixelated images of punk rockers minted on the Ethereum blockchain that remains a popular project today.[257] Soon after, a technical standard called ERC-721 was released that allowed users to easily spin up NFT projects that could be sold to the public.[258] As the ERC-20 standard did for the ICO bubble, the ERC-721 standard led to an NFT bubble. By its 2021 peak, there were more than $20 billion in annual NFT sales.

The NFT marketplace is its own ecosystem that is, in many ways, distinct from much of the financial side of crypto. A few video primers on the process of obtaining NFTs are provided below, but in short, NFT platforms are typically accessed by connecting a web-based digital asset wallet, such as MetaMask or Phantom, to an NFT platform like Magic Eden or OpenSea, which allows you to create, buy, or sell NFTs directly to your browser wallet. NFTs can be minted across all major blockchains that enable smart contracts, with the most popular chains being Solana and Ethereum. In recent years, NFTs inscribed to Bitcoin's blockchain, called "Ordinals," have also gained popularity.[259] Because NFTs are transferred between sellers and purchasers on a blockchain network, transactions must be made with the network's native currency and are subject to gas or network fees.

One question that often comes up when one purchases an NFT is what exactly is being bought? In some cases, the art being purchased is stored "on-chain," meaning the art is embedded within, and

---

257 Marcobello, Mason. *CryptoPunks, CryptoCats and Cryptokitties: How They Started and How They're Going,* CoinDesk, 19 Aug. 2022, coindesk.com/learn/cryptopunks-cryptocats-and-cryptokitties-how-they-started-and-how-theyre-going.

258 Tran, Ki Chong. *What Is ERC-721? The Ethereum NFT Token Standard,* Decrypt, 13 Dec. 2022, decrypt.co/resources/erc-721-ethereum-nft-token-standard.

259 Nelson, Jason. *What Are Ordinals? A Beginner's Guide to Bitcoin Nfts,* Decrypt, 8 Nov. 2023, decrypt.co/resources/what-are-ordinals-a-beginners-guide-to-bitcoin-nfts.

is indistinguishable from, the token itself. Because of technical limitations, on-chain art is usually pretty rudimentary, so in many cases, the art that is purchased is stored off-chain on a website, archive, or server. In this case, the NFT contains a reference to the image and is merely a digital ownership record, similar to a provenance or certificate of authenticity.

For off-chain NFTs, if the image is erased or corrupted, then the art purchased is lost, and all that remains is the record of its ownership. To some, this parallels the limitations of Colored Coins, which, because they were used to track real-world assets, were reliant on non-ledger databases or contracts to give effect to an asset transfer. For some NFT art collectors, this undermines the purpose of utilizing an immutable blockchain to record ownership in the first place since the art is still at risk should the database or server that is storing the art become compromised.

Despite its limitations, the NFT market has largely embraced projects in which the art is not stored on-chain. In that regard, there has been an effort by many to create projects that use NFTs as a way to record or track ownership of physical items like property or collectibles, under the theory that an immutable record of ownership that can be easily transferred is an improvement to current recordkeeping practices and title transfer processes. We have seen experimentation with using NFTs for things like supply chain management and land title transfers, leading to a broader theory that there will be a large market for "tokenized" assets that represent full or fractional ownership interests in physical or digital property, such as real estate, collectibles, art, or any other item, and which can be purchased and sold more efficiently than under current conditions.[260]

NFTs are a function of smart contracts and, therefore, are capable of representing complex, self-executing transactional arrangements. A programmable feature of many NFTs is to embed royalties or revenue shares to the creator of an NFT, such that they are automatically paid a royalty every time the NFT is sold. For many artists, the ability to receive proceeds from future sales is a primary motivator

---

260 "Creating NFTs for Physical Products." *YouTube*, Data Slayer, 29 Oct. 2022, y2u.be/awyUlPQD7Ng.

for creating NFTs in the first place. However, NFTs are capable of other embedded transactions, including acting as quasi-wallets that can store other digital assets (called nested NFTs) or grant holders individualized rights or permissions within DAOs or other online communities. There is an underexplored overlap between NFTs and decentralized finance, through which NFTs can be deposited on-chain as collateral for loans or other financial activity in a manner that parallels how real-world assets are leveraged for cash flow.[261]

Legal Considerations

The most common legal issues that have arisen with regard to NFTs are related to intellectual property rights. Intellectual property law contains considerable nuance and can vary between jurisdictions. Still, there is nothing to suggest that the traditional rights of a trademark or copyright holder are disturbed when someone misuses their intellectual property to create an infringing NFT.[262] Similarly, the question of whether a purchaser of an NFT is conveyed intellectual property rights to the associated content mirrors traditional considerations regarding the transfer of art or other property and is largely a function of the contract between the issuer of the NFTs and its first purchasers. Such sales, particularly with respect to larger issuers or corporate brands, are typically governed by terms and conditions that disclaim any right to the ownership of the underlying intellectual property, although some projects do purport to convey ownership or grant its holder a license to use the underlying image for profit.[263]

The other legal issue that tends to come up with respect to NFT sales is whether they were sold as investment contracts and, therefore, subject to registration requirements under the Securities Act. There

---

261 "What Are Nfts and How Can They Be Used in Decentralized Finance? Defi Explained." *YouTube*, Finematics, 29 Sept. 2020, y2u.be/Xdkkux6OxfM.

262 *See e.g., Yuga Labs, Inc. v. Ripps*, 2023 U.S. Dist. LEXIS 192487 (C.D. Cal. Oct. 25, 2023) available at shorturl.at/sFK78 (granting summary judgment in favor of the creators of the popular Bored Ape Yacht Club NFT on claims that another project misappropriated its intellectual property by creating a competing NFT project),

263 For a survey of different licensing models, see Thorn, Alex, et al. "A Survey of NFT Licenses: Facts & Fictions." *Galaxy*, galaxy.com/insights/research/a-survey-of-nft-licenses-facts-and-fictions.

is already a legal framework around the sale of art and its interplay with securities regulations under *Howey* that tends to create a distinction between the purchase of art and the purchase of a share or interest in the art that does not convey physical ownership.²⁶⁴

The SEC has not prioritized NFT issuer cases in the same manner as it has enforcement against cryptocurrency issuers, although it has brought a pair of cases that suggest it believes NFTs may be within its jurisdiction to a greater degree than sales of comparable physical art or collectibles:

SEC v. Impact Theory, LLC - Impact Theory, a media and entertainment company, issued "Founder's Keys" NFTs that offered holders benefits like ad-free content, digital collectibles, and discounts on products. Impact Theory promoted them with statements suggesting a potential for profit, directly linking the success and enrichment of the company, its founders, and the NFT holders. The SEC, applying the *Howey* test, determined the Founder's Keys were sold as investment contracts due to the expectation of profits from the efforts of others, as inferred from Impact Theory's promotional activities. Impact Theory settled the matter with the SEC for $6.1 million in disgorgement of profits and penalties. They also agreed to destroy any remaining Founder's Keys to ensure they would not receive any future royalties.²⁶⁵

In a dissent to the settlement, SEC Commissioners Hester Peirce and Mark Uyeda questioned the application of the *Howey* test and argued that promotional statements by Impact Theory did not constitute promises of profit typical of an investment contract.²⁶⁶

---

264 Von Appen, Antonia. "The Legal Framework of Art Investments: The Applicability of EU and US Investor Protection Regulations to the Art Market." Ph.D. Thesis, *Università Bocconi*, iris.unibocconi.it/retrieve/a5e02674-40b7-440c-8813-462925967446/PhD%20Thesis_AntoniavonAppen_finalized.pdf.

265 "SEC Charges LA-Based Media and Entertainment Co. Impact Theory for Unregistered Offering of NFTs." *SEC*, 28 Aug. 2023, sec.gov/news/press-release/2023-163

266 Peirce, Hester, and Mark Uyede. "NFTs & the SEC: Statement on Impact Theory, LLC." *SEC*, 28 Aug. 2023, sec.gov/news/statement/peirce-uyeda-statement-nft-082823.

SEC v. Stoner Cats 2, LLC - Stoner Cats 2, LLC sold 10,320 cartoon "Stoner Cats" NFTs for approximately $8.2 million to fund an animated series set to star Ashton Kutcher and Mila Kunis. The company's promotional efforts included promises to establish a DAO with Stoner Cats NFT holders and to develop new animation projects annually if all NFTs were sold. The SEC alleged the sale of Stoner Cats constituted the sale of an investment contract under *Howey* based on the economic reality of the offering. The company agreed to a $1 million civil penalty and to undertake actions including the destruction of the NFTs.[267]

SEC Commissioners Hester Peirce and Mark Uyeda again dissented, arguing that Stoner Cats NFTs were collectibles that should not be treated as securities. They criticized the SEC's broad application of securities laws, suggesting it might hinder creative efforts in content creation. As Commissioners Peirce and Uyeda noted in their dissent, applying securities rules becomes more challenging when the Securities Act is applied to the issuances of art or other media rather than purely financial instruments.[268]

I encourage you to review the background on securities regulations and digital assets discussed in Chapters 13-15; however, note that, like many cases in the digital asset space, much of the guidance has come from enforcement actions brought by the SEC that concluded in non-precedential settlements. Accordingly, it is still unclear where the line exists between a freely traded collectible and a collectible security that must be registered with the SEC.

So far, only one court has opined on the circumstances under which NFT collectibles may be considered securities, albeit only on a motion to dismiss standard where all of the allegations of the plaintiffs were accepted as true. In ***Friel v. Dapper Labs, Inc.***, plaintiffs had purchased digital NFTs called "NBA Top Shot Moments," which represented basketball highlights in the form of short video clips that

---

[267] "SEC Charges Creator of Stoner Cats Web Series for Unregistered Offering of NFTs." *SEC*, 13 Sept. 2023, sec.gov/news/press-release/2023-178.

[268] Peirce, Hester, and Mark Uyede. "Collecting Enforcement Actions: Statement on Stoner Cats 2, LLC." *SEC*, 13 Sept. 2023, sec.gov/news/statement/peirce-uyeda-statement-stonercats-091323

fans could collect. The NFTs were minted on a private blockchain called FLOW, which was controlled by Dapper Labs and could only be traded in a marketplace controlled by Dapper Labs. The plaintiff filed a class action alleging NBA Top Shot Moments were securities that Dapper Labs had sold without registration.

Dapper Labs moved to dismiss, arguing that the NFTs were not securities but just tradeable collectibles similar to analog baseball cards. On February 22, 2023, the court, in denying Dapper Labs' motion to dismiss, concluded that plaintiffs had convincingly argued that NBA Top Shot Moments could be classified as investment contracts.[269] The court based its decision on the relationship between Moments and the Flow blockchain and FLOW tokens—both controlled by Dapper Labs—asserting this interdependence was crucial for the operation and value of Moments. The Court highlighted that the economic interests of Moments' purchasers were closely tied to Dapper Labs' performance, given its control over the blockchain and its exclusive Marketplace for trading them. The defense's argument, that the ownership control over NFT portfolios negated any expectation of profits driven by Dapper Labs, was dismissed by the court. It pointed out that the value of Moments depreciated following trading halts by Dapper Labs and underscored Dapper Labs', and the NBA's control over the intellectual property and Marketplace operations.

The court emphasized that its ruling was limited to these facts and not a blanket statement that all NFTs are securities, underlining the necessity for a "case-by-case" assessment to determine whether a digital asset or NFT constitutes a security. The case has proceeded to discovery, with Summary Judgment briefings not expected to be concluded until 2025.

---

[269]   *Friel v. Dapper Labs, Inc.*, No. 1:2021-cv-05837, Doc 43 (S.D.N.Y. 2023), Order Denying Motion to Dismiss, *Justia*, shorturl.at/jwxJU.

Supplemental Resources - NFTs[270]

- "What Is an NFT? (Non-Fungible Tokens Explained)." *YouTube*, Whiteboard Crypto, 20 Mar. 2021, y2u.be/4dkl5O9LOKg.

- "Crypto Explained: What Are NFT or Non Fungible Tokens? Why Should I Care?" *YouTube*, Aantonop, 14 Apr. 2021, y2u.be/Y-i9Jsm95ro.

- Platform Tutorials: "How to Use Magic Eden (Easy Tutorial 2023)." *YouTube*, Seb Montgomery, 17 Sept. 2023, y2u.be/1TXtyLG3kz8; "Opensea Tutorial: How to Sell Your NFTS (2024) - Complete Opensea Tutorial to Sell NFT." *YouTube*, Tech Express, 8 Dec. 2022, y2u.be/GzhnkYbcvqQ.

- "Are NFTs Securities? With Securities Lawyer Brian Frye." *YouTube*, Bankless, 2023, y2u.be/jo1ZuhuCVZE.

- "IP Lawyers Answer Your Questions about Nfts." *YouTube*, Bankless, 18 Aug. 2022, y2u.be/velJ8LsIY4E.

- "Non-Fungible Tokens and Intellectual Property: A Report to Congress." *United States Patent and Trademark Office and U.S. Copyright Office*, 12 Mar. 2024, shorturl.at/xyGJ7.

Supplemental Resources – Web3

- "All About Web3." *MetaMask Learn*, learn.metamask.io. Digital asset wallet MetaMask put together a free 11-part lesson on Web3. While some of the lessons cover crypto, many are designed to teach you about broader uses beyond finance and practical approaches to using Web3 technologies.

---

270 For ease of reference, all Supplemental Resources and footnote links are available at www.TheCryptoLegalHandbook.com/resources.

- **Dixon, Chris.** *Read Write Own: Building the Next Era of the Internet.* **Cornerstone Press, 2024.** A16 partner Chris Dixon provides a vision for what the next "Web3" iteration of the internet may look like. For a preview of this vision, *see* **"Chris Dixon, Building the Next Era of the Internet."** *YouTube*, Kevin Rose, 4 Mar. 2024, y2u.be/l_0vpLfIjmo.

CHAPTER 17

Tax, International Considerations, and Other Legal Intrigue

As we near the end of this book, it should be clear that the subjects of legal relevance to a lawyer working in crypto are broad and in a state of constant development and fluctuation. This book touched upon what I believe are the most directly relevant topics, although there are certainly other areas of law implicated. In this final section, I want to address and provide additional resources for other areas you should be aware of but which I don't think warrant a dedicated chapter in this book.

If you believe there are specific areas I should address in future editions, please send me a note at www.TheCryptoLegalHandbook.com.

I. Taxes

The Internal Revenue Service (IRS) has provided general directions as to how to treat digital assets for tax purposes and maintains a Frequently Asked Questions page that incorporates its most recent guidance.[271] As you'll see from the short summary provided below, while the IRS has been proactive in providing guidance, it has done so in a fairly generalized and piecemeal manner, leaving numerous questions unanswered that would benefit from additional guidance or new regulations. I encourage you to talk to a tax attorney familiar with digital assets before making any tax decisions, as there is a growing body of strategies and best practices that are developing in the space.

---

271 "Frequently Asked Questions on Virtual Currency Transactions." *IRS*, irs.gov/individuals/international-taxpayers/frequently-asked-questions-on-virtual-currency-transactions.

Digital assets earned as income are subject to ordinary income tax at the fair market value of the asset when it is received. Digital assets, which include cryptocurrencies, stablecoins, and NFTs, are treated as property and subject to general tax principles for reporting capital gains and losses.[272] This means taxpayers must pay a capital gains tax on any profit realized at the time of sale due to the value of the property having increased. For those who receive crypto as part of their income that do not sell immediately, the taxpayer must still pay capital gains on any increase in value that is realized between the time the crypto is received and sold. This applies both ways, meaning if a digital asset is received as income and its value subsequently falls, the income tax is calculated at the higher price of when the asset was received, regardless of its present value. To the extent one sells an asset at a loss, the taxpayer may claim a capital loss deduction, which is capped at a $3,000 deduction against ordinary income.

Taxable events occur not only when a digital asset is sold for fiat but also when it is exchanged for a different digital asset since the §1031 "like-kind" exchange rule, a tax deferral mechanism that permits, for example, real property owners to exchange one property for another without triggering a taxable event, has been deemed not to apply to most digital asset transactions.[273] A taxable event also occurs when a digital asset is used to pay for goods or services, with no exception for small transactions. This means somebody who uses a digital asset to pay for a coffee would need to keep a tally of their basis for obtaining the digital asset and calculate any potential capital gain or loss relative to the few dollars spent on the beverage. Legislative efforts have been made to create an exemption from reporting small-value or de minimis capital gains, similar to the existing exemptions applicable to foreign currencies, but as of this writing, no exemption has been enacted.[274]

---

272 Notice 2014-21: IRS Virtual Currency Guidance." *IRS*, 2014, irs.gov/pub/irs-drop/n-14-21.pdf; "Notice 2023-27: Treatment of Certain Nonfungible Tokens as Collectibles." *IRS*, 21 Mar. 2023, irs.gov/pub/foia/ig/sbse/notice-2023-27-nft-as-collectibles.pdf.

273 Goldstein, Ronald J. "Applicability of Section 1031 to Exchanges of Bitcoin (BTC) for Ether (ETH), Bitcoin for Litecoin (LTC), and Ether for Litecoin." *IRS*, 8 June 2021, irs.gov/pub/irs-wd/202124008.pdf.

274 Zinda, Landon. "A Simple Legislative Fix to Complicated Tax Rules for Personal Cryptocurrency Transactions." *Coin Center*, 2 Oct. 2023, shorturl.at/bdpHL.

The IRS issued guidance in 2023 stating that revenue received from a network for staking assets is gross income and subject to ordinary income tax based on the fair market value of the digital asset at the time of receipt.[275] This mirrors guidance that bitcoin or other digital assets that are mined are similarly considered ordinary income as valued at the time the network awards the bitcoin.[276]

The IRS has also issued guidance regarding the tax treatment of hard forks and airdrops. In Revenue Ruling 2019-24 and subsequent guidance, the IRS made clear that digital assets received as a result of a hard fork of a network or an airdrop are deemed taxable income that is valued at the time the taxpayer takes dominion or control of the asset.[277] The IRS's guidance has been criticized as being difficult to practically apply in a fair manner, as airdrops can often occur without one's awareness, and determining the basis of a newly issued token is practically impossible because there has not been time for price discovery to occur in the market.[278]

The IRS has prioritized going after digital asset owners who do not report capital gains. In 2016, a federal judge in California broadly approved the IRS's ability to obtain financial records from centralized trading platforms, and the IRS has prosecuted numerous actions against individuals for failure to report crypto income and capital gains.[279] A reflection of this priority is that the IRS requires all taxpayers to declare on their U.S. individual Income Tax Return, or Form 1040, whether they have received, sold, exchanged, or

---

[275] "Notice 2023-14: Gross Income." *IRS*, 2023, irs.gov/pub/irs-drop/rr-23-14.pdf.

[276] Taxpayers Should Continue to Report All Cryptocurrency, Digital Asset Income, *IRS*, 22 Jan. 2024, irs.gov/newsroom/taxpayers-should-continue-to-report-all-cryptocurrency-digital-asset-income.

[277] "Rev. Rul. 2019-24: Gross Income." *IRS*, 2019, irs.gov/pub/irs-drop/rr-19-24.pdf; Goldstein, Ronald J. "Bitcoin (BTC)/Bitcoin Cash (BCH) Hard Fork." 22 Mar. 2021. *IRS*, irs.gov/pub/irs-wd/202114020.pdf.

[278] Chason, Eric. "Cryptocurrency Hard Forks and Revenue Ruling 2019-24." *Wm. & Mary Law School Scholarship Repository*, 2019, shorturl.at/fjtD2.

[279] "Court Authorizes Service of John Doe Summons Seeking the Identities of U.S. Taxpayers Who Have Used Virtual Currency." *DOJ*, 30 Nov. 2016, justice.gov/opa/pr/court-authorizes-service-john-doe-summons-seeking-identities-us-taxpayers-who-have-used.

otherwise disposed of digital assets during the previous tax year.[280]

In 2021, as part of the Infrastructure Investment and Jobs Act, new reporting requirements for digital asset businesses were enacted, including a requirement to report receipts of digital assets greater than $10,000. This rule technically went into effect on January 1, 2024, although the IRS has stated that the requirements will not be enforced until further guidance is published.[281]

The Jobs Act also set forth new requirements for digital asset "brokers," which are defined broadly to include not only centralized trading platforms and money services businesses, but potentially also decentralized exchanges and wallet providers, to report on their users' digital asset gains and losses through a new 1099-DA (digital asset) form. These rules will not go into full effect until January 2026. The expanded reporting requirements are controversial in that they expand the Treasury Department's ability to financially surveil digital asset use and many questions remain as to how to comply with these new requirements, including how and whether it is possible for something like a decentralized exchange or self-custodied wallet provider to comply.[282] Additional regulations will need to be enacted before these new requirements can be implemented, so it is possible the effective date may be delayed, or the requirements may change.

II. International Considerations

This book is admittedly styled as a guide to the laws of crypto within the United States, and I do not want to spend too much time on the laws of other jurisdictions except to note that they exist and should be considered when you are working on a project whose scope reaches beyond our borders. Similarly, even for those trying to bring a product to market that *excludes* the United States because of regulatory risk,

---

280 "Form 1040." *IRS*, irs.gov/instructions/i1040gi.

281 "Treasury and IRS Announce That Businesses Do Not Have to Report Certain Transactions Involving Digital Assets Until Regulations Are Issued." *IRS*, 16 Jan. 2024, shorturl.at/jluAH.

282 Van Valkenburgh, Peter. "Treasury's Proposed 'broker' Rules Expand Surveillance Well beyond a 'Third Party Doctrine' That's Already Stretched Thin." *Coin Center*, 14 Sept. 2023, shorturl.at/cowyI.

you should be aware that there are instances where U.S. laws can be enforced extraterritorially, such as with certain FinCEN regulations or sanctions as discussed in Chapter 10. Additionally, although other U.S. regulations such as securities laws do not, according to the Supreme Court in *Morrison v. National Australia Bank*, 561 U.S. 247 (2010), have extraterritorial application, depending on the facts of the case, U.S. regulations can apply to foreign entities if there is a nexus to U.S. persons or activities.[283]

Every year, PricewaterhouseCoopers (PWC) publishes a report on the state of global crypto regulations that provides a helpful snapshot of how different jurisdictions craft regulations for digital assets. The 2024 Report is linked in the footnote.[284] I encourage even those with an entirely domestic practice to give it a read in order to be aware of what other countries are doing in the space.

As you can imagine, there is probably a lawyer like me in just about every country who should probably write a version of this book.

---

283 In March 2024, the Second Circuit reversed the dismissal of a class action against Binance. The lower court found the sales were not U.S. transactions. The Second Circuit reversed, holding plaintiffs had sufficiently alleged transactions were "domestic" because orders were matched on U.S. servers and U.S. persons could use the exchange. *Williams v. Binance*, No. 22-927 (2d Cir. 2024) t.ly/nHrW7.

284 PwC. "Navigating the Global Crypto Landscape with PwC: 2024 Outlook." Dec. 2023, shorturl.at/wFMY7.

CHAPTER 18

Conclusion and a Plan for Keeping Up

The thing about rabbit holes is that once you think you've reached its bottom, they keep going. If you've stuck with me on this journey, you should have a pretty good idea of the basics of how the digital asset space has evolved and roughly where things sat at the point where I sent in the last version of this manuscript. The challenge is that almost none of the topics you have just read about are static. Crypto is evolving concurrently with the law meant to regulate it. Current efforts in Congress and cases pending before courts could fundamentally change how crypto is regulated and how the digital asset industry develops in the United States.

Keeping up with everything is very difficult. It is made more challenging by the fact that there really isn't a single source of news within the crypto industry that you can follow to stay up to date. Unfortunately, that means that those who wish to remain current have to keep up with many news sources, podcasts, YouTubers, and hundreds of Twitter/X accounts that, taken together, are needed to stay up to speed with everything going on in the wide world of crypto.

Below are some of the resources I typically use to stay current. I recognize that this is a lot for someone to keep track of, so if you would benefit from a curated, weekly update of the most important events impacting crypto and its laws and regulations, sign up for my newsletter at www.TheCryptoLegalHandbook.com.

Crypto Twitter. Most of the debate within the industry occurs on Crypto Twitter. Even if you do not plan on posting, I encourage you to create an anonymous account to follow the most prominent voices in crypto.

- Several helpful lists of the most vocal crypto legal voices have been compiled. The two bests are "$crypto law" and "crypto legal/regulatory." If you follow those, you should have the most prominent lawyers, organizations, and policy folks in crypto in your feed.[285]

- You should also follow at least some of the prominent non-legal voices in the space. A website called Twitter Score produces a list of the "Top 100" crypto Twitter accounts by engagement. *See* twitterscore.io/topScored. Be warned that some of the people in the Top 100 are insane. Still, if I were building a follow list from scratch, I would add these folks and then start unfollowing them when I realize they aren't providing me any value.

Podcasts/YouTube Channels. Besides Twitter, I tend to keep up with news about crypto technology, law, and policy through podcasts and YouTube channels. Some of my favorites are listed below. There is probably not a topic you can think about in the space that isn't covered through at least one of the following, including very complex legal questions. I encourage you to follow these accounts for new episodes, but I also believe you will be well served by exploring their archives for past episodes on the historical topics discussed in this book.

- **Bankless Podcast (@BanklessHQ)** - podcast.banklesshq.com. This started out as a podcast focused on DeFi and still is the best source for DeFi-related conversations, but has expanded in scope to include more general interest topics, including law and policy.

- **Unchained Podcast (@Unchained_Pod)** - unchainedcrypto.com/podcasts. Hosted by reporter Laura Shin, the Unchained Podcast is, in my view, the most dependable place to find discussion on crypto current affairs.

- **Law of Code Podcast (@JacobRobinsonJD)** - podcasts.apple.com/podcast/law-of-code/id1578287932. Jacob Robinson is

---

285 *See* "$crypto law", x.com/i/lists/913370305187471361; "crypto legal/regulatory", x.com/i/lists/1550854976754356225.

an attorney who hosts sophisticated conversations with the industry's top lawyers. For those looking to dive deep into a specific crypto-legal topic, search Jacob's archives. It has almost certainly been covered.

- **Andreas Antonopoulos' YouTube Channel** - youtube.com/aantonop. In my view, Andreas Antonopoulos (@Aantonop) is the best educator in the space. He has a way of explaining digital asset technology that is very easy for a beginner to digest. He tends to focus mostly on Bitcoin issues, although there are playlists and resources on Ethereum and, to some degree, other "Web3" topics.

- **Whiteboard Crypto's YouTube Channel** - youtube.com/WhiteboardCrypto. In my view, Whiteboard Crypto provides the most accessible explanations for complex crypto issues. I cite many throughout this book, and while these won't provide you with expertise on these topics, they are very good starting points for new topics that can give you the vocabulary needed to explore them more on your own.

- **DeFi Dad's YouTube Channel** - youtube.com/@DeFiDad. Very in-the-weeds tutorials and discussions on advancements in decentralized finance.

News Organization/Newsletters/Other Websites to Bookmark

- **CoinDesk.com** – CoinDesk is the most prominent crypto news organization.

- **CoinTelegraph.com** – Another crypto media outlet.

- **TheDefiant.io** – Focused primarily on DeFi news.

- **CoinCenter.org** – CoinCenter is the premier crypto advocacy group in the United States. Their website provides a number of educational tools and resources for the policy minded.

- **CapHillCrypto.com** – A valuable newsletter by a former Congressional staffer that documents political and policy news related to digital assets. I also encourage you to follow the Blockchain Association (@BlockchainAssn) on Twitter for up-to-the-minute policy updates.

- **Messari's Crypto Thesis** - Every year, digital asset data provider Messari's CEO, Ryan Selkis (@TwoBitIdiot), produces a robust report on the state and direction of the crypto industry. It is an impressive work covering developments in technology, markets, and regulations. The 2024 Report is available for free at messari.io/crypto-theses-for-2024.

If you think I am missing anything that should be added to future editions, let me know at www.TheCryptoLegalHandbook.com.

Printed in Great Britain
by Amazon